MW00616380

Project Mayflower

PROJECT MAYFLOWER
Building and Sailing a Seventeenth-Century Replica

RICHARD A. STONE

Essex, Connecticut

An imprint of Globe Pequot, the trade division of
The Rowman & Littlefield Publishing Group, Inc.
4501 Forbes Blvd., Ste. 200
Lanham, MD 20706
www.rowman.com

Distributed by NATIONAL BOOK NETWORK

British Library Cataloguing in Publication Information available

Library of Congress Cataloging-in-Publication Data
Names: Stone, Richard A., author.
Title: Project Mayflower : building and sailing a seventeenth-century replica / Richard A. Stone.
Description: Essex : Lyons Press, 2024. | Includes bibliographical references and index.
Identifiers: LCCN 2023043425 (print) | LCCN 2023043426 (ebook) | ISBN 9781493084364
  (cloth) | ISBN 9781493084371 (epub)
Subjects: LCSH: Sailing ships—Reproductions. | Mayflower II (Ship)—History. | Mayflower II
  (Ship)—Design and construction. | Project Mayflower, Ltd. | Historic ships—Massachsetts—
  Plymouth. | Ships, Wooden—Great Britain—Design and construction. | Charlton, Warwick
  M. J., 1918–2002. | Villiers, Alan, 1903–1982—Travel. | Transatlantic voyages—History—20th
  century. | Historical reenactments.
Classification: LCC VM17 .S766 2024 (print) | LCC VM17 (ebook) | DDC 623.822/4—dc23/
  eng/20231108
LC record available at https://lccn.loc.gov/2023043425
LC ebook record available at https://lccn.loc.gov/2023043426

♾️™ The paper used in this publication meets the minimum requirements of American National
Standard for Information Sciences—Permanence of Paper for Printed Library Materials, ANSI/
NISO Z39.48-1992.

For Joan

CONTENTS

FOREWORD

As a young teen on June 13, 1957, I was standing in Pilgrim costume on the Cole's Hill bleachers above Plymouth Rock watching *Mayflower II*'s masts and sails proceeding beyond Long Beach toward the harbor entrance. "SHE'S HERE," blared the largest headline in the *Old Colony Memorial* newspaper's 135-year history. Excited onlookers burst into jubilant cheers, only to be slightly taken aback to see the valiant little ship being *towed* around the beach point by a tug rather than sailing free—unavoidably, given the shallow harbor's torturous channel. That unexpected measure in some ways exemplifies the expedients and challenges involved in successfully bringing *Mayflower II* to America.

Mayflower II's improbable adventure—skeptics gave the voyage itself only a 50–50 chance of success—captured the imagination and won the hearts of an international audience. This was in large part due to the public relations wizardry of the undertaking's mastermind and dogged promoter, Warwick Charlton. It was his dream, conceived in North Africa during World War II, of a tangible memorial in honor of the Anglo-American wartime coalition. His vision took shape in the form of a replica of the Plymouth Pilgrims' *Mayflower*.

But how to make this vision a reality? Charlton had some useful professional contacts but no real resources of his own. He also had a regrettable knack for irritating the powers-that-be, which viewed him as an implausible huckster with an embarrassing stunt to sell. Undaunted by the political headwinds, Charlton and his public relations firm partner, John Lowe, plowed ahead soliciting funding and raising public awareness about "Project Mayflower Ltd."

The primary breakthrough came with the serendipitous discovery of a corresponding intention to build a full-scale re-creation of the *Mayflower* by the fledgling outdoor museum Plimoth Plantation in Plymouth, Massachusetts. Charlton contacted Plantation founder Henry Hornblower II in March 1955 to see if the museum would be willing to receive and maintain the ship after its arrival, and also share the meticulous design plans that had been commissioned of naval architect William A. Baker (no relation). The resulting agreement was a matter of mutual benefit, and with that in hand, Project Mayflower Ltd. recruited the venerable J. W. and A. Upham shipyard in Brixham, Devon, to undertake *Mayflower II*'s construction.

Both parties were equally determined to have the reproduction be as historically accurate as possible. Although modern components and temporary navigational equipment were employed in a few instances, *Mayflower II* was constructed using painstaking traditional methods and materials. Retired shipwrights, sail makers, and riggers shared outmoded skills on hewing and shaping the oak timbers, hand-stitched real linen canvas sails, treated the Italian hemp rigging with Stockholm pine tar, and caulked the seams with oakum and pitch to achieve a credible authenticity. A similar care for historical verisimilitude was exercised in the selection by Captain Alan Villiers of a crew with a core of veterans with square-rigged deep-water experience who would sail the little "barque" to America without an auxiliary engine of any sort.

Launched on a rainy afternoon on September 22, 1956, while English affairs were in the throes of the Suez Crisis, the new *Mayflower* began her fifty-five-day voyage on April 20 (the original *Mayflower* took sixty-six days to reach Cape Cod) that climaxed in the ebullient June 13, 1957, reception in Plymouth, Massachusetts.

A great deal has been written about that *Mayflower II* voyage—including first-person memoirs replete with fascinating facts and anecdotes—but these depictions were singular and limited. What Richard Stone has done is produce a superb synthesis from an impressive number of diverse accounts to deliver, among other things, a revealing survey of previously unidentified individuals instrumental in supporting (or disparaging) Project Mayflower Ltd., and its temporary American successor, called the "Mayflower Foundation" or "Mayflower, Inc." The Foundation retained possession of the ship in an effort to meet their financial obligations by exhibiting *Mayflower II* in New York, Washington, DC, and Miami before returning her to Plymouth on June 30, 1958, and assigning ownership to Plimoth Plantation as agreed.

The supporting narrative here centers on two figures: the irrepressible Warwick Charlton and his American counterpart, Plimoth Plantation's Henry Hornblower II. Both men were romantic visionaries who found the legend of the *Mayflower* Pilgrims irresistible and took the challenge of re-creating a substantive representation of the 1620 vessel with unreserved ardor. However, the professional relationship was not without its tensions. Charlton had a single-minded disregard for anyone else's needs and resources, be they financial or pragmatic, that did not solely further the *Mayflower* project as he conceived it. It also must be said that "Harry" Hornblower was not actually the rich, powerful, and austere establishment figure that Warwick's and Randal Charlton's perspectives present. Admittedly, there are few equivalent published accounts about Harry and his ambitions for Plimoth Plantation, but for we that knew him, there is never a fair balance. Similarly, the fiscal shenanigans Charlton indulged in, which even John Lowe regretted, looked rather different from the debtors' perspective. Many of the fully listed contributors were left unpaid until the Plantation took over the $190,000 liability that paid some at fifty cents on the dollar and took years to account for in cooperation with the vessel's disgruntled British financial supporter, Felix Fenston.

In *Project Mayflower*, Richard A. Stone has comprehensively documented this complex and fascinating accomplishment in a magisterial account of the re-creation of the Plymouth Pilgrims' famous transatlantic vessel. It is concise and accessible in style, revealing the unexpected vicissitudes of expectation and frustration, triumphs and setbacks that make *Mayflower II*'s annals resemble a novel of suspense.

What's more, he clarifies the project's contemporary political and cultural context, and does what no other author has attempted in extending the narrative to cover the ship's post-voyage travels to New York, Florida, and so on up through the laudable multi-million restoration that ensured the longtime survival of Charlton's quixotic achievement—even as it put paid to *Mayflower II*'s original painstaking quest for historical authenticity. The substitution of English oak, linen canvas, pitch and tar that had suffered the ravages of time in favor of durable Dyneema cordage, Oceanus polyester sailcloth, bronze bolts and trunnels became an evolution that mirrors the public perception of the formerly hallowed Pilgrim Story in today's revisionist cultural milieu.

Stone's wide-angle conceptual lens locates the Project Mayflower enterprise in its cultural context, from the financially fraught successes of the mid-1950s up to today. It is hard to imagine that *Project Mayflower*'s exposition will ever be surpassed. As Richard Stone concludes:

> *The impossible had been done: a lost seventeenth-century ship had risen from the past, ignored doubters, crossed the Atlantic, survived a storm, and captured global praise. In the halls of achievement—in which there are many pretenders but few originals—*Mayflower II *was now primal.*

—James W. Baker, retired Director of Research, Plimoth Patuxet Museums; author of *Thanksgiving: The Biography of an American Holiday* and others

October 2023

PROLOGUE

One of the world's most famous ships, the *Mayflower*, died ingloriously in 1624. No towering flames. No watery grave. Just shipyard wolves, dirty hands, and sweaty men devouring her skin and ribs to pay debts. She had run her course, served her purpose. The end. But destiny had other plans. Her spirit lived on, grew, and eventually carried the square-rigger's reincarnation through a time portal that opened centuries later in a strange harbor on a beautiful summer day. It was New York in 1957, and while the vessel was surely not the first to arrive unexpectedly in those waters, it had been 348 years since a remarkably similar craft sailed up the river that one day would become known as the Hudson in search of a New World.

The *Mayflower* reincarnation was a triumph made possible through the tenacity of a British war veteran named Warwick Charlton, who was viewed with suspicion by the British government as well as by social elites on both sides of the Atlantic because he refused to follow their rules. He liked making his own. The idea of building the ship could be traced back to the 1942 battlefields of North Africa, where the young soldier witnessed the unalloyed generosity of the United States in the form of Sherman tanks delivered to the British Eighth Army as it was being pushed backward across the desert by superior German forces. Once the war ended and the veteran returned to his prewar life as a London journalist, he continued to believe that America played the pivotal role in defeating antidemocratic forces. The more he reflected on this act of brotherhood, the greater his desire to thank the US military veterans who had stood beside him in war. But what do you give a country that seems to have everything?

Figure 1. *Mayflower II* sailing into New York Harbor on July 1, 1957. *(B. Anthony Stewart/National Geographic Creative)*

As he considered the American soldiers' families back home, who had given the nation moral strength and courage as their husbands, sons, and fathers fought beside him, an idea came to mind: Why not give the United States a piece of her own lost history—the ship that famously transported the Pilgrims in 1620, inspired Thanksgiving, and was then lost to the scrapyard: the *Mayflower*. Before he knew it, the craft became a passion that wouldn't be satisfied until its replica was built and delivered.

What Charlton didn't know was that the son of a powerful New England financier had the same idea. His name was Henry Hornblower II—"Harry"—and he needed the vessel as badly as Charlton wanted to proffer it, though for a different reason: as the star attraction for a new museum he was building in Massachusetts, where the original *Mayflower* had landed centuries before. Dubbed Plimoth Plantation, the enterprise sought to transform the way colonial history was taught to the public by allowing visitors to walk back in time as they entered period exhibits animated by specially trained docents dressed as early American colonists.

Despite clearly differing personal motives, Charlton and Hornblower agreed to join forces when they met by chance in 1955. Warwick would be responsible for financing, construction, and the ship's safe passage across the Atlantic, while Harry promised mooring, maintenance, and exhibition. The partnership was a big relief to the Bostonian because the building expense exceeded what he was willing to pay, while the Londoner considered cost secondary to the duty of honoring his country's ally.

Neither man could imagine what would happen next. Events beyond their control nearly scuttled the ship, and matters in their own hands pulled in unexpected directions. Both dreamers ultimately made good on their promises, and *Mayflower II* went on display for all the world to see. But as with any tale worthy of its sea legs, there was more to the story.

PART I
SHIPBUILDING

Chapter 1

Fighting Editor

Nicknames. They often say more about a person than those given at birth and can be meant to honor or belittle. For *Time* magazine, the one it bestowed on Warwick Charlton in May 1944 was a gesture of earned respect: "Monty's Fighting Editor."[1] That same month, *Life* recited "The 'Monty' Legend" to Americans and put Sir Bernard Montgomery on its cover. The British general had gained acclaim with troops, senior officers, and Allied forces with his proven courage, charisma, and battlefield victories. "Gather round me," he told troops preparing for D-Day. Thousands of men broke ranks and came near. "I never put an army into action until I know it can win. We're going to give the enemy one hard blow and that will finish him." Then cheers erupted: "Monty! Monty!"[2]

Time had been informing the world about current events since its founding in 1923 by Henry Luce, who in 1936 expanded his publishing enterprise with the photojournalism weekly *Life*. A decade later *Life* had become one of the most popular and widely read magazines in America. As for *Time*, its news editors prided themselves on clear writing that made complex topics understandable to everyday readers. One well-read section, called Press, hailed "Monty's Fighting Editor" as a man who was not afraid to champion a cause with determination and courage to the highest level and to ignore hierarchy:

Probably the only editor in uniform who has attacked his own Government again & again and got away with it is Warwick M.

J. Charlton, editor of the British *Eighth Army News* . . . the testy, grip-
ing pal-in-print [voice] of the "desert rats" who followed Monty from
Egypt to Italy[, which began publication] in September 1941, during
the siege of Tobruk.

To tall, slim, 26-year-old Captain Charlton, onetime *London Daily
Sketch*–man, Monty gave free rein and backed him up when the War
Office was howling for the suppression of the paper, and even Winston
Churchill was making known his disapproval. . . .

Editor Charlton prodded soldiers to write him letters about the
slow mail service, editorialized on it, finally stirred the House of Commons to action. There was a campaign on the low pay of British combat
troops—and Parliament moved again. . . .

Last October Charlton's *News* attacked [Britain's war policy] in
Yugoslavia. Again Parliament seethed, later came around to switching
sympathies (and supplies) to Communist Marshal Tito.

Through all this, Monty defended Charlton. . . . Captain Charlton
wrote Monty's first Order of the Day in the Desert. Thereafter the
General wrote his own, but Charlton edited some of them. Said the
Captain of the General: "He kept using the same old trite phrases."

When the War Office sent an emissary to warn Montgomery about
his press man, the general replied, "Charlton is not a bad man. He is a
funny man." Monty liked him and was loyal.[3]

The soldier's willingness to challenge established orthodoxy was
part of his basic character, and he did it fearlessly. After the war, that
personality was essential when Charlton organized a group of dedicated
men and women to build a replica of the 1620 *Mayflower* to honor
democracy and the United States. The magazine remembered him well—
as did members of the British government, who did not forget the way
he brazenly challenged authority. Given the chance to knock him down
a notch or two, they would happily take it if the right opportunity came
along.

Two years later, former British prime minister Winston Churchill
introduced a pair of powerful terms that would define the postwar
world and capture the public's imagination: "iron curtain" and "special
relationship." Churchill used those words to describe seismic forces

exerting pressure in the new atomic age when he spoke at Westminster College in Fulton, Missouri, on March 5, 1946, with President Truman and the international press corps in attendance. England's wartime leader said that an "iron curtain" had fallen across Europe as communist governments sought to seize totalitarian control and crush democracy. He then added that there was a counterweight to that challenge, a "special relationship between the British Commonwealth and Empire and the United States," that would stand up to that evil and defend freedom. His address was officially titled "The Sinews of Peace" but became popularly known as "the Iron Curtain speech."[4]

Figure 2. Winston Churchill introducing "iron curtain . . . special relationship" to the world. *(America's National Churchill Museum, CH.07.058a)*

A year later, Charlton was still wearing government-issued clothing. He looked forward to getting back into civies, but first he needed to get home. It was during that period of limbo, while returning from war on a US Navy frigate, that Warwick first learned of the *Mayflower*. He had served on the personal staffs of the British Empire's best-known generals: first with Monty and then with Lord Louis Mountbatten in Asia. Montgomery was most famous for his victory over Field Marshal Erwin Rommel, the "Desert Fox," at the Second Battle of El Alamein in November 1942. That triumph marked a turning point in the war because the Nazis' Afrika Korps was denied access to the Suez Canal and Middle Eastern oil fields. Mountbatten was Supreme Allied Commander South East Asia Command and later became the last Viceroy of India. He was a favorite of Winston Churchill and the second cousin once removed of Queen Elizabeth II, who enjoyed calling him "Uncle Dickie," even though he was Prince Philip's uncle, not hers. Because of Charlton's proximity to these great leaders, he witnessed America's pivotal role in defeating global tyranny and came to believe that his country owed its ally a debt of gratitude. How it might be repaid, however, was anybody's guess.

Then something fortuitous happened. Charlton came across a book in the ship's library that sparked his curiosity and imagination: *Of Plimoth Plantation* by William Bradford. He had never heard of the author and didn't know much about seventeenth-century English immigrants in the New World, but after "I turned the first few pages . . . I did not put the book down until I had read [the] last." He was totally captivated and found it "one of the great works of the English language."[5] The author was the second governor of Plimoth and a signer of a document called the Mayflower Compact. The work's only description of the ship that carried Bradford, 101 other passengers, and a crew of about thirty across the Atlantic in 1620 was a mention of its size—180 tons of burden—and the presence of at least one topsail.[6]

As a good Englishman who had been taught the nation's seafaring history, the soldier knew that Sir Walter Raleigh died two years before the Pilgrims set sail and that the adventurer had been granted a royal charter by Queen Elizabeth to explore and colonize North America. Although Raleigh never traveled there himself, others made the voyage on his behalf and founded Roanoke Colony, which ultimately failed but inspired the establishment of Jamestown in Virginia, England's most famous foothold on the continent. Raleigh's knowledge of the sea was outstanding, and after traveling to what is now Venezuela, he told stories of a land with vast riches and a city of gold called El Dorado. At times adored by royalty, he eventually fell into disfavor with Elizabeth and her successor James I and was accused of plotting treason against the Crown. Raleigh disputed the charges for fifteen years, during which time the Tower of London was his home. He left there only after an axman removed his head in 1618.

England was also home to Sir Francis Drake, who circumnavigated the globe between 1577 and 1580, providing inspiration to Raleigh and other British mariners. *Mayflower* captain Christopher Jones was almost certainly one of those nautical acolytes, which made his troubles in late 1620, when he landed far east of his planned destination, so intriguing to Charlton. Had the crew known how to calculate longitude, the little ship would have had a much better chance of hitting its target, the mouth of the Hudson River. But that maritime calculation would not be available until the next century, so it made landfall on Cape Cod rather than Long Island. While his passengers had survived a harrowing voyage, they were clearly not expecting to land on barren, unknown shores. Realizing the depth of their predicament, the Pilgrims' decision to bind themselves together in a written agreement for their "better ordering" was impressive. No one back home in the land of royals dared to even imagine "just and equal laws . . . for the general good."[7] Indeed, their monarch, James I, had made clear in 1609 that he did not like being contradicted or challenged when he delivered before Parliament his lecture "On the Divine Right of Kings," declaring: "The state of monarchy is the supremest thing upon earth. . . . Kings are justly called Gods, for that they exercise a manner or resemblance of divine power upon earth . . . so it is sedition in subjects, to dispute what a king may do."[8]

Charlton knew firsthand that the world had just concluded a global war to uphold the principles articulated in the Pilgrims' declaration, and he was awestruck. No one shivering on that old boat could have imagined the long-term consequences of their decision to memorialize their hopes for governance in the New World on a piece of parchment. They just wanted to make it through the winter to a fresh start in the spring.

Beyond his theological interests, James I supported the performing arts. He was particularly fond of a young bard named William Shakespeare. While history often inspired the playwright, current events also caught his attention. One particular news story had London abuzz and his creative juices flowing because it was about a shipwreck, a wondrous island, and the vessel's survivors.

The *Sea Venture* had set sail in 1609—the same year the king gave his "Divine Rights" speech—as the flagship of a seven-vessel fleet of armed merchantmen bound for the New World. During a mid-Atlantic storm, the craft was blown off course, separated from the group, and crashed on the coast of Bermuda. The island was a garden paradise with fresh water, animals, and exotic birds that kept the men alive for nine months while they built two new boats from the remains of their wrecked vessel and local Bermuda cedar. They set out again and ultimately arrived at Jamestown, where they stayed until returning to England. Shakespeare was almost certainly thinking of those events when he penned a quickly popular play called *The Tempest*.

One of the characters was a drunken, power-hungry sailor named Stephano who tried to depose the island's ruler. To many he seemed to be a caricature of real-life seaman Stephen Hopkins, who fomented an insurrection against the *Sea Venture*'s captain, was condemned for treason, and then spared in an act of clemency. Upon repatriation to England, the troublemaker's thoughts returned to the New World. He wanted to go back. Eventually he found passage on an old merchantman called *Mayflower*.

Once again, his ship went off course. While not crashing, the result was nearly as bad. Yet unlike the first mishap, which resulted in wreckage, fueled an insurrection, and inspired a popular theatrical drama, the second ending prompted survivors to seize the day with quills drawn rather than swords. The passengers knew what they wanted and were not about to let a navigation error dash their dreams. Here is what they wrote:

In the name of God, Amen. We whose names are underwritten, the Loyal Subjects of our dread Sovereign Lord King James, by the Grace of God, of Great Britain, France, and Ireland, King, Defender of the Faith, etc.:

Having undertaken, for the Glory of God, and advancement of the Christian faith, and honor of our King and Country, a voyage to plant the first colony in the northern parts of Virginia, do by these presents, solemnly and mutually, in the presence of God, and one another, covenant and combine ourselves together into a civil body politic, for our better ordering, and preservation and furtherance of the ends aforesaid; and by virtue hereof do enact, constitute, and frame such just and equal laws, ordinances, acts, constitutions, and offices, from time to time, as shall be thought most meet and convenient for the general good of the colony; unto which we promise all due submission and obedience.

In witness whereof we have hereunder subscribed our names at Cape Cod the 11th of November, in the year of the reign of our Sovereign Lord King James, of England, France, and Ireland, the eighteenth, and of Scotland the fifty-fourth. Anno Domini 1620.

John Carver	William Bradford
Edward Winslow	William Brewster
Isaac Allerton	Miles Standish
John Alden	Samuel Fuller
Christopher Martin	William Mullins
William White	Richard Warren
John Howland	Stephen Hopkins
Edward Tilley	John Tilley
Francis Cooke	Thomas Rogers
Thomas Tinker	John Rigsdale
Edward Fuller	John Turner
Francis Eaton	James Chilton
John Crackstone	John Billington

Moses Fletcher	John Goodman
Degory Priest	Thomas Williams
Gilbert Winslow	Edmund Margeson
Peter Browne	Richard Britteridge
George Soule	Richard Clarke
Richard Gardiner	John Allerton
Thomas English	Edward Doty
Edward Leister	

Among those signing the parchment and publicly challenging authority again was Stephen Hopkins, Shakespeare's muse-of-sorts. An additional forty names were also inscribed, but within a year, twenty-two of them were dead. Most perished during their first few months in the New World, but their visionary writing lived on to inspire countless

Figure 3. *The Mayflower Compact 1620*, by Jean Leon Gerome Ferris, oil on canvas, 1899. *(Pictorial Press Ltd./Alamy Stock Photo)*

generations, including the authors of a 1787 document that began "We the People." Hopkins (naturally) survived, living a long life, and the text he endorsed has been described as "the first written American constitution."[9]

CHAPTER 2

Big Idea

ONCE BACK IN LONDON, CHARLTON RESUMED HIS LIFE AS A FREELANCE writer, building a career strengthened by wartime relationships. The country was still suffering the psychological aftershocks of battle and eagerly sought stories that captured the imagination and provided relief from daily drudgery. Norwegian Thor Heyerdahl provided such a tonic in 1947 with the voyage of *Kon-Tiki*, a simple raft made of balsa logs, proving that early humans could have sailed with the trade winds from Peru to Easter Island and thus have been the first settlers of Polynesia. The raft, built with materials the ancients might have used, was named after the Incan god of creation, Viracocha, also known as Kon-Tiki. The expedition inspired Heyerdahl's bestselling book of the same name, as well as an Oscar-winning 1950 documentary.

Three years later, a New Zealand beekeeper named Edmund Hillary joined Nepali Indian Sherpa Tenzing Norgay to become the first men to reach the top of the highest mountain on earth, Mount Everest. They stood at the summit on May 29, 1953, and the world cheered their daring as a tribute to man's undefeatable spirit. The trek, part of the British Everest Expedition, gathered climbers from around the Empire to achieve a goal that seemed nearly impossible to George Mallory in the early 1920s when he said Everest needed to be conquered "because it's there."[1] Charlton read every story he could find about the feat, and as he did, an idea materialized: I should also organize a great adventure. Before he knew it, Bradford's journal was retrieved from that corner of his mind in which it had been tidily stowed. A craving developed to learn as much as he could about the Pilgrims and their quest. As he studied that history, two individuals and one special event struck a chord.

The first was a Native American called Squanto. He was Wampanoag, and his people had lived in New England for thousands of years before the first European explorers began arriving intermittently after 1524. That was the year France's king François I commissioned Italian explorer Giovanni da Verrazzano to examine the east coast of North America. Upon returning to the Old World, Verrazzano described an unknown region of vast fields, "open and free of any obstacles or trees, and so fertile that any kind of seed would produce excellent crops."[2]

The news of this wonderous land spread quickly as European powers sought to establish footholds in the New World, and by the early 1600s ships began to appear on the New England coastline with growing frequency. In 1614 one of those vessels was captained by Thomas Hunt, who landed in Cape Cod Bay near Patuxet seeking furs—but he departed with far more than pelts as cargo. Hunt kidnapped twenty-seven Wampanoag and took them back to Europe to be sold as slaves in Malaga, Spain, along with other "goods."[3] Luckily for one of the captives, the transaction was stopped by local Catholic priests, who cited a routinely ignored Spanish law prohibiting the sale of North Americans into slavery. An indigenous man named Tisquantum—shortened to Squanto—was thus spared and transported to London, where he would sharpen his English skills and come to be employed by Sir Ferdinando Gorges, a merchant actively involved with schemes to monetize the continent.[4]

In 1619 Gorges financed an expedition led by Captain Thomas Dermer and had Squanto join him because he thought it might give his group a competitive advantage. Thus the nearly enslaved Wampanoag returned to Plymouth Bay as an interpreter, working for men similar to those who had captured him five years earlier. But this irony was far less shocking than what Squanto witnessed upon his return to his native land. During his absence, more Europeans had arrived in his homeland, bringing with them diseases previously unknown to the region and its people. Where there had been as many as twenty-four thousand of his kin, epidemics annihilated that population. Squanto's people were nearly wiped off their sacred earth.[5] Tribes further inland, like the Narragansett, had been spared, but those having close contact with the white men had perished, leaving virtually no one to greet Dermer's ship when it arrived in Patuxet, as he later wrote: "I passed alongst the Coast where I found some ancient Plantations, not long since populous now utterly void."[6]

The following year, the *Mayflower* landed, and its passengers were likewise greeted by few local inhabitants. The ones who did emerge must certainly have had mixed feelings about the new arrivals, knowing from experience that strange travelers brought enslavement, disease, and grave misfortune. The Wampanoag also knew that inland groups posed a threat because they had survived the deadly sickness and now wanted coastal land. Perhaps these new arrivals, the Pilgrims, could become allies of Squanto's kinsmen in defending what was theirs. If so, the immigrants would have value. Accordingly, his people helped the lost voyagers and changed the course of history. The interpreter went on to play a key role in the interactions between the new arrivals and the Wampanoag, becoming a central actor in America's early story. Charlton kept studying.

Caleb Cheeshahteaumuck, another Wampanoag and the first Native American to graduate from Harvard, captured Charlton's attention as well. Touted as America's answer to Oxford, Harvard was established in 1636, and its Charter of 1650 made a commitment to "the education of the English and Indian youth of this country."[7] From 1655 to 1698 an "Indian College" operated from the school's first brick building, which also housed its printing press and was near the spot now claimed by a student dormitory, Matthews Hall in Harvard Yard. Caleb and his classmate Joel Hiacooms were the first indigenous students to matriculate following entrance exams they passed when they were about fifteen years old.[8] Joel would have been valedictorian, but he died in a shipwreck off Nantucket Island when returning to school after visiting his family in Martha's Vineyard before the ceremony. Because attending the commencement was a requirement for graduation at the time, Caleb walked alone. He had a bright future but was struck down shortly thereafter by consumption—tuberculosis—so neither Charlton nor anyone else would ever know what impact he could have had on American history.

Not many years after Caleb's tragic passing, tensions began growing between the indigenous tribes of Plymouth Bay and the English colonists. It was inevitable. Since 1620, more and more ships had been arriving annually with settlers eager to start a new life. Their population growth outpaced the regional tribes, and they were hungry for land, territory occupied and rightfully owned by New England's native people. Pushing and shoving eventually grew into something much worse—King Philip's War, or the First Indian War (1675–1676). It was one of the deadliest conflicts in US history. When comparing the carnage to other well-known wars, the death rate per thousand was nine times greater than the American Revolution, twice that of the Civil War, and seven times higher than World War II.[9] In just over a year, a dozen towns in southern New England were destroyed and more than half of the region's ninety settlements were embattled. One in five Native Americans was killed in the fighting. Hundreds of Wampanoag and their allies were publicly executed or enslaved, and the people who welcomed the Pilgrims—quite likely the biggest contributors to the colonists' survival—were left landless and defeated. It was a catastrophic moment that emboldened the colonists, who had fought without foreign military or government support. They did it themselves, for good or evil, and out of that pain came new feelings of North American identity that were separate from England and the Crown. As he read the history of this pivotal moment, Charlton felt the seeds of the American Revolution may have been planted in the rubble of that conflict, and he wondered what unforeseen sprouts would emerge from the debris of his recent war.

In addition to Squanto and Caleb, Charlton was captivated by the first Thanksgiving. In 1621 Edward Winslow described the gathering in a letter, saying the colonists were joined by the Wampanoag's "greatest king Massasoit, with some ninety men, whom for three days we entertained and feasted."[10] Charlton was struck by the grandeur of the occasion because it celebrated the harmony that could prevail when people of different backgrounds worked in unity for a common purpose. Was there a message here for the modern world? He discovered that in 1789 America's first president, George Washington, declared November 26 as the new nation's first "Day of Publick Thanksgiving." This national directive generated some political criticism, and except for a victory celebration following the War of 1812, no more Thanksgivings were held until the Civil War.

In an irony of history, both the North and the South liked the idea of Thanksgiving and wanted to make it their own. The Confederacy made the first move. Following its victory at Bull Run in 1861, a Thanksgiving holiday was declared by Jefferson Davis and the Confederate Congress, repeated the next year after the Second Battle of Bull Run.

Then in October 1863, President Lincoln made Thanksgiving a national holiday. It was a useful reminder to all citizens, Yankee or Rebel, that the nation was built on shared democratic values dating back to 1620. The following month, Lincoln stood before a crowd in Gettysburg, Pennsylvania, lamenting that the nation that "our fathers brought forth, conceived in liberty, and dedicated to the proposition that all men are created equal" was "now engaged in a great civil war testing whether that nation [could] long endure."[11] When reelected a year later, Lincoln asked citizens to move forward "with malice toward none, with charity for all, with firmness in the right, as God gives us to see the right, . . . to finish the work we are in, to bind up the nation's wounds."[12] Before he could put those words into action, however, Lincoln was assassinated, and the arduous task of reconstructing the nation had to go on without him. A president lay dead, but the spirit of Thanksgiving was reborn throughout the reunified nation.

As his research continued, the Fighting Editor learned that the holiday's date wandered until 1939, when FDR issued a presidential proclamation declaring the last Thursday in November as Thanksgiving. Unfortunately, sixteen states refused to follow his orders. Two years later an act of Congress resolved the matter, setting the fourth Thursday as the day, and the president signed it into law on December 26, 1941. While FDR's tinkering helped clarify the holiday's future, what lay ahead for the nation was unknown. After years of sitting on the sidelines of history, watching in isolation as the war Hitler started on September 1, 1939, continued to expand and Imperial Japan's brutality in Asia grew by the day since it began in 1937, two vast oceans would no longer be sufficient to quench the hot winds of war blowing toward the United States. The country needed to brace itself for what lay ahead, and Thanksgiving offered a practical expression of national unity in the face of adversity.

Charlton, too, recognized the connection between communal gratitude and triumph over strife, and he wanted to share it with others—but was it relevant to his big idea of creating an adventure to rival the conquering of Everest, one that would capture the world's imagination? He would soon find out.

Like a shoot in fresh earth, the *Mayflower II* concept took root and began to grow. Now all the veteran had to do was transplant his excitement to others. As the thought became an all-consuming drive, Charlton realized the story he wanted to tell was more than just words written in an old style of English. After spending years in the European and Asian theaters of war as both a soldier and a writer, he understood the power of symbolism when spreading ideas. Personal experience had taught him that images reached more people than text because their propagation was independent of the ability to read. Coca-Cola, Lucky Strike cigarettes, and other global consumer brands took advantage of that to evoke positive reactions when people saw their logos. The Germans had also mastered advertising, or propaganda, with their potent symbol of Aryan supremacy, the swastika. What Charlton needed was a visual statement that could tell the *Mayflower* story and be instantly understood, regardless of one's language, location, or national origin. The medium itself needed to be the message, and he began to realize that the vessel he was obsessing about could deliver that communication. If a replica could be built and sailed across the sea, it had the potential of becoming an international news sensation—one that would require reporters to describe the ship's history to a worldwide audience. That could even include a description of the Mayflower Compact and its aspirational goal of "just and equal laws" for the general good.

Because Americans already knew the Pilgrim story, Charlton's growing desire was to tell the world via a new messenger. To test the idea, he engaged with two media barons he knew. Would they see the same potential? He first spoke with Lord Beaverbrook, the owner of the *Daily Express*, and he got a positive response. However, the publisher then discussed it among his associates and changed his mind. Charlton next approached Edward Hulton, the owner of the *Picture Post*, the British equivalent of *Life* magazine, and described it as a big photojournalism story that could bolster circulation. While initially expressing support, Hulton also changed his mind.

Undeterred, Charlton shifted focus to prestigious groups like the Pilgrims Society and the English Speaking Union (ESU),[13] which were founded to further Anglo-American relations. The British upper class proudly backed both. Queen Elizabeth II was herself a patron of the ESU, and its vice presidents included Winston Churchill and former prime minister Clement Attlee. Unfortunately, those bastions of cultured Anglo-Saxon wealth and privilege had little interest in the plan. Indeed, the Pilgrims Society, "not to be confused with the Pilgrim Trust," presented itself explicitly as having "nothing whatsoever to do with the *Mayflower* and the Pilgrim Fathers of 1620."[14]

The veteran eventually discussed his brainchild with an old army buddy, Hugh Cudlipp, who had become editor of the *Daily Mirror*, which sold five million copies a day. Cudlipp was intrigued but, like the others, found a way to say no. However, one of his most popular columnists, Bill Connor, got wind of the idea, liked it, and ran a short piece in the paper that many readers also liked. With that amorphous, general public vote of approval, Charlton felt his daring plan had been validated by the people who mattered most: everyday readers. To heck with the wealthy elites and naysayers. From that point on, he was not letting go of the idea of building a second *Mayflower*.

Good fortune then struck when he was introduced to a London property developer named Felix Donovan Fenston in late summer 1954. A self-made millionaire, not from the British gentry, Fenston had lost a leg in a motoring accident early in the war, returned to civilian life while others remained in uniform, and developed an active interest in property speculation. In 1939, London had a population of 8.6 million, making it the second largest city in the world after New York. Then the German Luftwaffe, Adolf Hitler's air force, bombed it ruthlessly, destroying more than seventy thousand buildings and damaging another 1.7 million from 1939 to 1945.[15] The city was decimated, but Fenston knew instinctively that residents would eventually come back and rebuild.

He had little doubt that property owners would be willing to make a devil's bargain for desperately needed cash. That cunning allowed him, and other aggressive speculators, to make tax-free fortunes while most English households struggled financially. To many, Fenston personified postwar greed.

As Charlton peddled his big idea to anyone who would listen, the speculator's company was quietly finalizing plans to buy a parcel of land in Central London so it could erect an office building. There might be a problem, however. The structure currently occupying the space was the historic St. James's Theatre, which had stood majestically for over a century. During the Nazis' relentless London bombing from September 1940 to May 1941 that killed forty thousand civilians and became known as the Blitz, the St. James's Theatre miraculously survived while other theaters suffered direct hits. Then came Felix Fenston. Even though his

Figure 4. Warwick Charlton with Felix Fenston, Project Mayflower's first investor. *(Keystone Press/Alamy Stock Photo)*

father had been a theater impresario, the developer seemed to care less about what was already there. Others could disagree, however, and merely having the law on his side might not be enough this time around, particularly if faced with public outrage. Fenston needed to develop a counterweight that could silence potential protests. Enter Warwick Charlton.

When Monty's Fighting Editor described his plan to build a second *Mayflower*, Felix quickly recognized an opportunity that could benefit his Central London scheme. Specifically, if Charlton succeeded, his new maritime creation might neutralize negative press coverage generated by the St. James's destruction. Thus the entrepreneur agreed to contribute £500, then the equivalent of $1,400,[16] to the project, saying, "It's not much, but it is a start," suggesting there could be more. The sum was pocket change to him and a fraction of the iconic theater's value—a paltry investment that could deliver an enormous return as a public relations buffer in the event his plans generated a national outcry. In effect, *Mayflower II* was an insurance policy that would allow him to claim involvement in a noble enterprise. It was definitely worth a shot. The donation from a wealthy individual was just the kind of support Charlton had been seeking. He later described the prime investor as "a small, bearded man with powerful shoulders in his early forties. He struck me at once as a younger version of Ernest Hemingway." Fenston was "a connoisseur of the arts, yachtsman, a big-game hunter, classical pianist, 'a jolly good chap,'" and would become "one of the important names in the story of the second *Mayflower*."[17]

Within months, Warwick formally established Project Mayflower Ltd. with John Lowe, his business partner in the public relations firm Lowe, Charlton and Associates. Both were excited about creating their own escapade to lift British spirits. Unlike Charlton, who could be boisterous and flamboyant, Lowe was low key, circumspect, and stood six-foot-five. Warwick was a mere six-two. Instead of knowing media men and the publishing arts, Lowe understood the British power structure and upper class.

Lowe had graduated from Cambridge University with a double first—the equivalent of achieving summa cum laude at Harvard or Yale in two separate majors. It was a signal accomplishment that left

Figure 5. The St. James's Theatre, facing destruction while *Mayflower II* sought creation. *(Look and Learn/Peter Jackson Collection)*

no doubt about his intellectual prowess. During the war, he worked at Britain's top-secret Code and Cypher School at Bletchley Park, where Germany's Enigma Code was broken. Afterward, he was a member of the European League for Economic Cooperation and served as secretary to a committee of the House of Lords. Lowe's work with these groups gave him credentials earned through hard work, intelligence, and trust. While this postwar background was generally known, his secret service was not discussed.

The two were Project Mayflower's sole shareholders, and they never lost sight of the principles expressed in their venture's Articles of Association:[18]

> a. To raise any sum required, by public or private subscription, in order to build, equip, and maintain a replica of the *Mayflower*.
> b. To sail the ship across the Atlantic and present her to the people of the United States.

   c. To promote, support and encourage Anglo-American relations in any form whatsoever, and to remind English-speaking peoples of their common heritage.

   Nothing herein shall be construed as giving the right to the Company to carry on any of its primary objectives for the purpose of profit and that it is a fundamental part of the construction of the company.

In short, the replica was to be built for the general good and not personal gain. Accountants would describe Project Mayflower as a nonprofit enterprise. Political pundits, on the other hand, might call it a nongovernmental organization whose purpose was to strengthen the "special relationship" Churchill had described in his "Iron Curtain" speech.

Figure 6. John Lowe and Warwick Charlton. (© *British Pathé*)

Chapter 3

Scoop

Unbeknownst to Charlton and Lowe as they composed their Articles of Association and dedicated their energies to Project May-flower, someone in New England had the same idea. His name was Harry Hornblower.[1] Unlike the British duo, he was not scrounging for money because his family had plenty of it. They had been in the securities business since 1888 when his grandfather founded Hornblower & Weeks, which by the 1950s was one of Wall Street's top financial houses. Harry and his father both knew he would join the family business after graduating from Harvard, and they also understood that the scion had an outside interest that would fill his nonwork hours: archaeology. Since adolescence, Harry was drawn to stories of colonial America and tales of life along the shores of Cape Cod Bay, particularly those told via the discovery of ancient artifacts hidden underground. The primary focus of his time away from the financial world would not be yachting, golfing, and partying but rather exploring Pilgrim history. And he had a plan.

Harry envisioned an outdoor museum that would be innovative in its approach to teaching archaeology and history. When tourists walked through its gates, they would step back in time to 1627. Well-trained docents dressed in Pilgrim costumes would introduce themselves to guests and provide them with topical information and demonstrations of life in colonial times, using the same format other outdoor museums were successfully deploying.

As a boy, Harry read about living history parks being built across the country by affluent families like his. These included Colonial

Williamsburg in Virginia (funded by the Rockefellers and opened in 1926); Greenfield Village in Dearborn, Michigan (backed by the Fords and opened in 1933); and Old Sturbridge Village in western Massachusetts, which had been in the works since 1936 (supported by the Wells family, owners of the American Optical Corporation). The Commonwealth of Massachusetts even got into the act in 1930 when it built Pioneer Village in Salem to celebrate the state's three hundredth anniversary. Why not emulate those attractions and build his own? Although Harry did not think that he was a *Mayflower* descendant—his genealogical connection to Stephen Hopkins would not be discovered until 2014[2]—what he later described as "my teen-age dream" began to take shape.[3]

But where should it be built? One idea was to raze Leyden Street in downtown Plymouth to build it there, but the land area available was not large enough. Another thought was to build it on the south side of the Eel River on land that the Hornblower family owned and that would eventually become the site of the Plymouth Country Club. Then in 1955 Hattie Hornblower died and bequeathed her estate to her grandson Harry's dream. It was perfect for Plimoth Plantation, consisting of 130 acres of land she owned near Plymouth Harbor with its "beautiful natural planting" that included azaleas, rhododendrons, and "garden paths wind[ing] down over a hillside to the Eel River."[4] The site of those flowing waters also serendipitously matched the settlement's original location on a hillside north of the stream. A "sprawling summer estate . . . with sea view and English garden and Rolls Royces," it had a chief gardener named Jesse Brewer, who would become a contributor to the bulletin of the Massachusetts Archaeological Society, and who sparked Harry Hornblower's youthful curiosity.[5] As a high school student at Milton Academy, "Harry wrote about his desire to create a new England Native American museum" and the noted scholar "Samuel [Eliot] Morison encouraged him to take up historical archaeology." Milton was followed by a "finishing year" at Phillips Academy.[6] At Harvard he was taught by Professor John Otis Brew, the director of the Peabody Museum and widely known as one of the foremost archaeologists of North American Indian civilizations.

Harry loved "arrowheading," which involved the exploration of fields and overgrown hillsides in search of "odd-shaped rocks" that were in fact arrowheads, "remnants of 7000 years of native American life before the Pilgrims." His orderly young mind prompted him to create notebooks that recorded where the stones were found, their depth below the surface soil, and careful drawings that detailed shape and dimensions. When scholars rediscovered them decades later, Douglas George, a professional archaeologist, described Harry's original writings as "very important in terms of showing the distribution of the Indian population" in the region because "many sites represented in the collection no longer exist." In fact, carbon-14 dating showed that some of Hornblower's finds range "from about 5000 BC to 1675 AD."[7]

When this interest—let's call it motive—was added to his family's means, a clear opportunity for an act of archaeological and historical passion presented itself. Conveniently, his grandmother's property was just a few miles from Plymouth Rock. The family estate would be perfect. Bradford's book would then be honored, as the outdoor museum would be named Plimoth Plantation.

Now all Harry had to do was convince his dad to fund the idea. Ralph obliged in 1945 by giving $20,000 to Plymouth's Pilgrim Society, a group of men who might or might not be able to trace their lineage back to the first Thanksgiving. It was fourteen times the seed money Fenston would contribute to Charlton. As for the Society, it was led by a descendant of *Mayflower* passenger William Brewster, Ellis Brewster, who liked the idea of erecting "a Pilgrim and Indian Village . . . where Indian relics might be displayed" and had no objection to the requirement that "some kind of an appropriate 'trading post' should be provided where handicrafts, pictures and other suitable things, especially with a Plymouth flavor could be sold" to earn money for operations once the start-up funds ran out. Unfortunately, the effort proved to be a much bigger challenge than the men expected, so the trustees of the Society created an independent corporation in 1947 to take over and support young Hornblower's dream of building a "memorial to the . . . influence of the Pilgrim Fathers throughout the world."[8]

Figure 7. Ralph Hornblower (left) and Harry Hornblower, with portrait of Henry Hornblower, founder of Hornblower & Weeks. *(Courtesy Hornblower & Company)*

"First House" was built near the harbor two years later and opened to the public in May 1949. It was a small wooden building that let people see how the colonists might have lived in 1627, which was when most of them were free from charges incurred getting to the New World. Until then, virtually everything produced was pledged as repayment for the 1620 transit. Debtor colonists were not allowed to work for themselves or own the houses they might build. The dwelling was thus an example of what life might have been like for the Pilgrims after being released from travel debts.

More than three hundred thousand people visited the exhibit that year, and by 1951 the "reproduction of an early Pilgrim house near Plymouth Rock" attracted more than six hundred thousand.[9] Harry's backers considered this volume a confirmation of public interest in early seventeenth-century history. Within two years, however, it dawned on them that the true attraction was the grand Doric portico that stood above the place where tradition had William Bradford and the *Mayflower* Pilgrims stepping ashore for the first time. The dramatic structure allowed visitors to have a panoramic view of the harbor and gaze down upon the town's famous rock. Erected in 1921 by the National Society of the Colonial Dames of America,[10] to commemorate the three hundredth anniversary of the Pilgrims' landing, it was now one of the state's most popular tourist attractions. People were not traipsing out of their way to see a small rustic abode, they were coming to see the Rock.

Additionally, the oldest public museum in America, Pilgrim Hall, was just a few blocks away. Built in 1824, it housed an unmatched collection of Pilgrim possessions and historical artifacts,[11] including a beautiful model of the 1620 *Mayflower* that was sixty inches long, forty-five inches high, and thirteen inches wide. Its creator, Dr. Roger Charles Anderson

Figure 8. Dr. R. C. Anderson's 1926 *Mayflower* model. *(Courtesy Pilgrim Hall Museum)*

of England's Greenwich Museum, described his work in 1926: "The model is now in the Hall of the Pilgrim Society at Plymouth, Massachusetts. It was ordered in their name by their late President, Mr Arthur Lord. Unfortunately he did not live to see it finished and delivered, but died quite suddenly about two months before the model reached Plymouth. I shall always be grateful to him for the confidence he showed in giving me an entirely free hand to produce the best model I could and I can only hope that the result is not unworthy of his trust."[12]

Those were the proven stars. When Harry's museum eventually relocated to the Hornblower estate a few miles from town, it would need its own tourist magnet, perhaps a life-size replica of the *Mayflower*. Why not build one? It could take advantage of the existing entertainment offerings, and it would not require a land-based concession. It would sit in the water. The idea had merit and would allow Harry to crash the party, so to speak. On top of that, he had access to the financial resources to make it happen.

Across the Atlantic, challenge and convention never deterred Warwick Charlton, nor did repeated rejection. Although conceding "I had no knowledge of sailing or of the sea except what I had read,"[13] he continued to press forward, making self-education a top priority. His first stop was the Society for Nautical Research, which was instrumental in the founding of the National Maritime Museum in the London borough of Greenwich. He knew exactly who he was looking for: its president, Dr. R. C. Anderson. The scholar wholeheartedly welcomed Charlton and took the ex-soldier under his wing, acting as a mentor and teacher. A regular reader of the premier maritime journal *American Neptune*, Anderson noticed two articles published in January and October 1954 about the efforts of a New England group to build a life-size reproduction of the Pilgrim craft. Their author, a renowned naval architect, described the careful research and detailed drawings he had produced.[14] Because the effort sounded similar to what Charlton wanted to do, Anderson gave his student the name of someone to contact in Massachusetts. They just might be interested in his Project Mayflower idea.

When Arthur Pyle, Plimoth Plantation's first employee, received a phone call from England out of the blue, asking if his organization would be interested in an oceangoing replica that a London team was planning to build, he was shocked. Because the call came via Anderson, he certainly wanted to know more, and a meeting was arranged. Charlton sent his polished, well-tailored, thoroughly British partner John Lowe to meet with the Americans, and if their interest was confirmed, Lowe was to ask them for assistance in securing a home for the duo's tribute. The best outcome would be for the museum to offer residence.

Those initial discussions may have been unexpectedly aided by Harry and John's clandestine service during the war, which neither man described publicly. While Lowe hunkered down at Bletchley Park, Hornblower served in the US Army's cloak-and-dagger branch—the Office of Strategic Services. After finishing basic training at Fort Belvoir, Virginia, he was initially assigned to Washington and "then went overseas" to "England, France and Germany."[15] In Europe, he would have interacted with other intelligence men, including those in His Majesty's service, as the war came to an end and a new era on the continent began. He was discharged as a first lieutenant, and his secret branch soon evolved into the Central Intelligence Agency. John's unit operated under British Military Intelligence, Section 6, commonly referred to as MI6. When Plimoth Plantation's founder and Project Mayflower's cofounder realized they shared a common, yet unusual, wartime history, that background gave the two strangers something in common, and perhaps an unspoken bond.

Lowe discovered that in the spring of 1951, the Plantation's governors had hired the naval architect William A. Baker to prepare plans and specifications for a second *Mayflower* in his free time, when not designing modern cargo ships, passenger liners, and tankers for the maritime division of the Bethlehem Steel Company.[16] After graduating from the Massachusetts Institute of Technology in 1934, Baker had joined the shipbuilders as the world prepared for war. When the global conflict entered its final phase, he was transferred from their Quincy, Massachusetts, operation to San Francisco. There he was assigned to work on the restoration of the 1872 Norwegian sloop *Gjøa*, as a consultant. *Gjøa* had earned international acclaim as the first ship to navigate the legendary sea route between the Pacific and Atlantic through the Arctic Ocean, the Northwest Passage.[17] That shortcut had been sought since the time of Sir

Francis Drake but wasn't successfully navigated until 1906, when explorer Roald Amundsen finally did it. The single-masted seventy-foot craft was then donated to the Golden Gate city. Baker was enthralled with the assignment, carefully documented every step of the 1947–1949 undertaking, and published his findings in *American Neptune*.

With the completion of that work, Baker was transferred back east and resumed engineering new hull designs for the shipbuilders. In the evenings and on weekends, however, his mind stayed in the past, focused on ancient vessels. When he was approached by Plimoth Plantation and asked if he would be interested in producing plans for a full-scale reproduction of the Pilgrim ship *Mayflower*, his answer was an enthusiastic yes. Designing the ship, he later wrote, "was for me a form of 'busman's holiday.' My vocation involves the designing of modern cargo ships . . . [but] as an avocation, I have for many years studied all manner of things concerning old ships."[18]

The museum's initial charge was to design a vessel that would float but not necessarily sail because the crooked channel of Plymouth Harbor could not accommodate a seventeenth-century ship. Unfortunately, getting large numbers of tourists from shore to an anchored ship and back made this plan impractical, and public safety issues had to be considered in the event of major storms or hurricanes such as Carol and Edna in 1954. Design thus shifted to building a "concrete foundation at a convenient waterfront location." A "dry-land ship" would then be created with the exterior shape of the Pilgrim craft. Walt Disney did such a thing in 1955 when the full-size Chicken of the Sea Pirate Ship and Restaurant began entertaining visitors and telling the Peter Pan story at his amusement park in Anaheim, California.[19] Harry's boat would likewise be a "place of public assembly" and satisfy the museum's desire to have a large artifact available for retelling the Pilgrims' tale.

Baker's first challenge was finding reliable source materials because the current standard was William Bradford's *Of Plimoth Plantation*, which was written about ten years after the voyage and only mentioned the vessel's size, 180 tons of burden. Bradford didn't even give the ship a name. That bit of information came from other colonial records around 1623 that said the English colonists "came first over in the

May-Flower."[20] Taking that snippet, Baker soon discovered that there were about twenty ships named *Mayflower* in the early seventeenth century. Which one was his? He researched ancient records from the London Port Books and found a merchant ship captained by Christopher Jones listed from 1609 to 1621, with a gap corresponding to the 1620 crossing. The last mention of the vessel appeared in the High Court of the Admiralty when her owners petitioned to have her declared "in ruins" in 1624 so they could be compensated by having the remnants sold.

Identifying what appeared to be the ship he was seeking, Baker then focused on her size and shape. Could he accurately determine dimensions based on water displacement? The answer was yes. Thanks to a 1582 formula developed during the reign of Queen Elizabeth I, a ship's weight could be calculated using its keel length, hull breadth, and below-water reach. Working backward, Baker reasonably concluded that the original *Mayflower* most likely had a keel length of fifty-eight feet, a breadth of twenty-five feet, and a depth of twelve feet six inches.[21] But what did she actually look like?

A year into the assignment, Baker traveled to Europe with his wife to visit maritime museums in London, Paris, Amsterdam, and Stockholm so he could meet with experts in seventeenth-century ship design for insights and guidance. To determine exterior framing from centuries earlier, he studied the skeletal remains of twenty-five seventeenth-century ships that were wrecked in Kalmar Harbor, Sweden, in the manner a paleontologist might look at dinosaur bones to determine the creature's shape.[22] Then a circa-1586 manuscript titled "Fragments of Ancient Shipwrightry" was uncovered in Cambridge University's Magdalene College Library and attributed to one of Queen Elizabeth's master shipbuilders, Mathew Baker (unrelated to the current architect). The notebook, which would have been compiled over several decades, provided the basic data for *Mayflower II*'s design.[23] With these foundations, the Steel man moved forward with his vision of the historic ship.

When the architect submitted his completed construction guide to Plimoth Plantation, he knew it was capable of producing much more than the stationary harborside attraction being contemplated. How would they react? Harry and his directors liked what they saw, but before spending any money to realize the plans that they had commissioned for $2,400 and now owned,[24] a cost-benefit analysis was performed to determine the scope of work and to gauge financing costs. One quotation put the price at $800,000,[25] which the museum directors dismissed as outrageous. That alone might have made them reluctant to move forward. But another reason may have been the initiative's complexity. After opening First House, it had taken four years to build a second structure, and then another two years for a third. This record suggested that project management skill may have also played a part in the museum's indecision. If the nascent enterprise had been challenged by these three small units, erecting a complex transatlantic sailing ship would likely have seemed out of the question, which could explain their continued focus on building a Disneylandish replica that would simply be a tourist attraction. Baker may well have understood their reluctance to do more, but disappointment was probably the best word to describe his feelings as he contemplated the dust his wonderful design would collect sitting in a library archive.

Then "fate intervened in the shape of 'Project Mayflower Ltd.'" via telephone from England.[26] It was unexpected good fortune for both Harry and Baker, who later wrote, "In return for the use of [my] plans, the English group . . . proposed to [build, sail, and then] present the ship to the American people."[27] It was a win for everyone, and negotiations began at once to work out the arrangements.

After months of discussion and bargaining that ran from fall into spring, the British and American groups felt comfortable with each other yet could not agree on next steps. It occurred to Charlton back in London that a third-party news story about the Englishmen's plans might add a sense of urgency to the talks. So he decided to give the Reuters news service a scoop. The result was an article that appeared in the *New York Times* under the headline "New *Mayflower* to Sail with Goodwill for U.S." It said a team in England was building a square-rigged ship that would "foster better British–United States relations and provide scholarship funds for American students in Britain." The keel was to "be laid in a British shipyard later this year," with a target departure date of September 1956. Supporters of the project reportedly included "leading

British members of Parliament, prominent British business leaders, and United States Ambassador Winthrop W. Aldrich, himself a descendent of the original *Mayflower* voyagers." The writer said that the "180-ton craft" would cost "more than $300,000" and added: "Most of the money already has been pledged."[28] The story also ran in multiple English newspapers the next day and emphasized the Atlantic bond, Anglo-American scholarships, and the fact that, of the project's estimated cost, "most of the $308,000 has been promised."[29]

The strategy definitely got the negotiators' attention, and within weeks an agreement was reached. In exchange for the UK enterprise financing, building, and sailing a second *Mayflower* to America, the Plymouth nonprofit would provide ongoing housing, maintenance, and exhibition. As an additional incentive, Plimoth Plantation contributed Baker's plans and promised his advice during construction. Relieved of any financial obligation and assured that it would receive the tourist attraction it sought at no cost, the museum shut down its own efforts. The architect later wrote: "It is difficult to believe that in the mid-twentieth century there would be any group seriously interested in re-creating a full-size seventeenth century ship. That there should be two such groups with the same ship in mind is almost inconceivable—this is the fairy tale part of the project."[30]

As for the actual status of the Britishers' efforts, no significant money had been raised, nor had a shipyard been chosen. Charlton and Lowe had a huge task ahead, but their undertaking was now public on both sides of the Atlantic, and they hoped it would generate interest in the endeavor, along with free-will contributions. While the Englishmen would not have described themselves as the underdogs, they most certainly were, because the group with direct access to the financial pipelines that fueled America's economic engines, Wall Street, had just unloaded a daunting undertaking and its accompanying funding burden onto a group led by a man who until recent years didn't even have a bank account.[31] On top of that, Hornblower already had a backup plan in case Project Mayflower failed: he would simply build an amusement park–style boat for tourists to visit. His bet was covered.

Before his return to England, a photograph was taken of Lowe with Hornblower and Baker, plus others, looking at a model of the ship the naval architect had made, and the *Illustrated London News* published it on April 16, 1955.[32] In a remarkable juxtaposition of nautical antiquity with modern instruments of war, other articles on the same page of the weekly newspaper included reports that USS *Nautilus*, America's first atomic-powered submarine, had completed sea trials, and that Britain's crescent-winged Victor bomber was capable of "very high sub-sonic speeds at a height of nearly ten miles."

Although the war had ended ten years earlier, readers were still drawn to stories about conflict and the instruments of battle. The *Mayflower* news fit nicely into that narrative because the original ship's departure point, Plymouth, had a long history of being vital to Britain's national defense. Early in World War II, before America's entry, the Nazis brutally bombed the city for five terrifying nights, leaving the harbor and its town in ruins. As a result, many of His Majesty's soldiers and warships were sent off to fight from smaller ports around the country, and one of them was a southern harbor in Devonshire named Brixham. The village itself sat high above the water and could be reached by steep roads that led up from the dock areas, where fishing and construction provided employment for generations of residents. One of the most respected local firms was J. W. & A. Upham Ltd. Its craftsmen had been building wooden ships for nearly two hundred years, with records showing that their first vessels were fruiters—fast boats of about 150 tons that had a foremast, a mainmast, and a small trysail—designed to bring oranges, lemons, and other delights to England from the Mediterranean. When duty called, however, they could quickly be converted into warships. That pedigree came to the fore a dozen years earlier when the yard made thirty-five wooden minesweepers and motor torpedo boats, all more than one hundred feet long.[33] The name Upham was well known to the Admiralty. Given that history, it was not surprising when the wife of the current generation's leader, Stuart Upham, brought the photo to his attention immediately upon reading the newsweekly.

"When, by chance, I saw the model in an illustrated paper and read of the proposal to build and sail her to America," Upham wrote later, "I

Figure 9. *Mayflower II* model pictured in the *Illustrated London News*, left to right: William Brewster, Harry Hornblower, Mrs. A. E. Saunders, William Baker, and John Lowe. *(© Illustrated London News Ltd./Mary Evans Picture Library)*

could not resist the temptation to offer my services."[34] Within days he was welcoming Warwick Charlton to Brixham and giving him a tour of his family's shipyard. No one in the United Kingdom was more experienced or better qualified to take on the project than Stuart Upham, but the task would not be easy. While his craftsmen were accustomed to working with timber in the age of steel, this assignment was unique. "There's a mighty difference between planning a model and building a galleon that's going to sail the Atlantic, that's got to steer and be stable and handle well, and that men can live in." Stuart did not want anyone to forget that "it's been 300 years since ships like this were laid down and fitted out along this coast."[35]

So what was going to be the biggest challenge? John Lowe had told Warwick that Harry's group thought it would be getting enough oak timber. That task might take two years. "No, that won't be the problem. It's the men," Upham responded. He needed to assemble a crew of workers for building, just as the ship's future captain would have to do for sailing. "But we have got a nucleus of them. They are old ones, but they are the ones with the craft and they will teach the others."[36] For example, sixty-two-year-old sailmaker Harold Bridge knew men in their eighties who had taught him those unique skills and could give him advice on teaching a new generation, should one want to step forward, and it did. Similarly, chief rigger Bill Gregory had a younger man, Jim Gempton, who would help him rig the ship when the time came. Meanwhile, ship's carpenter Edgar Mugridge would be able to train and lead younger men in the major task of shaping the wood. Those three were in effect Stuart Upham's first mates. He knew they could do the job and manage a ship-yard workforce that might swell to thirty men, including those needed to run a small foundry and blacksmith shop for casting and shaping the iron fasteners that would be needed to secure the lines and rigging. But there were practical matters to be resolved. Where was the money coming from? Who would be willing to insure the ship? Upham could build her, but Charlton needed to indemnify the product and provide financing.

The builder's first task was getting the lumber. The yard needed tons of it, and Stuart knew where to look: Wistman's Wood on Dartmoor, the forbidding forested country that Sir Arthur Conan Doyle used as the setting for his Sherlock Holmes novel *The Hound of the Baskervilles*. The story was inspired by local tales of a supernatural, murderous beast that lived among the region's moss-covered boulders and ancient twisted oaks, which could rouse the imagination and strike fear in the hearts of lost hikers. Indeed, the 1939 MGM motion picture starring Basil Rathbone as Holmes was prefaced with a warning to viewers: "In all England there is no district more dismal than that vast expanse of primitive wasteland, the moors of Dartmoor in Devonshire."[37] Stuart Upham, however, was not afraid.

The west branch of the River Dart ran through the wood, eventually emptying into Dartmouth Bay on the Devon coast just a few miles south of Brixham. Arborists loved the region's beautifully contorted great oaks, so the shipbuilder wisely decided to undertake his exploration under cover of night to avoid conflicts with local naturalists. It was reported that a particular stand of distinctive, sturdy oaks vanished about the same time a large supply of wood appeared in his shipyard. No comment from

Upham. Those moss-covered, heather-entwined prizes had all grown in every shape except straight, and many were "crooked as a donkey's hind leg,"[38] which was perfect for the task ahead because every major piece save the masts was curved. Thus a tree with multiple large, twisted limbs was ideal. Crotches could be hewn into V-shaped and L-shaped pieces used for structural support belowdecks, and long curving branches were destined to become ribs for the giant sea creature that would soon rise along the shore.

All wood was cut and shaped using tools and skills from centuries past because the journalist-turned-promoter had convinced the yard chief that the replica had to be as historically accurate as possible—right down to the axes, hammers, and saws, plus dozens of other shipwright instruments. "I got so involved in it," Charlton noted, "that I would say to people, 'Bradford wouldn't have liked that,' as if he was around the corner. The minute you start changing, it devalues what we are doing."[39] Exceptions were made, however. The saw pit method of cutting timber, where one man would stand above a massive tree trunk holding one end of a long saw blade while the other was in an open pit below pulling and pushing, was replaced with a power saw. That modern device was also employed to create decking. Similarly, thousands of nail holes were bored with an electric drill because, as architect Baker observed with a smile, "the use of hand augers can be very boring in hard oak."[40]

The shape of each piece to be created was outlined in French chalk on a huge loft floor painted black to make a giant blackboard, and then patterns were cut or molds crafted for the woodcutters to replicate. It was the same approach a dressmaker might take when cutting pieces of cloth before stitching them all together. From high above, it looked like a huge jigsaw puzzle that would eventually be assembled to create a ship, not a picture but the real thing.

In the matter of insurance, the venerable Lloyd's of London provided coverage, credibility, and historical gravitas when it underwrote the ship the following June. The group had been founded by Edward Lloyd at his coffeehouse in the City of London sometime around 1686, when he provided coverage for merchant craft trading in the Far East. His angle on the insurance game was having multiple independent groups self-organize into syndicates to spread the risk, which proved quite successful and earned Lloyd's a name as an up-and-comer in the business of underwriting. News of his operation soon spread, and shippers engaged in the slave trade were drawn to the company. Like its competitors, Lloyd's of London insured the vessel and its cargo, but it wrote policies in a manner that equated humans with livestock—perishable items that would not receive a payout if the transporter sank. Only the boat and hard goods were covered. Eventually such methods helped Lloyd's capture nearly 90 percent of the maritime insurance market between England, Africa, and colonial America. The group benefited from these practices until President Lincoln abolished slavery, after which it sought alternative sources of revenue. In the shadow of this disgraceful chapter in the company's history, Lloyd's was glad for the opportunity to join in the noble enterprise of insuring *Mayflower II*.

The Brixham builder had specifically asked Charlton about insurance when they met, and Upham was relieved to see £80,000 ($224,000) in coverage provided by a special syndicate. Not to be left out, the New York–based Insurance Company of North America provided an additional token policy of $5,000.[41] For both groups, Upham's pledge to be on board during the Plymouth-to-Plymouth transit was reassuring because it would allow him to keep track of every leak and squeak during the voyage.

Ancient penmanship was then used to write the policies on parchment reminiscent of the seventeenth century. Lloyd's policies for the *Tiger* (1613–1614), the *Three Brothers* (1656–1657), and the *Golden Fleece* (1680–1681) were used as guides for wording. In the United States, archivists found the policy for the *Experiment*, a two-masted square-rigger requiring coverage for trips between Philadelphia, Havana, and New Orleans, for North America to emulate.[42] The period-accurate policies were further examples of the meticulous detail and historical accuracy that Project Mayflower demanded in every aspect of the replica's creation.

CHAPTER 4

Ties That Bind

WARWICK CHARLTON WAS A MARKETING AND PROMOTION MAESTRO. His power play back in March 1955, prior to solidifying a partnership with Hornblower, proved that. When those transatlantic talks stalled, the story Warwick took to the press about a second *Mayflower* was irresistible. That report, as he hoped, pushed the Lowe–Hornblower negotiations across the finish line. But it was pure serendipity that it also resulted in Stuart Upham stepping forward on behalf of his Brixham shipyard. Three months after taking on the assignment, the builder was ready to lay the keel, the vessel's spine, and the promoter in Charlton wanted to make it a newsworthy event. Based on the results of his previous effort, he felt confident that fresh reporting would produce positive results.

The ceremony took place on July 28, 1955, in a roofed, open-air work area with views of Brixham Harbor and neighboring boats that provided many local residents with a source of income. Two giant wooden beams measuring fifty-eight feet each had been carved by hand from ancient Devon oaks. Both had sharp ninety-degree edges and measured twelve by fourteen inches.[1] One end of each beam turned upward, making the pair look like giant snow skis or sled rails. The opposite ends were shaped to create overlapping scarfing that allowed them to be fitted together and fastened with iron bolts, driven in place by a hand-held hammer. When unified, the individual segments created a single giant keel. Perched on wooden sawhorses facing the harbor, the backbone infused the air with anticipation and thoughts of the future. "We had now laid the foundations of *Mayflower II*," Upham later wrote, "and it was heartwarming to see the old crafts resurrected and old tools dusted and re-sharpened for the task ahead."[2] Suspended above were large British and American flags, joined at their flying ends in symbolic unification. Young women dressed in Pilgrim costumes stood among the guests to provide theatricality, as the choir of Brixham's All Saints Church sang hymns and national anthems.[3] Among those in the congregation was William Baker, who made sure he did not miss the birth of his nautical creation. Clearly elated to see his designs coming to life through Project Mayflower, he congratulated Charlton by telling him, on reaching this milestone, "I feel sure that you are the right man to build her."[4]

Lieutenant Commander Douglas Kenelm Winslow, Royal Navy (Ret.), was the guest of honor and officially commenced construction of the replica when he hammered the first nail into place, as guests and the news media looked on. His ancestor Edward Winslow was not only a passenger and first Thanksgiving witness, but he also saved the *Mayflower* when its main beam cracked during a storm. William Bradford in *Of Plimoth Plantation* said a "great iron screw" was used successfully to lift and straighten the cracked timber.[5] A legend subsequently grew saying, "it was part of the dismembered printing-press from Leyden" that Winslow brought with him to the New World. If true, Kenelm's ancient relative "deserved a vote of thanks. It might equally well have been brought for a wine-press or some similar purpose, but there it was." Whatever "the workings of Providence," that ancient equivalent of the modern device used to lift a car when changing a flat tire saved the ship and all on board.[6]

US ambassador Winthrop Aldrich was extended an invitation but was unable to attend, as was Harry Hornblower, who sent a congratulatory telegram that was read to those gathered. At the very mention of his name "a pleasant ripple of chuckles spread through the assembled crowd."[7] Spontaneous, yes, but no disrespect intended, because a famous high seas adventurer shared the same last name, fictional hero Horatio Hornblower. It was he who came to mind before a wealthy museum man in need of a boat.

Activities that day were reported in newspapers on both sides of the Atlantic, and Pathé Television sent a camera crew to produce a newsreel

Figure 10. The keel-laying ceremony of *Mayflower II*. (© *Illustrated London News Ltd./Mary Evans Picture Library*)

episode titled "Britain Starts Building a New 'Mayflower,'"[8] which ran on the BBC and in English theaters. The *Illustrated London News* again provided special coverage and ran a story about the event with a photo captioned: "The Laying of the Keel of Mayflower II: The Start of the Construction of a Replica of the Original Ship, in which the Pilgrim Fathers Sailed."[9] In the United States, the *New York Times* published a lengthy story under the headline "New Mayflower Is Begun in England,"[10] with the image of a painting titled *The Mayflower at Sea*. It described the project as ambitious, "the brainchild of two London public relations men, John Lowe and Warwick Charlton." The paper noted that the replica's crew and passengers would be dressed in period costumes and that navigation would be done without modern instruments, relying instead on what was available to the original voyagers. The article was upbeat and said the estimated construction cost was $280,000, with funding coming from England. It was exactly the kind of free publicity the journalist sought, and he was sure it would stimulate interest.

Charlton's instincts were spot-on. Just as the bugle call for a great British adventure that promised to conquer the world's tallest mountain, Mount Everest, had been heard by a New Zealander climber named Edmund Hillary several years earlier, this time the cry was answered by a man with an unquenchable thirst for the open seas. Reading press reports of the high-profile voyage was *National Geographic Magazine*'s president and editor Dr. Melville Grosvenor. Grosvenor thought the project sounded fascinating and addressed a personal letter to someone he knew would also be captivated, the Australian sea captain Alan Villiers: "No doubt you have read in the papers over there about the building of a new *Mayflower* at Brixham, and the plan for sailing it across to America. . . . Would you size up the project for us and let us know if you'd be interested in covering it for *National Geographic?*"

The deepwater mariner, who had thrilled readers with his exploits from aboard the windjammers *Eagle* and *Joseph Conrad*, quickly responded: "I think the Mayflower project would be a good piece for The Magazine. I had better go down to Brixham and look over the setup on the spot. I hope they realize that it is a difficult thing to sail that ship across in this day and age."[11]

The captain set out immediately to learn more about what promised to be the top high seas challenge of the decade, and perhaps the century. He introduced himself to Warwick Charlton and quickly discovered what was driving the Englishman. Warwick told him about his wartime experience and his desire to thank America with a new expression of gratitude. The French, he said, had created and delivered the Statue of Liberty, but what about the Brits? He wondered what could be done to honor their common heritage. "Then I hit upon an idea that was really worth while. The *Mayflower*, of course! I knew nothing whatever about ships, but I did know the Pilgrims' story. And what an inspiration that is! I'll build a new *Mayflower*, I thought. Not a model—the actual ship."[12]

As they kept talking, the sailor soon found the Englishman's enthusiasm infectious, and he concluded that Project Mayflower was well organized and legitimate. So he had to ask: "Who's going to sail the ship across for you?"[13]

It was not the first time the query had been made, and Charlton's mentor at the Maritime Museum in Greenwich, Dr. R. C. Anderson, had been advising him on suitable candidates for the job. "As a matter of fact, we were thinking of you," was Charlton's quick reply, and the deal was done on the spot.

A few days later, while America celebrated Thanksgiving, Villiers penned a short message to Grosvenor on November 24: "I went down to Brixham and looked over the Mayflower. They want me to be captain of the ship!" *National Geographic*'s role in Warwick's drama was thus cemented as "a great sailor became the captain of a great adventure,"[14] and the famous magazine's handpicked writer would soon be holding a pen in one hand and the ship's wheel in the other. It was a journalistic coup of the first order.

Villiers immediately started thinking about a crew, which could prove a challenge because the men had to be British, in compliance with regulations. But he had organized just such a group several years earlier when Hollywood director John Huston hired him to captain the whaler *Pequod* in the Irish Sea during his filming of *Moby Dick*, starring Gregory Peck and Orson Welles. The Aussie had stayed in contact with those sailors and quickly began organizing his team.

In addition to having strong nautical credentials, Villiers was a prolific writer. His first book, *Whaling in the Frozen South*, was published in 1925, and by the time Project Mayflower hired him in 1955, twenty-six more had been penned. In the two years needed to complete construction of the replica, four more of his books were published by major houses. That energy was not lost on *National Geographic*. Once Villiers was confirmed as the voyage's leader, the magazine immediately put him under contract to write two exclusive accounts that would become instant classics: "We're Coming Over on the *Mayflower*" and "How We Sailed the New *Mayflower* to America."

The legend's presence at the helm guaranteed global interest in the quest because of the powerful media groups that profited from the captain's creativity and sold his stories to eager readers worldwide. Editors at the *New York Times* knew their subscribers would also be hooked. To give them a preview and tease the story, news of Villiers's selection was carefully placed the day after the 1955 Macy's Thanksgiving Day Parade, which had thrilled millions. Photos of its famous balloons and celebrating crowds were published adjacent to an image of the Aussie.[15] The editors wanted to be sure the public saw the announcement of the *Mayflower II*'s master—who himself was about to be woven into an important storyline that would sell papers in the months ahead:

> The directors of the Mayflower Project announced today that they had selected the man who would captain the copy of the Pilgrim fathers' ship when it crosses the Atlantic Ocean next year.
>
> He is Cmdr. Alan Villiers, a 52-year-old sailor, yachtsman and author from Australia. In 1934 Commander Villiers bought the famous sailing ship *Joseph Conrad* and sailed it around the world.
>
> The copy of the *Mayflower* is under construction at Brixham, Devon. The 183-ton ship will sail across the Atlantic as a goodwill gift to the American people. Her departure date is tentatively set for Independence Day, next year.

While Charlton later said that Villiers brought the scent of the sea with him when they first met, it was the ink under his fingernails—and the media's high esteem for him—that would put wind in the replica's sails. The project's founders, as well as *Nat Geo*'s Mel Grosvenor, fully understood the importance of words when lifting spirits or sparking imaginations. The Englishmen also knew texts could provoke anger and enflame citizens. That knowledge derived from their professional backgrounds in publishing and public relations, as well as the lessons of World War II, when Nazi propaganda and Churchill's oratory roused the peoples of countries around the globe to arms, for better or for worse. It was Charlton and Lowe's belief that education offered the best defense against tyranny and the demagogues and rabble-rousers who foment it. For that reason, they planned to use a portion of the revenues generated by their tribute to support college students. Their idea was to complement high-profile graduate school programs with Project Mayflower scholarships that targeted undergrads as they began their academic journeys. The partners were in total agreement on this, and the actions of governments on both sides of the Atlantic reaffirmed the wisdom of their thinking.

American foreign policy in the postwar years recognized that a country's ability to influence other nations was based on two broad forces: hard power and soft power. Hard power was coercive, used military might, and had been applied successfully by the Allies to achieve victory over Germany and Japan. Keeping the peace, however, required a different set of strengths and sought to avoid conflicts by persuading nation-states that their common interests outweighed their differences. To do that, perceptions of shared culture and heritage were used tactically by the United States and Britain to maintain the spirit of Churchill's "special relationship." Nationalism and my-country-first policies would be replaced with shared interests and common solutions.

US senator William Fulbright championed soft power via "cultural diplomacy" in 1945 when he introduced a bill to Congress that proposed using surplus war property to fund "the promotion of international goodwill through the exchange of students in the fields of education, culture and science."[16] The legislation was passed, became law, and created Fulbright Scholarships, the country's flagship international educational exchange program. A few years later the British Parliament mirrored that effort by passing the 1953 Marshall Aid Commemoration Act. Its Marshall Scholarships would hopefully strengthen Anglo-American ties for "the good of mankind in this turbulent world."[17]

The approach for both countries relied on music, arts, and lifestyle to increase their credibility on the world stage. Hollywood movies, for example, were used to increase the appeal of American values in postwar Europe. Likewise, the Emergency Fund for International Affairs was established specifically to promote dance, theater, and music to audiences around the globe. Jazz played a critical role during this period because it was unstructured and hopefully evoked images of free-spirited individuals, a hallmark of American youth.

The British Foreign Office and its Washington embassy discussed the use of creative expression in response to President Eisenhower's demonstrated interest in this method of building a nation's nonmilitary influence. Unfortunately, identifying artists, actors, and musicians who would be malleable to diplomatic designs was extremely difficult, and funding them could be risky if their message or political views differed from the government's. Britain had the added challenge of a stubbornly rigid social order that often held family ancestry in higher regard than an individual's talents and abilities. It should have been rendered obsolete by the changing political tides, but it lingered nonetheless. Although the English rock band the Beatles was still a decade away, the ministry started thinking about how the nation might benefit from the international success of British artists from any genre. Early in 1955 the idea of "namesake towns" was considered,[18] but it was ultimately rejected because the program's impact on the sale of British goods in America—a key success metric—would be hard to calculate. The plan could falter if the leaders of shared-name locations, such as Boston, New Haven, or Essex, had disputes regarding trade, politics, or social issues.

Soon after, unexpected news of a *Mayflower* replica being built in a small harbor in Devonshire came to the ministry's attention, and officials began contemplating how the little ship might be employed to achieve the country's cultural diplomacy goals. Any enterprise that could benefit Britannia, did not require government funding, and promised to buttress initiatives to strengthen Anglo-American ties was worth a closer look. Because Project Mayflower met those criteria, it had special appeal, but there were also concerns. While Charlton focused on promotion, securing a shipyard, and hiring a first-rate captain, his partner John Lowe concentrated on generating support among England's wealthy elite—an activity that created a conflict with British diplomats, who considered that very group essential to their own efforts to curry favor in Washington. To execute that strategy, regular meetings were held between bureaucrats and prestigious groups backed by the British aristocracy, including the English Speaking Union and the Pilgrims Society. Then came news reports of a second *Mayflower*. That unsanctioned parallel program seemed to compete with the Foreign Office.

The Pilgrims were formed in 1903 to encourage Anglo-American good fellowship, and fifteen years later the ESU was organized because "the peace of the world and the progress of mankind can be largely helped by the unity in purpose of the English-Speaking democracies." The group pledged "to promote by every means in our power a good understanding between the peoples of the USA and the British Commonwealth."[19] After four decades it was known across the globe, had substantial financial resources, and boasted twenty-two thousand members in the United States. A diplomatic initiative supported by a trifecta of the Foreign Office, the Pilgrims Society, and the ESU would have an excellent chance of delivering positive results.

In organizational contrast, Project Mayflower was merely a big idea led by two men with drive and determination. When Charlton gained widespread media exposure for his enterprise in April and July, it was only natural that officials would become interested because the undertaking focused on a seminal moment in the two nations' common history: the 1620 voyage and its Protestant passengers. No other event connected them so tightly, which lent the effort an unparalleled appeal. It had the precise optics and messaging the British government sought to promote—except that the two men behind it were not aristocratic. Despite good resumes and intentions, the duo at the helm of Project Mayflower simply did not possess the requisite social pedigree to represent Her Majesty. So while the Americans might look favorably on the effort, the ministry approached it with suspicion. In Lowe's case, he may have had access to influential people, but he was considered an outsider among them. In cruder terms, the gentry likely pigeonholed Lowe as the scholarship kid at a tony prep school, applauded during the week for his abilities (and in recognition of their own charity) but never invited to the weekend parties.

As the Foreign Office learned more about Lowe's achievements, it became increasingly agitated—particularly when officials in Whitehall (the thoroughfare that lends its name to British government in general) realized he had an agreement with a new American museum funded by a patrician Boston family named Hornblower. If anything went wrong, there might be blowback that could complicate London's strategy of cultivating the upper class. The dilemma and a possible solution were articulated in December 1955 when Foreign Office staffer R. L. Speaight wrote a memorandum noting that because the government did "not want to appear as active opponents of the Project now that it has gone so far . . . *ad hoc* warnings seem better."[20] The ESU and the Pilgrims Society were thus quietly advised that the *Mayflower* venture had limited financial support and the men behind it were questionable. In Boston, the consul-general received the same warning and shared it with Plimoth Plantation.

As a result, efforts to raise funds from wealthy Anglo-Saxons were fruitless, and it would be difficult to build the replica without such resources. The dynamic duo behind Project Mayflower might have expected powerful headwinds out at sea, but not on shore from political forces intimidated by a meager nonprofit that wanted only to thank Britain's World War II ally for her sacrifices in defending freedom and democracy. The men's good intentions were now producing unintended consequences that made their task more difficult and their Everest ever taller and increasingly steep.

CHAPTER 5

Mother of Invention

NECESSITY HAS BEEN CALLED THE MOTHER OF INVENTION, AND AS 1956 began with no money, little construction, and enormous obstacles, she was standing at the entrepreneurs' door. According to a report secretly obtained by the Foreign Office from Price Waterhouse, the venture's financial picture was bleak, with liabilities of £10,000 ($28,000) and just £3 in the bank.[1] Harry Hornblower also happened to receive an unsolicited copy of the report via an attorney for Project Mayflower's ostensible partner, Felix Fenston, who delivered it without explanation.[2] The action was likely intended to be a door opener for future opportunities the British real estate speculator might develop with an American genetically connected to the financial arteries of Wall Street. Despite his donation of £500 as *Mayflower II*'s first investor, Fenston now had little time for Warwick Charlton and a project opposed to profit making,[3] but he knew instinctively that a direct connection with Hornblower could reap benefits.

Unaware of this surreptitious activity, the Fighting Editor remained upbeat and optimistic, despite his company being essentially broke and only a single rib having been added to the ship's keel since its creation in July 1955. His positive attitude was rewarded when *Life* magazine offered to pay £1,000 in advance for the exclusive rights to photograph the ship during its Atlantic crossing, should that event ever occur.[4] If it didn't, *Life* agreed to let Project Mayflower keep the money—a gesture the entrepreneur interpreted as confirmation of the vessel's news-making potential.

As for Charlton's prediction on construction costs, it was now clear the original estimates were way off. Hornblower surely realized this, and that knowledge was probably the deciding factor when his museum planned to build a stationary waterline model instead of the real thing. Once they were offered an actual ship, it was easy to propose permanent anchorage for it, assuming the craft would ever be delivered. Harry was careful to keep Plimoth's investments low risk, particularly during its start-up. While the Englishmen still thought they could erect and deliver the replica for £100,000 ($280,000),[5] the final cost would be more than twice that, and Plimoth Plantation's only contribution thus far was the set of architectural plans it had commissioned William Baker to produce—though a grand contribution it was.

The blueprints—the result of many years' groundbreaking research—became a bible for the craftsmen at Upham's yard as they transformed tons of unhewn wood into an exacting replica of a 1620 cargo carrier. To honor its commitment, Plimoth had the architect travel to Brixham five times during construction to provide technical support. This included converting his measurements from US to English standards because the American Bureau of Shipbuilding's "Rules for Construction and Classification of Wooden Ships" had been used for the drawings based on Baker's assumption that *Mayflower II* would be built in the United States.[6] He also used seventeenth-century drafting techniques to add authenticity, just as Upham's workers were using tools from a bygone era, and this meant the plans did not have the smooth lines of modern manuals.[7] It was a sight to behold as imagination and designs were transformed into reality. The architect later praised "the work of Stuart A. Upham and all hands at the yard" for "faithfully translating my plans into a living ship—to them it was more than just a job of building another vessel,"[8] it was a labor of love.

An example of that devotion could be found in the ship's outer planking, which was fixed to the ribs with wooden pegs called treenails, or trunnels. Pounding in these slender pieces of timber, which could be as long as twenty-four inches, required skillful strokes with a mallet or maul. Each thin shaft had to be hewn from very dry and well-seasoned oak, which was a problem because all the timber in the yard was freshly

Figure 11. Stuart Upham and Warwick Charlton inspecting a model of the *Mayflower*. (© *Illustrated London News Ltd./Mary Evans Picture Library*)

cut. Treenails crafted from new wood could shrink after being driven in and cause leaks. Upham found an innovative solution when he happened upon a large cache of 120-year-old cider barrels that were no longer in use. The crafty builder realized they could be repurposed and become his treenail source. Not only was it a practical answer to a critical challenge, the casks paid indirect homage to the original *Mayflower*'s job of carrying wine for European customers.[9]

Back in the hard, temporal world of finance, it was a different story. No support was forthcoming from the British government, which watched quietly from the sidelines but did nothing to help. Charlton had no illusions in that realm and knew his venture would have to get creative if it hoped to survive. Revolutionaries are disruptive by nature, and the PR man's avant-garde approach to problem solving would make construction of the replica possible by ignoring convention. Today his methods are widely employed and regarded as essential for bringing complex undertakings to fruition. At the time, however, they were criticized as crass, commercial, and embarrassing by both the Foreign Office and transatlantic aristocrats.

The first Pilgrim ship and her progeny *Mayflower II* were built as merchant carriers using designs, materials, and craftsmanship found in the seventeenth century. In 1620 the cargo consisted of 102 individuals financed by investors eager to profit from the fur trade and other opportunities. Three centuries later, the reproduction replaced humans with freight loaded into special shipping crates called Treasure Chests. These unique boxes could trace their inspiration to Robert Louis Stevenson's 1883 adventure novel *Treasure Island*, a tale of buccaneers and buried loot. In 1950 the Walt Disney Studios produced an action movie based on the story and it became such a hit that public perceptions of pirates, sailing ships, and hidden treasure were greatly influenced. It resonated so much with Warwick Charlton that the idea of leveraging the public's imagination and having the second *Mayflower* carry sought-after items in its own Treasure Chests was irresistible.

To help execute the strategy, Warwick engaged S. J. Lethbridge Ltd., a Plymouth furniture maker located in the general vicinity of the Pilgrims' departure point near the Barbican. (The current quay and steps down to the harbor did not exist in 1620, but tradition has made this the place where passengers boarded the ship that would take them to the New World.) They discussed designs, and the head of the company offered to manufacture a few chests to get the ball rolling.[10] As anticipated demand increased, however, the need for a second builder quickly became apparent, perhaps one with a well-known name that could add credibility to the scheme. Morris of Glasgow then stepped forward.

Neil Morris, the son of the founder, had joined the company in 1938 with ambitions of transforming it into a global leader in design and craftsmanship, but his plans were interrupted by World War II. With the arrival of peace, it was back to fine furniture for well-heeled patrons. A special bedroom suite was commissioned for crown princess Elizabeth and Prince Philip, the company's iconic Cloud table won numerous design awards, and its creations went on display in New York. For Neil Morris personally, the maritime industry was an area of special interest, and his company eventually became a supplier of choice for opulent ocean liners, including those of Cunard. When Morris learned about Project Mayflower's idea, it seemed a natural fit.

The luxurious coffers produced in Scotland were designed in the manner and style of 1620 and built to be historically accurate. Accordingly, each was made of English oak and measured fifty-four inches wide, twenty-four inches deep, and thirty inches high.[11] The top was hinged so it could be lifted up to reveal the sponsor's name or logo. The front dropped forward to rest on the floor. Handles on each side facilitated lifting, and interiors could be customized.

Charlton invited a thousand British exporters identified by the Dollar Export Council to join the quest, but the response was pitiful. In fact, most were not even interested in buying small ads in his promotional newspaper the *Mayflower Mail*, conceived in December 1955 and first published in January 1956. Consequently, many spaces were given away in exchange for construction materials as the chests lay empty. While not producing cash, Charlton hoped they would generate credibility among prospects who simply could not see how a seventeenth-century sailing ship could fit into their marketing plans. It was unlike anything ever offered before, and there was no measurable relationship between what companies were being asked to pay and what they might reasonably expect in return. While Project Mayflower felt £460 (roughly $1,300) per chest was a fair price and "the cost of a week's building less materials" at that time,[12] British companies had a different opinion and were undoubtedly concerned about the damage their brands might suffer if the voyage failed. No one wanted to risk being associated with a losing effort. The Sunday worship services held at the shipyard sought heavenly intervention, but prayers for corporate support went unanswered. Thinking beyond convention was not something postwar executives tended toward, and the hard truth was that if any sales were going to be made, the two Englishmen had better come up with a different approach.

The Bletchley Park code-breaking school taught John Lowe how to anticipate hostile activity. A decade earlier, he had used that skill to

Figure 12. Sunday worship service at Brixham shipyard. *(Lee Israel/Mayflower Studios)*

predict German intentions, but now the expertise helped him recognize a possible effort by the Foreign Office to engage in sabotage. Diplomats exchanged memos throughout 1955 discussing how to warn the ESU and Pilgrims Society to steer clear of their perceived rivals. "Unsatisfactory and obscure" is how the foreign minister, Lord Reading, described Charlton and his partner to groups the duo might approach.[13] They just weren't the right sort. Additionally, the ministry was in "daily communication" with both groups asserting that Project Mayflower did not seem capable of delivering transnational "initiatives that would encourage American administrations and the Congress to treat Britain with more consideration in N.A.T.O., the I.M.F., and the United Nations."[14] Only trained diplomats had the skills necessary to get the United States to "see the world through British eyes."[15]

Given the size of the opponent, exposing its efforts seemed the best way to push back. Thus on January 11, 1956, Project Mayflower held the inaugural meeting of its council, important individuals who were supporting the undertaking, such as Felix Fenston and admiral of the fleet the Lord Fraser of North Cape. A private report called "Preparation, Progress and Plans" described the "irritation which the officers of the Project have from time to time felt at the malice and misrepresentation" directed at the undertaking by unnamed individuals in the government and the pressure applied against those who wished to support the project's efforts. The Foreign Office subsequently obtained a copy of the meeting's official minutes and, not surprisingly, feigned ignorance of any such intent. Nonetheless, the nonpublic report was added to an expanding file on the two men.[16]

That was not the end of it, as officials quietly looked deeper into their backgrounds. The Fighting Editor was a known troublemaker since his days in North Africa, when he challenged government policies via the *Eighth Army News*. Those attacks had prompted a transfer to Asia, where he continued to prod and push on behalf of the underdog. He seemed to enjoy being a provocateur and maintained many of his wartime connections, including a friendship with Randolph Churchill, whose father was succeeded as prime minister in 1955 by his former secretary of state for war, Anthony Eden. The new leader knew Mountbatten and Monty, while members of his staff were familiar with Charlton's resume, his pugnacious personality, and his craftiness at circumventing authority. A decade earlier, the *Mayflower* man was partially controlled because he was in uniform, but that kind of direct action was impossible now, which only made his courage, competence, and combative nature more of a threat. There was no question the rogue needed to be monitored closely because his activities were competing with the Foreign Office's own efforts to strengthen ties with the United States.

As for his partner Lowe, it took some digging, but they eventually found someone who could sow doubt about his character and modus operandi. Nigel Gaydon was now first secretary for information at the British embassy in Washington, but during the war he had been John Lowe's commanding officer. He wrote to London and described John as confounding and having "a very complicated personality." For example, Gaydon authorized him to form a special "section" at Bletchley Park and discovered at the war's end that the analyst "had done a superb job of persuading the War Office . . . that he was vital to our local authorities, and the local people . . . that the War Office would disintegrate if it did not receive the fruits of his labours!" The US-based diplomat told his London colleagues that such an achievement "took a good deal of skill and ballyhoo." He believed his former subordinate had great enthusiasm and strong persuasive abilities. Lowe was also "beguiling" and sometimes "lacking in common sense," which might be expected of an intellectual, and he was "prone to advancing cockeyed schemes that always failed because someone else let him down."[17]

This final assessment startled London. What if Project Mayflower failed? How would it impact their internal efforts to cultivate transatlantic opinion leaders? The wooden tribute was clearly an outstanding idea, but little was known about who was backing it financially. One thing was certain: the diplomats needed to keep track of the project and its shaky financials, and wake up Plimoth Plantation to the ministry's belief that "the reputations of its organizers [were] none too savory."[18] This put Harry Hornblower's museum in a very awkward position. On the one hand, it had been impressed enough with Lowe and Charlton the previous year to abandon its own construction plans and hand over responsibility to the Englishmen. Then it received an advisory from the British government suggesting that that decision might have been made in haste—reinforcing what Harry likely suspected upon reading the unsolicited Price Waterhouse report sent by Fenston. Getting the document from the financier was already shocking, but this Foreign Office notice was alarming. In response, the museum quickly dispatched one of its governors, Herbert Boynton, to investigate the matter, gather information, and report back regarding the project's viability. As a cover story, Harry told Warwick Charlton that the museum representative was traveling to London to check on construction progress. If Boynton agreed with the diplomats' suspicions, the New England group would take defensive action in short order.

On March 16, 1956, Lord Reading met with US ambassador Winthrop Aldrich, Plimoth Plantation representative Herbert Boynton, Pilgrims Society chairman Sir Campbell Stuart, and ESU director-general F. O. Darvall to discuss Project Mayflower.[19] The ambassador was thus compelled to be involved with the venture's outcome as a matter of protocol. Ironically, Aldrich had devoted a major part of his professional and private life to strengthening transatlantic ties, and the tribute Charlton was building was also praise for those acts.

Plimoth's man met with all available parties, including representatives from Lloyd's of London, who told him that Hornblower's English partners had already generated £25,000 ($70,000) in cash donations. It was heartening news because, although only a third-party report on the construction effort, it was coming from a maritime insurance provider with three hundred years' experience assessing risk. Charlton and Lowe were now apparently taking in an average of £1,000 or more each week, chiefly from the sale of so-called Treasure Chests.[20] These, Boynton learned, would carry British products destined for display in major department stores, such as Filene's in Boston. Boynton subsequently told the Foreign Office that he was "pretty certain" the group building the Plantation's much-desired entertainment attraction was not in financial trouble, contrary to ministry suspicions that it might be on the verge of collapse. In other words, the competition was not going away, as some had quietly hoped. Being meticulous, the bureaucrats took notes at the meeting and added them to the project leaders' expanding dossier.

Sir Ivone Kirkpatrick, permanent under-secretary of state for foreign affairs and a senior advisor to Prime Minister Anthony Eden, was briefed on Boynton's conclusions and noted a sense of disappointment among the presenters when he filed a report a few days later. His involvement with matters related to Project Mayflower made it clear to officials that the venture was important at 10 Downing Street, the official residence of the prime minister.

Chapter 6

Next Steps

London continued to monitor the boatyard and in May noted that, despite internal predictions of failure, it was thriving. Diplomats in London, Boston, and Washington exchanged memos,[1] reporting that with the arrival of spring, lines had begun to form in Brixham as excited visitors sought a glimpse of the craft. It was the largest wooden shipbuilding project of the century, and after five months of hard work there was tangible progress. "There's nothing parallel in the ship," Stuart Upham told the *New York Times*. "She's all shape, like a wineglass." The twelve-ton keel now had ribs all around it, and the craftsmen would soon build a "shelf" of heavy timber that would eventually support the decks and superstructure, while the hull below would hold the finest British goods and the ship's crew.[2] With its completion, Upham reported that the most difficult part of the build was done. It was a sight to be seen, and journalists from around the world raced to Devon to take pictures and write stories for their readers. In fact, so much interest was shown that it was decided to make a charge for admission to the yard and to mount a small exhibition.

Thousands of tourists were lining up each week to pay two shillings for a view of the emerging craft, plus a display of seventeenth-century tools and other facets of craftsmanship from a bygone era when England ruled the seas. Eventually "a quarter of a million people associated themselves in a particularly spontaneous and genuine way with *Mayflower*'s work of education in Anglo-American history and common heritage."[3] They could imagine Sir Walter Raleigh's *Ark Royal* being built or

Admiral Lord Nelson inspecting his fleet before it defeated the French and Spanish armadas at Trafalgar. Tours of the shipyard and a nearby Pilgrim house replica were given by guides dressed in seventeenth-century garb to add theatricality.[4] Executives from Plimoth Plantation came to visit and returned to Massachusetts with fresh ideas about how the museum might promote the replica once it was delivered. Upham even noted in his diary, "There comes a time in all great undertakings that Providence takes a hand," and this was what seemed to be happening to his creation, "which was no ordinary ship, whatever view critics—and there were many—held."[5]

While the government continued to look for ways to sway America's rich and powerful, the replica was rousing pride in everyday Britons—similar to what they had felt in 1953 when the country celebrated the coronation of Queen Elizabeth II. To capitalize on this groundswell of enthusiasm for *Mayflower II*, souvenirs reminiscent of that hallmark event were offered. Large gold, silver, and bronze coins were crafted by artist Paul Vincze, renowned in England following his designs for the young monarch, which were described as having "a charm and regal quality whilst avoiding the somewhat stereotyped images of previous official issues."[6]

Vincze's works have a Renaissance quality. The *Mayflower II* medals picture a father standing tall and pointing toward the future—a distant horizon—while holding a Bible in his lowered left hand. His wife stands under his benevolent gesture with a baby in one arm and a small boy holding her hand. Over the patriarch's shoulder is an older woman looking in the same direction. The group fills half the coin and is balanced by two shirtless workers with slightly bent knees lifting a heavy chest. All seven are standing on a wharf, suggesting their departure in the year inscribed: 1620. Printed around the edge are the words "Thus out of small beginnings greater things have been produced. Bradford." The reverse side contains allegorical figures of the United States and Great Britain, kneeling with their respective shields and joining hands across the ocean, with the Statue of Liberty and the historic ship in the background. Connecting their separate docks is a draping banner with the words "1620 MAYFLOWER 1957."

Figure 13. Stuart Upham and a Pilgrim mother looking at a ship that's "all shape, like a wineglass." *(Lee Israel/Mayflower Studios)*

The coronation ceremonies also inspired the production of commemorative china plates. In America, historic moments were likewise immortalized in special porcelain artwork intended for display on a wall or small stand. Charlton knew such items confirmed the prominence of an event, so he commissioned William Adams and Sons of Staffordshire to create a series for the replica. Each pictures the ship in full sail with frothing sea and billowing clouds. The inscription below the image reads *Mayflower II Crosses the Atlantic, Spring 1957*. A description of the voyage is found on the reverse side: "Mayflower II was built and sailed across the Atlantic as a goodwill gift from Great Britain to the United States of America in the Spring of 1957. This plate commemorates this historic second sailing."

For visitors seeking a simpler memento, the wood shavings produced when each piece of oak was handcrafted were collected, trimmed, shortened, and sold. These became rustic yet elegant tokens of history. Octogenarians could recall childhood memories of how the Statue of Liberty had also drawn large crowds during its construction as French citizens and international tourists sought a glimpse of the colossus before it was disassembled into 350 pieces and shipped to America. That same sense of excitement was in the air of County Devon, and people were traveling from near and far to breathe it in.

Warwick Charlton had no doubt that Upham would complete construction in a timely manner, and with that confidence he turned his attention to the ship's arrival on American shores. Lowe and he were well aware of Foreign Office efforts to create doubt about the venture's viability, and he wanted to counter that messaging with his own. New York City and Washington were destinations pondered after Plymouth, and it was important that the vessel's welcome in those cities be as spectacular as possible. With that goal in mind, he dispatched Alan Villiers

Figure 14. Artist Paul Vincze commemorative medallion. *(Courtesy Medallic Art Collector)*

to the Big Apple to meet with Mayor Robert Wagner, Bernard Gimbel of department store fame, and the Convention and Visitors Bureau. The captain was glad to go because, in addition to planning ahead, it gave him a chance to look back and recall memories from the three years he lived on Bay Ridge Parkway in Brooklyn "on and off before the war."[7] Charlton armed his captain with a model of the ship to present during his meetings, hoping it would stimulate conversations about how to maximize excitement for the tribute. The Australian additionally gave a lecture for the National Geographic Society to boost interest in the voyage.[8]

Reaching out to the US government required subtlety, however, because the capital was full of British diplomats who enjoyed a close working relationship with the Eisenhower administration. Charlton was not quite sure what he was seeking, but he knew whom to call for advice: Sir Francis de Guingand. Freddie, as he was known to friends, had served as Montgomery's chief of staff from El Alamein to the surrender of the unified armed forces of Nazi Germany in 1945, and he was known to the president. Freddie possessed considerable diplomatic skills that had served him well as primary liaison between his temperamental boss and the Americans. Charlton had had regular interactions with de Guingand during the war and kept him advised of his plans to build a *Mayflower* replica and present it to the people of the United States. Although he was no longer in uniform, Freddie's military service record provided him with a unique calling card, one that could be used to quietly support his former comrade-in-arms.

Neither of the initiatives to grease the wheels in New York and Washington was disclosed to Plimoth or the Foreign Office, but they both found out about them nonetheless. For the Americans, the discovery most likely came from David Longfellow Patten, a New Englander with connections similar to de Guingand's. During the war he served on General Douglas MacArthur's staff, stood aboard the USS *Missouri* when the Japanese surrendered, and was awarded the Legion of Merit by his country. The State Department then recruited him for diplomatic service with the rank of minister at the US embassy in Portugal, where he oversaw the Marshall Plan. Now he served Harry Hornblower's Plimoth Plantation as its first executive director. When he uncovered the Villiers and Charlton visits, and learned that his organization would receive only 20 percent of admissions revenues in those two ports of call and nothing from souvenir sales—both of which seemed to be fairly lucrative, based on Boynton's London investigations—he was not pleased. Patten wanted a larger share, even though the asset belonged to others. A free seventeenth-century sailing ship was apparently not enough, and according to the Foreign Office, he called Charlton a "crook" and recommended that Plimoth stop working with him.[9] Luckily, cooler heads prevailed, but discontent was growing.

As for the diplomats, they were concerned that the White House might support Project Mayflower in some way, which could interfere with Britain's quiet hostility. To their relief, the US embassy in London reported that it felt the effort was "something of a commercial publicity stunt,"[10] and the government had little enthusiasm for the private undertaking. All this was duly noted, memorialized, and added to the project's file, which continued to grow. However, so did public enthusiasm for the venture on both sides of the Atlantic.

Despite these rumblings, Project Mayflower was clearly upholding its side of the bargain,[11] and Felix Fenston contributed another £4,500 to the venture in August,[12] as Charlton flew to Massachusetts to give a progress report to the Town of Plymouth and the Plantation. During that trip, Harry Hornblower showed Charlton the large parcel of undeveloped land along the Eel River that would eventually become the museum's new home. It was a few miles from town and, centuries earlier, had been Wampanoag territory. Most recently, his grandmother owned it. Money to dredge Plymouth Harbor and make it navigable for the second *Mayflower* was coming from the state, which recognized the tourism and tax revenue potential of the museum's new prize and the impact it could have on the greater Cape Cod area. In 1893 the narrow channel connecting Plymouth Bay to the inner harbor, plus a two-acre turning area and the boat basin in front of the town's wharf, were dredged to a depth of nine feet.[13] Sixty years later, however, the natural shoaling process, storms, and shifting sands had reduced clearance, making the passage hazardous at low tide, particularly for a craft like the *Mayflower* replica. When

William Baker first met with Plimoth, he had raised this concern, which was a factor in their deciding to build a model on a concrete slab—until the advent of Charlton and his bold proposal. As in Plimoth's deal with Project Mayflower, someone else would do the heavy lifting while the Plantation harvested rewards.

Though many considered Warwick Charlton a master in the art of salesmanship, Harry was no slouch. As a director of the Cape Cod Company real estate firm, he knew the value of location, location, location. Applying this mantra to "my main hobby . . . Plimoth Plantation," the proximity of his museum's three modest structures to Plymouth Rock enabled them to be "visited by more than two million people since we opened the first unit in 1949." That foot traffic spelled opportunity, particularly because "the *Mayflower* has been promised to us by a British group" at no cost and the Commonwealth of Massachusetts was footing the bill to make the harbor ready for its arrival. To ensure the state's unwavering support, Harry arranged a meeting between Governor Christian Herter and Charlton before he returned to London. As Hornblower, David Patten, and William Brewster looked on, Project Mayflower's leader described his vision and action plan as only he could. It was a triumphant performance. As a result of those two initiatives, "we are now planning to enlarge and move our exhibits to another site which will make it possible for us to build the entire Plantation as it was in 1623, as well as a trading post, an Indian Village and an archeological laboratory-museum." The combined efforts of Project Mayflower and the state were now putting Harry's boyhood dream within reach. "All that's needed is $500,000," he wrote, and he was confident he had the skills to climb that financial Everest. Since 1941 he had served as the chief fundraiser for his Harvard class and multiple large undertakings. Surely he could find the money to build a replica of the colony the original *Mayflower* voyagers eventually called home, Plimoth Plantation.[14]

Following Charlton's visit, the governor of Massachusetts sent a personal note on September 14:[15]

To the Sponsors of the Mayflower Project and the People of Great Britain:

I salute your magnificent effort to re-create a moment in history in which your nation and mine share special pride. In bringing back the Mayflower as it was in 1620, you are reliving an immortal story of heroism in the face of adversity that cannot help but make its imprint on the world.

As Governor of the Commonwealth of Massachusetts, in which the Pilgrims chose to settle, I am particularly pleased by what you have done. We owe a great debt to the Founding Fathers. They gave us the concept of constitutional liberty on which we built the Declaration of Independence and the American Constitution.

I am stirred by the spirit of good will that prompted your people to give so generously to a craft that will soon sail far away. God speed your valiant ship to our shores! We shall take loving care of it and treasure it always as a living monument of friendship between our nations.

[SIGNED]CHRISTIAN A. HERTER

Not everyone in New England shared the governor's full-throated embrace of the venture, however. Harry was concerned that dirty commercialism was creeping onto an American icon and into the retelling of the nation's history.[16] Just look at the huckstering going on at Brixham and how Warwick Charlton was shamelessly selling souvenirs and promoting "Treasure Chests." How dare private enterprise and public companies sully the waters of cultural preservation? Funding for museums and the arts was the purview, within the tradition of *noblesse oblige*, of well-heeled patrons and individual citizens with sensibilities more refined than the average person. Plimoth's founder was not pleased, but he needed the tourist magnet the Englishmen were building for him—without the replica, his Plantation would be missing its star attraction. If Harry Hornblower had been responsible for construction instead of berthing, he likely would have used his business expertise to the fullest. But the task of raising money was on Warwick Charlton's slate, and he employed the skills he knew best: marketing and promotion. Just as the 1620 voyage introduced new concepts of governance that had a lasting impact, the 1957 voyage introduced new thinking about marketing, promotion, and event sponsorship that would endure. For now, Harry would be wise to keep his personal feelings to himself and avoid public criticism of Warwick's methods. He knew better than to rock the boat.

CHAPTER 7

Big Splash

BACK IN ENGLAND, WORKMEN WERE CAULKING AND PITCHING THE hull, essential tasks for assuring watertightness. The cider barrel treenails were used to fasten the ship's exterior planking, its outer oak skin, to the interior ribs by hammering each one into its own hole, which historically would have been made with a long-shafted pod auger but was now made by an electric drill with a nod from Baker. If a wooden fastener protruded through the planking, it would be trimmed off with an adz. Inside the hull, slits were made in the treenails and small wedges were hammered in to ensure very tight fits. Then the excess would be trimmed, just as done on the outside, to complete the process. Hemp—old mailbags or rope—was teased back to its original fiber to make oakum that became caulking to be wedged between the planks with a mallet and a hauseing iron, which looked like a small hand ax.

Next came the pitching, a horrible task. Stockholm tar, made from sticky sap that would ooze from pine trees, was melted in a large vat and then rubbed into the plank seams with a mop. If the slop splashed on the worker, it would stick to his arms, face, and hair, and then become brittle and very difficult (and painful) to remove. In the olden days, pitchers would lather themselves in harbor mud, consisting of who-knows-what but easy to wash off along with any muck it attracted. Upham's men thankfully had a modern solution: old oilskins worn head to toe and cinched tightly around the neck and wrists. Hands and faces were then covered in a thick body cream, a modern harbor mud replacement and much more hygienic. Historian James W. Baker notes, "After a woman in a white dress walked under falling tar during the tarring of the mizzen brace and visitors were tracking it from deck seams on hot days, the real tar was replaced with a rubberized compound" when the deck seams underwent maintenance in the late 1960s.[1]

With *Mayflower II* now watertight, the day of triumph Charlton and Lowe had dreamed about for the last two years finally arrived on September 22, 1956. Dignitaries, news media, and tourists gathered in Brixham to witness an important moment, the launch of a historic seventeenth-century replica. It was tangible evidence that this special gift to America was becoming a reality, and the promise of a grand seafaring adventure was one step closer to being fulfilled.

In circumstances befitting her troubled upbringing thus far, *Mayflower II* splashed into the water for the first time in the midst of a hearty storm.[2] Ten shipwrights stood on each side of the replica with long-handled mauls and simultaneously struck wooden wedges that would lift the hull off blocks under the keel, allowing gravity to take over and pull tons of timber to the harbor. It was an age-old tradition that followed the rhythm of a shantyman's shouted cadence:

"Stand by."
"One blow, two blows, three blows, up she rises.
Inch a blow, Down she goes."[3]

If the strikes were not in unison, he would pause, cry "Together," and start over again. As the wedges did their jobs, the crowd held its breath, then "with no hesitation, the new *Mayflower* skipped down the ways, gave a graceful curtsy as she took to the water, and skittered out across the harbor, scattering a fleet of small sightseeing boats and yachts."[4]

The honor of christening the ship was given to Reis Leming, a US Airman Second Class from Yakima, Washington. He had won the love of England in 1953 when he risked his life to save twenty-seven people from drowning in the violent waters of a massive North Sea storm. He could not swim but leapt into the waves anyway because it was the right thing to do—a selfless act that earned him Britain's George Medal for bravery. Warwick later told his son that he believed the courage, good character, and moral fortitude exhibited by Reis gave him hope for the future:

> He and his wife represented the missing decent American young people. They were almost too good to be true; modest, charming and possessed of a quiet dignity. The people of Plymouth (Massachusetts) wanted me to invite one of them or perhaps the state Governor to do the job and the patrons (in England) thought we should invite an admiral or a member of the cabinet but I thought "what would the pilgrims have wanted if they had been making the choice?" They would have been proud of Mr. and Mrs. Reis Leming.[5]

John Allen May from Boston's *Christian Science Monitor* wrote a front-page story for the launch edition of the *Mayflower Mail*, "G.I. Hero Launches New *Mayflower* Sailing in the Spring. None of those who were there are likely to forget the launching of the new *Mayflower*."[6] Prominent witnesses included Harry Hornblower's friend William Brewster; USAF General Roscoe Wilson, commander of the Third Air Force; and the ship's architect, William Baker. Massachusetts governor Christian Herter sent a message that was read to the crowd, and Warwick Charlton announced that his team had accepted an invitation from New York City mayor Robert Wagner to exhibit the tribute before it went on permanent display in Plymouth. The boat was now complete up to the first deck, the 'tween deck, which was at the waterline when floating, and Stuart felt the most difficult work had been done. Now his attention shifted to finishing the exterior planking from the 'tween to the main deck, plus all the other construction, and this would be done in a nearby drydock that had a small crane for lifting heavy items.

The shipyard owner also focused on securing timber for the masts and yardarms that would hold the sails. This presented a different challenge than procuring the Devon oaks for the hull, which were plentiful in England's mossy southern forests. Upham's team looked to Canada for mighty Oregon pines that grew straight, could reach a height of two hundred feet, had diameters greater than four feet, and could be hewn for the replica.[7] Once identified and cut, these natural wonders were shipped

Figure 15. The hull of *Mayflower II* launched. *(© British Pathé)*

to Manchester, transferred onto specially built long trucks, driven to a nearby water access, put on a barge, then towed to the shipyard. After this journey, special cranes lifted the towering poles into the hull, where they were secured and became the ship's three propulsion pillars: the mainmast, foremast, and mizzen. Fitted near the top of the main and foremast, but below their respective topmasts, were round platforms called tops, on which crewmen worked when handling the sails and rigging. The mizzen, stepped aft, carried a triangular lateen rather than the square sails attached to the arms of the two taller masts. A fourth, shorter pole called a bowsprit was installed at the prow of the ship at about a forty-five-degree angle and held the square spritsail.

All sails were made of flax canvas that was cut and sewn by hand under the watchful eye of Francis Webster and Sons of Arbroath, Scotland, an outfit that had been making wind catchers for more than two hundred years. Flax is a long vegetable fiber, finer than human hair, exceedingly strong, and has been used by mariners since earliest times and through the days of the great tea clippers that connected London and Liverpool to Calcutta and Bombay. To seamen, the name Webster, which means weaver,[8] was synonymous with trustworthy craftsmanship, and having them involved gave the venture further credibility. Unlike modern sailing craft and America's Cup yachts, whose sails are pulled up, *Mayflower's* were dropped down for use and then hoisted up to be stowed. It was the operating signature of square-riggers and provided special drama for both the crew and those watching the replica power up.

To Warwick, John, and Stuart it was clear that the tide was turning in their favor at long last. An important milestone had been reached, and success seemed in sight. But that optimism was not shared by everyone. Two weeks after the launch, members of Britain's diplomatic corps continued to ridicule Project Mayflower's work despite its apparent success. Foreign officer A. N. MacCleary had been monitoring construction since it began, and on October 2 he noted that a decision needed to be made regarding his country's posture when "this somewhat embarrassing ship" arrived in American waters the following spring.[9]

D'Arcy Edmondson at the Washington embassy countered that Charlton's brainchild had become so popular on both sides of the Atlantic that the government should just get on board and take some basic actions to assure its safe arrival. The London office, however, believed that such steps would indirectly involve the ministry in a project over which it had no control. Better to stand on the sidelines and watch while continuing its own efforts to cultivate upper-class opinion leaders in both nations.

Hold on a moment! the consul-general in Boston, Robert Marett, cautioned on October 19: "Whatever . . . our private reservations about Charlton and Lowe . . . *Mayflower* is going to be presented to the American people as a great gesture of British friendship."[10] The project's success was fast becoming as predictable as the tides, and the government should just embrace the effort, not only because it would highlight the special relationship but also because British companies and products were being promoted. As diligently as bureaucrats had tried various cultural diplomacy schemes, none had the potential of *Mayflower II*.

Just days before Marett sent his note to London, the Massachusetts commissioner of commerce wrote a personal message to the everyday Englishman:[11]

Mr. Warwick Charlton, whose vision and friendship have charted a new course for the *Mayflower* and all that she represents to our two nations. We look forward keenly to her re-arrival!

RICHARD PRESTON, MASSACHUSETTS
COMMISSIONER OF COMMERCE—
BOSTON—16 OCTOBER 1956

That handwritten note of appreciation from an important New England state official was clearly at odds with the US embassy in London, where the replica was still considered a publicity stunt.

To an impartial observer, it was starting to look like pride and prejudice were interfering with sober assessments. The men behind the effort to build the new symbol of democracy had spent their formative years working directly for Britain's top generals, breaking Nazi codes at Bletchley Park, and building wooden minesweepers for the Admiralty. The trio had grit, undaunted courage, and were in no way run-of-the-mill. It would be a mistake for anyone to underestimate their resolve. They saw a bright future for the second *Mayflower*.

PART II

HIGH SEAS ADVENTURE

CHAPTER 8

Upside Down

Feelings of optimism at Project Mayflower were to be short-lived. Less than two weeks after Commissioner Preston's congratulatory message and the bickering Foreign Office memos, Charlton, Lowe, and Upham watched helplessly as their country turned the world upside down. On October 29 England joined forces with France and Israel to start a war in the Middle East. The "special relationship" *Mayflower II* hoped to honor was summarily dismissed, threatened with destruction, and replaced with a new era of global politics.

Whitehall's goal was to seize control of the Suez Canal, the strategic passage that delivered two-thirds of Europe's oil from Arabia, a fundamental shift in purpose from its original objective of providing Britain with a "shortcut" to India when India was the jewel in Her Majesty's colonial crown. The current trouble began in July 1956, when Egyptian president Gamal Abdel Nasser abruptly nationalized the waterway in an effort to force a confrontation with England for regional leadership and demonstrate to other Arab nations his unflinching resolve to remove European colonial powers from the Middle East. At the same time, the French were waging a ruthless war with Algerian rebels fighting for national independence with the unofficial support of Egypt. Both European countries had been colonial powers in the region for more than a century, and Britain had a garrison of eighty thousand soldiers near the canal, while French troops in North Africa numbered four hundred thousand. Simultaneously, Israel was the target of escalating military attacks from Gaza, which was under Egyptian control. Adding further complexity to the moment, Nasser had preceded his nationalization pronouncement by pulling diplomatic cords in Washington that positioned his plan to modernize Egypt's economy via construction of a dam across the Nile River at Aswan as a bargaining chip. In return for US financial support, he offered to limit his growing relationship with the Soviet Union, which Washington considered a threat to regional governments and a challenge to its global leadership ambitions. Unfortunately, US policy analysts had little faith in Egypt's ability to manage such a massive construction project, and the US offer of monetary support was withdrawn, prompting the British to step back as well. Thus, when Nasser made his nationalization move, he did so on the pretext that the money generated from canal operations would be used to fill the revenue gap caused by the loss of Anglo-American funding. The French and English thought otherwise and saw the action as a direct threat to their colonial control, not only in the Middle East but also in Africa.

Recognizing what was at stake for the two European powers, Israel approached the French with a proposal to regain control of the passage, which was a source of pride for Paris because it was designed by the Frenchman Ferdinand de Lesseps. Of course, the success of that plan could also result in greater security for the Jewish state from its Muslim neighbor across the canal. US officials analyzed the situation and concluded that such an action was both possible and dangerous, so they took immediate steps to defuse tensions by engaging the United Nations in an effort to find a diplomatic solution that would keep the waterway open to all traffic and avoid bloodshed. Unfortunately, and unbeknownst to the Americans, the British had already accepted an offer from Paris to join the French in military action and, choosing not to inform Washington, girded for battle. While the Americans were seeking a noncombative solution, planners in London, Paris, and Tel Aviv picked up their weapons.

For a world still reeling from global war and hoping the UN could become an instrument for conflict resolution, London's decision proved disastrous. It blindsided the United States just six days before the 1956 presidential election in which Eisenhower was running as the incumbent "peace" candidate. He was incensed by the unfolding events and told his aide and speechwriter Emmet John Hughes in the White

Figure 16. Bombing of the Suez Canal, sparking a crisis that would change Europe. *(Crown Copyright/Imperial War Museums)*

House, "I've just never seen great powers make such a complete *mess* and *botch* of things. . . . My God!"[1] Britain had made a grave mistake in underestimating America's reaction, and the consequences were severe, threatening the future of the Anglo-American alliance. Just hours before the start of hostilities, Britain delivered a final warning to Egypt and dispatched Sir Ivone Kirkpatrick to the American embassy in Grosvenor Square. Kirkpatrick was the same official who, seven months earlier, spent a good deal of his highly valuable time observing and reporting Foreign Office frustration about Project Mayflower. Ambassador Aldrich was stunned by what the permanent under-secretary told him, as he later wrote:

> I asked if the ultimatums had been made public and he answered, "Yes. The Prime Minister is making the announcement in the House at the present moment."
>
> "In that case," I said, "the only thing I can do is telephone the contents of these documents to Washington immediately, but of course the President and the Secretary of State will have already learned of this action taken by Her Majesty's Government on the news services."

... The effect on our Government of this sudden and unexpected
British and French move and of the actual opening of hostilities against
Egypt two days later was catastrophic.[2]

President Eisenhower and Secretary of State John Foster Dulles
wanted no further contact with Prime Minister Eden.

Egypt responded to the aggression by sinking forty of its ships, boats,
and barges in the 120-mile-long canal, blocking all traffic including oil
carriers destined for the United Kingdom and Europe. It would be April
before the passage was fully reopened. The Mediterranean-based US
Sixth Fleet commanded by Vice Admiral Charles R. Brown had to take
immediate action to protect and evacuate US citizens in the war zone.
That involvement "is not so generally known" and "endangered the whole
of" the special relationship, according to British general Charles Keightley.[3] The American oil industry quickly began diverting tankers around
the Cape of Good Hope at the southern tip of Africa and redirecting
fuel carriers to Britain, and the United States released petroleum from its
strategic reserves to aid the effort.

Eisenhower interrupted campaigning and on October 31 reported to
the nation: "The United States was not consulted in any way about [the
British and French] actions. Nor were we informed of them in advance."
He said America did "not accept the use of force as a wise or proper
instrument for the settlement of international disputes"—which was
precisely what the Soviet Union was positioned to do in Hungary, where
an uprising was gathering force in the face of Soviet oppression. Peace,
he declared, "means much more than mere absence of war. It means the
acceptance of law, and the fostering of justice, in all the world."[4] The Cold
War era's spread of communism had been a central focus of the president
since taking office, and it remained a top national security concern—now
exacerbated by the Suez Crisis.

The Middle East was a high-value region, and the United States had
been working hard to improve relations with Egypt, which was a key
player because of its location, size, and charismatic leader. Britain's action
jeopardized these efforts because it forced America to make "the most
difficult decisions," Vice President Richard Nixon later explained. The

United States "couldn't on one hand complain about the Soviets intervening in Hungary and, on the other hand, approve of the British and the French picking that particular time to intervene against Nasser."[5] If Washington was seen as supporting the invasion, it could spark a regional backlash and embolden communist efforts in the Middle East, Latin America, and Southeast Asia, notably Vietnam.

Sure enough, on November 4, Soviet troops and tanks viciously crushed the Hungarian Revolution—a spontaneous citizens' uprising against Moscow and the first major nationalistic challenge to the Soviet Union since the end of World War II. Thousands were killed or wounded, and two hundred thousand people fled the country. Then, on November 6, Eisenhower was reelected, and domestic issues immediately took a backseat to the international crises demanding his attention. The newly established United Nations High Commissioner for Refugees was notified of the humanitarian crisis, and the General Assembly heard the plea within days of the invasion but was unable to make a specific call for international help until November 21 because it was preoccupied with the Suez Crisis. Within two years a total of thirty-seven countries from around the world stepped forward to provide assistance and new homes, including the United States, where more than thirty-six thousand Hungarians were resettled. It was a remarkable achievement for the fledgling UNHCR and became a model for future groups forced to leave their homelands as the result of war.

In financial markets, the Suez action subjected the British pound to such rampant speculation that the Bank of England was forced to deplete its US currency reserves to defend the fixed value of sterling against the dollar. Decades later, the International Monetary Fund said those events might have constituted "the first financial crisis of the twenty-first century" and remained in a destructive category all their own until the Mexican peso meltdown forty years later.[6] The chancellor of the exchequer, future prime minister Harold Macmillan, urged calm, but he knew a forced devaluation would have grave consequences for the United Kingdom and its Commonwealth of Nations.

The Americans understood this too, and it gave them leverage. If Whitehall wanted financial assistance, then Britain would have to

Figure 17. Soviet tanks in Budapest, November 1956. *(FOTO:FORTEPAN/Nagy Gyula/Public Domain)*

withdraw her troops from all occupied territories. To Ivone Kirkpatrick, his country's debacle meant there was a new reality: "No country can any longer pursue an independent foreign policy. The liberty of action of each is in varying degrees restricted by the need to obtain the concurrence of one or more members of the alliance."[7] Britain's status as a world power was irreversibly undermined by events the permanent under-secretary had hawkishly encouraged Prime Minister Eden to put in motion. The two men would rue the day hostilities began, and their misjudgment would haunt the nation well into the next century. Already in October 1957, General Keightley observed: "The one overriding lesson of the Suez operations is that world opinion is now an absolute principle of war and must be treated as such."[8]

Nations watched as the two great pillars of democracy stumbled. Britain lost prestige, and the wheels of independence were set in motion among Crown colonies in Africa and the Pacific. The United States lost ground to the Soviet Union in the Middle East, while communist military forces crushed the desire for freedom in Central Europe. It was not a good moment for either country, at home or on the international stage, and a demonstration of unity was needed to change course and redirect the global conversation.

Colonialism was fast becoming an anachronism, as the arc of history moved away from European empires and new democracies emerged around the globe. The Foreign Office hoped that a planned 1957 visit by Queen Elizabeth II to Jamestown, Virginia, to honor the former colony's three hundred fiftieth anniversary would be well received and demonstrate enduring ties—but there was a problem. Virginia's opposition to racial equality, public school integration, and the Supreme Court's decision in *Brown v. Board of Education* placed the state firmly on the wrong side of history, allying it with South Africa's policy of apartheid, which was a growing cancer on the integrity of the British Commonwealth. Led by US senator Harry Byrd Sr. and the Virginia General Assembly, a strategy of "massive resistance" to desegregation was set in motion and threatened to close public schools statewide. Virginia's Supreme Court and a panel of federal District Court judges eventually declared those efforts unconstitutional, but focusing world attention on the issue of racism risked more harm than good for both nations. As for efforts to increase the sale of English goods in America, such programs required spending money the exchequer simply did not have.

The insightful Robert Marett, consul-general in Boston—a city eager to welcome *Mayflower II* to her new home berth—sent another memorandum to D'Arcy Edmondson on December 15, 1956. He reminded his Washington-based colleague that Charlton's project focused on "our common roots" and that the replica was tailor-made "to boost Britain and British trade."[9] Their homeland colleagues again pushed back, but in the end they couldn't avoid the reality of their country's economic dependence on its former colony and the importance of the transatlantic bond. Why not use Project Mayflower to achieve Whitehall's goals? It would not require government funding and, if successful, had a good chance of achieving the elusive goal of increasing foreign revenues from across the Atlantic—not to mention easing the present tensions between the two world powers. Pride had not been prudent when it played a role in the decision to seize the passage to India, and it should not cloud sober evaluations of the benefits a new seventeenth-century reproduction could deliver.

The unexpected events of late 1956 were changing the gift's relevance and pulling it to center stage of a British drama about saving the "special relationship" and defending the pound sterling. Any private conversations among social elites and the Foreign Office before the invasion became trivial in its aftermath. If the tribute being built in Devon could help heal self-inflicted wounds, then Anglo-American diplomats should support it. The *Northern Daily Mail* reinforced that point of view when it reported, "The Eisenhower administration has completed stand-by plans to save Western Europe from an oil famine," and ran a photo of Captain Alan Villiers holding a model of *Mayflower II* adjacent to the article.[10] The converging stories suggested a diplomatic mission for the replica. No one

Figure 18. Alan Villiers holding *Mayflower II* model as the Foreign Office discusses the ship's importance. *(SWNS Picture Desk)*

seemed to notice the irony of proffering a gift that honored past sacrifices made during a war of necessity to heal injuries caused by a recently aborted war of choice.

As the year ended, Stuart Upham described the impact all this had on his operations. "When winter came and the visitors went, it was plain to see the dark clouds gathering and the heavy weather that lay ahead for the venture. Indeed, the one glimmer of hope lay in the fact that the ship was now a reality and not a dream and had already created worldwide interest." This gave him hope. "The thought came to me, as I stood looking up at the half-built skeleton of *Mayflower II*, that perhaps I was facing much the same problems as did those early Pilgrims—whether to go on or turn back. I decided that, come what may, the ship must be completed."[11] The die was cast. What "looked something like the backbone of a fish that one might find on a beach" or "the skeleton of a whale" would not be left abandoned on the shores of Brixham Harbor.[12]

CHAPTER 9

New Realities

THE FIRST FEW MONTHS OF 1957 WITNESSED THE INTRODUCTION OF major foreign policy doctrines and the birth of new institutions that would affect the world for generations. President Eisenhower told a joint session of Congress on January 5 that the United States would henceforth take a more active military role in the Middle East. Under the new Eisenhower Doctrine, any nation threatened with "armed aggression from any country controlled by international communism" could receive "American economic assistance and/or aid from U.S. military forces."[1] While originally intended to repel Russian aggression and reduce its influence in Arabia, the policy became a roadmap for future presidents as they developed strategies and rationales for handling wars around the world, such as in Vietnam.

Across the Atlantic, England and France were forced to reevaluate their strategic alliances with the United States because of the military actions in Egypt and Hungary. For France, that meant moving expeditiously to finalize a unity deal with other Continental nations who had been reluctant to move forward prior to Suez. The necessity of that formation came into clear focus the previous November 6 when the country's prime minister, Guy Mollet, received a call from Anthony Eden telling him that the British were abandoning their joint attack on Suez because of pressure from the United States. When the phone rang in his office, Mollet happened to be in a meeting with West German chancellor Conrad Adenauer, which was also attended by the French foreign minister, Christian Pineau. Pineau later recorded that when Mollet shared

Figure 19. Eisenhower Doctrine signed in the White House. *(Getty Images)*

the news with Adenauer, the German said: "France and England will never be powers comparable to the United States. . . . Nor Germany, either. There remains to them only one way of playing a decisive role in the world; that is to unite to make Europe. . . . We have no time to waste: Europe will be your revenge."[2]

To achieve that satisfaction, the Treaty of Rome was signed the following March to create a European Economic Community (EEC) consisting of Belgium, France, Italy, Luxembourg, the Netherlands, and West Germany. Their combined population of 160 million was only slightly smaller than the United States's 176 million, and more than three times larger than Britain's. While the British and French had suffered defeat in the desert, "Europe won on all fronts."[3] Trade barriers between members were to be reduced or eliminated, with the hope of generating peace and prosperity for future generations. Britain applied for membership in 1960 and again in 1967, but each time its application was rejected by France, which forced it to remain an isolated nation outside Europe until 1973, when it was finally granted admission along with Ireland and Denmark. The French denials were fueled by President Charles de Gaulle's fear that British entry into the EEC would weaken the French voice within Europe while strengthening America's influence because of its "special relationship" with England—its Trojan Horse. When de Gaulle left office, the door was finally opened for the United Kingdom, and it stepped forward, giving British companies access to millions of previously hard-to-reach consumers. Before then, however, and particularly in the late 1950s, the British government's primary trade focus was on gaining easier access to US markets because World War II left the United Kingdom with a national debt that exceeded 200 percent of GDP, and it was reliant on loans from its former colony. To pay down that debt, it needed to generate as many US dollars as possible.

Britain continued to hold firm to its tradition of national identity based on the English language and its Commonwealth of Nations—a

Figure 20. Europe's "revenge"—the EEC—being formalized as France (Christian Pineau, *left*), West Germany (Konrad Adenauer, *right*), Belgium, Italy, Luxembourg, and the Netherlands sign the Treaty of Rome in March 1957, with the United Kingdom excluded. *(Keystone Press/Alamy Stock Photo)*

decision that required strong transatlantic ties. The bond was crucial, and it needed to be repaired and then showcased to the world in a manner that would leave no doubt about its strength. It also needed to herald equal partnership, lest Britannia appear submissive to America's recent muscle flexing in its flurry of international policy development. The imbalance was starting to produce anti-American sentiment among Britons that the minister of state for foreign affairs termed "a form of madness,"[4] and it was rendering Project Mayflower sales efforts worthless. If only citizens and diplomats could find a way to see Brixham and Whitehall navigating in similar seas of uncertainty. Then the fog lifted when the *Sphere*, a publication of the *Illustrated London News*, told readers: "In recent months Anglo-American relations have suffered a serious rupture. Every effort is now being made by men of good will on both sides of the Atlantic to restore them and make them stronger than ever before. What finer contribution could there be to this vital task than this grand [*Mayflower II*] gesture on the part of Britain?"[5]

To make that sentiment a reality, Project Mayflower needed a new answer when companies asked, "What's in it for me?" because the prewar "low risk, high reward" response was not working. To solve the problem, Charlton ingeniously repositioned Project Mayflower as a maritime adventure story that could be marketed in the same way movies were sold to theater owners before their release. To help execute the strategy, he hired a successful young film publicist named Fiona McCrae-Taylor,[6] and he was confident she could sell the idea. Project Mayflower was, in effect, a high-stakes adventure featuring a charismatic star, Alan Villiers, who would captain an epic challenge to cross the North Atlantic in an untested wooden ship, *Mayflower II*. Instead of being seen in dark theaters, it would play out on television and radio and in newspapers and magazines whose enthusiasm for the project had already been verified when the ship launched in September. The visuals were so powerful that *Life* magazine, *National Geographic*, and other media were already planning major coverage. The promoter then took a page from American soap operas that were broadcast on the CBS and NBC networks and sponsored by leading consumer companies such as Procter & Gamble and Colgate-Palmolive—who happily associated their brands with episodic programs that evolved on a daily basis and were discussed by millions of viewers as plotlines emerged. If Warwick Charlton's team could convince English companies that each day of the voyage represented a day of original entertainment, then their products would benefit greatly by association. A new approach to multiday event marketing was thus invented for *Mayflower II* because the voyage represented an unscripted live drama that would unfold each day to eager followers in the United States and Britain.

At the same time and unbeknownst to Charlton, another force may have added momentum to the sales efforts. Winthrop Aldrich instinctively knew that the tribute could be used to repair the damage caused by the Suez Crisis, and his monitoring of the project had forced him to be aware of the minimal support offered by the British upper class, their government, and the Hornblower organization. The ambassador also knew how to apply lessons learned at sea: adapting to circumstances while keeping your eye on the objective and not taking unnecessary risks. In this moment, the goal was to restore and reaffirm an Atlantic alliance he fervently believed in. With the end of his appointment to the Court of St. James's approaching in February, he knew there was a final contribution he could make to that cause: quietly support the mission of unity ingrained in the seventeenth-century craft.

Aldrich's experience prior to becoming ambassador made him uniquely prepared for a moment in history that involved sailing, business, and politics. His love of the sea dated back to his childhood in Providence, Rhode Island. During World War I he combined that passion with his family's fortune to build the USS *Herreshoff No. 309*, which was leased to the US Navy for patrols along the New England coast. In 1923 his schooner *Flying Cloud* won the Astor Cup, second only in prestige to the America's Cup, which was won in 1930 by the *Enterprise*. Aldrich led the syndicate that built that champion and then served as navigator when it defeated Britain's *Shamrock V*, the only J Class racing yacht ever built with a wooden hull. Those experiences gave him great insight into the challenges and merits of building a ship to honor Anglo-American ties.

Future prime minister Harold Macmillan coincidently had such an exceptional relationship with Aldrich that Washington used the closeness to support his accession to the premiership.[7] When he assumed office, he told a Pilgrims Society gathering that his American friend had played a "remarkable and, indeed, historic role during those anxious weeks of strain" resulting from Suez. It was "largely because of what he did during this period" that Macmillan could "look forward with such confidence to the complete and successful re-establishment of our relations upon the old level."[8] That was all the British leader could say publicly about his friend, but there was more to be told.

Chapter 10

Moving Forward

Beyond the diplomatic uncertainty surrounding *Mayflower II* as 1957 got under way, the project faced hard internal realities. The government's behavior prior to the crisis had been effective in dissuading wealthy contributors from joining the effort. Only everyday people seemed willing to help as they stood in line to view a wooden ship being built at Upham's yard and perhaps buy a souvenir. Then came the Suez Crisis, followed by America's response, and any hope of significant donations evaporated.

John Lowe evaluated the situation and came up with a solution. Lowe believed the best course of action was to delay the departure to America for a year and exhibit the replica in England. The public had already confirmed its keen interest, so why not reap some reward? A tour might include visiting Southampton, traveling around the coast, and then sailing up the Thames into the heart of London and anchoring at St. Katherine's Dock, a prime location. An Elizabethan village could be erected there so tourists would get a better understanding of life in 1620. Lowe had little doubt that big money could be made. It seemed like a good idea to him.

Felix Fenston agreed. Bills were now piling higher by the day for extra ballast, food supplies, and wages. Where was the money to pay them? "If *Mayflower* leaves now we are going to disappoint hundreds of thousands of people in Britain who want to see her. Why don't you keep her here until next year?" he proposed, and "leave next spring with a healthy balance in the bank."[1] Unlike Lowe, he made his case with "a businessman's perspective and sharper tongue."[2]

What Fenston did not say was that delaying departure could also shine a positive light on him, personally, as his company moved forward with its Central London scheme. So far it had been a well-kept secret, but that wouldn't last. He knew it. Once the press learned the details of his plan to demolish the St. James's Theatre and replace it with an office building, public anger could explode. A *Mayflower II* exhibition might help counter that. His Project Mayflower insurance policy would finally pay him benefits.

In comparison to the risk and labor involved in generating funds from Treasure Chest sales, Lowe's proposal had great merit. Massachusetts was not going anywhere, and from what the three men could see, Plimoth Plantation would not have the promised berthing facilities finished for at least a year. The Englishmen were upholding their side of the deal, but there was no evidence the Americans would be ready on time, despite a barrage of urgent requests from Harry Hornblower that the replica sail in the spring of 1957.

Warwick Charlton sided with Harry. He had given his word. On top of that, Charlton had "foolhardly" told the public the ship would sail in the spring. Although a delay was "naturally tempting," he feared that waiting until 1958 "would be an anti-climax from which the Project would find it difficult to recover, and a bitter disappointment for our American friends." Harry Hornblower had not let up on his "constant insistence" that the vessel arrive as originally promised because "he must have had a hard date to help his [fundraising appeals] for the Plantation."[3] Investors might be understandably skeptical of his big plans when all they could see were three small structures near the waterfront. Two were one-room dwellings—First House, modeled on a 1620 structure, and the stone-chimneyed 1627 House—while the third was a larger, thirty-square-foot Fort Meetinghouse. Although the museum master would later berate Charlton and Project Mayflower for arriving with unpaid bills, Harry's focus was on his own financial needs and credibility, not his English counterpart's. Charlton later recalled that after the Egyptian invasion, as the pound collapsed, the "breach in Anglo-American relations did some material damage to us. A number of the firms who had promised financial support suddenly discovered reasons for withdrawing, and this happened when we needed every penny to meet mounting building costs."[4] Still, he held firm on the departure date and pleaded with his partner. "After a long discussion," he recorded, "Felix agreed that we should not postpone sailing."[5]

Years later, his biographer said he "probably got his way not so much by the use of hard-headed logic as by pouring every ounce of emotional energy into willing Felix to do it his way."[6] It did not change the financier's nature, however. Felix was a numbers man and would remember his acquiescing to Warwick should the ledger need to be balanced in the future.

Then, remarkably, sponsorships started to sell as executives and operations managers began calculating the negative consequences of a European common market that excluded Britain. Tariffs had not gone up yet, but in less than a year they almost certainly would when the EEC became operational. Trade barriers could be ruinous, and paths around them had to be found. But where, and how? Government efforts to secure stronger commercial ties with the United States continued to falter, and Foreign Office initiatives lacked strategic vision and adequate funding.

Companies then began unraveling the wordplay hidden in Charlton's tribute to the "special relationship." The wooden ship was powered by *sails*, and it was offering to deliver *sales* to British industry. Nothing fancy, just a different way to view a seventeenth-century nautical workhorse that would carry chests filled with English products to consumers in the New World—the largest market on earth.

While revenue-generating efforts began to gain traction, nothing could be delivered unless the ship was built and supplies for the voyage secured. Only four equipment-providing companies had publicly identified themselves as supporters, and many more were needed. In-kind commitments thus became a focal point because they would allow organizations to get involved by donating goods and services instead of cash. The approach was a game changer. By the end of March, Project Mayflower was able to secure commitments from thirty-five top construction groups that had previously resisted coming aboard. Companies now proudly signing on included International Paints, Kelvin & Hughes, Marconi International, and many others.

Construction Groups Supporting *Mayflower II* [7]	Product or Service
British Jute Trade Federal Council	[unspecified]
British Ropes	[unspecified]
Briton Brush Co.	brushes
Brixham Urban District Council	ship's bell
Chas. Early & Co.	blankets
Crompton Parkinson	[unspecified]
Fabric Combiners	life rafts
Francis Webster & Sons	sails
Gourock Ropework Co.	ropes
Healey Marine	Skimaster
Hollins Brush Co.	paintbrushes
International Paints	paint
John Griffiths & Son	[unspecified]
John Player & Co.	cigarettes
Kalamazoo	stores index
Kelvin & Hughes	navigational instruments
Lee, Howl & Co.	pump for lifeboat
Lloyd's of London	log
M. Berman	tailored costumes
Marconi International Marine Communications	wireless
Mobil Oil Co.	oil and lubricants
Munster, Simms & Co.	bilge pumps
National Wool Textile Export Corporation	costumes
Parker Pen Co.	pens and ink
R. A. Lister (Marine Sales)	engine for lifeboat
Richard Thomas & Baldwins	[unspecified]
Robert Stocks & Co.	tea towels
Seaboard Lumber Sales Co.	[unspecified]
Stewart & Maclennan	fire appliances
Thomas Mercer Limited	chronometer
Thos. Ross & Son (London)	prints for captain's cabin
Truman, Hanbury Buxton & Co.	beer

Tyrrell & Green	tea towels
W. T. Grover & Co.	cables
Watts Fincham	lamps

Next, the Project Mayflower team turned its attention to what would be coming out of the galley during the long voyage. To provide sustenance for the crew, eight internationally recognized food and beverage outfits stepped forward to join the project, including Heinz, Huntley & Palmer, and Nestlé.

Companies Providing Food to *Mayflower II* [8]	Food Products Delivered
Burnyeat Ltd.	[honorary ships stores agents]
Carson Drinking Chocolate	beverage
David Williams & Sons Limited	butter
H. J. Heinz Company	canned foods
Huntley & Palmer	ship's biscuits
Nestlé Co.	canned milk
Pearce, Duff & Co.	custard and curry
Smedley's	canned vegetables

Finally, it was essential that all members of the ship's company remain in good health throughout the transit, and world leaders in pharmaceutical products came on board. These included Burroughs Welcome, British Schering, Pfizer, and nine additional medical suppliers.

Companies Providing Medical Supplies to *Mayflower II* [9]	Medical Products Delivered
Benger Laboratories	drugs
British Schering	medical supplies
Burroughs Welcome & Co.	drugs and ointment
Dalmas	medical supplies
Down Bros. & Mayer & Phelps	surgical instruments
Duncan Flockhart & Co.	drugs
Ethicon	sutures
Evans Medical Supplies	transfusion solutions and dressings

Imperial Chemical Industries	drugs
Pfizer	drugs
S. Maw Son & Sons	dressings
Smith & Nephew	first aid equipment

The range of industry support was impressive, and because the Suez Crisis had been caused in part by the country's thirst for petroleum, the commitment from Mobil Oil was not surprising. Although the canal had been essential for connecting the United Kingdom to India when it opened in 1869, that imperative ended in 1947 when the subcontinent became independent. The waterway's value then shifted to shortening the distance from Middle East refineries to Southampton—from 11,000 miles via the Cape of Good Hope at the southern tip of Africa to 6,500 miles through the shortcut. By 1955 most canal traffic was devoted to petroleum, making the passage uniquely important in economic and geopolitical terms. British holdings in Arabia were also a major source of foreign revenue, and if Middle East oil were cut off for a prolonged period, the impact on the United Kingdom and its economy would be catastrophic.

With this perspective, it made sense for Mobil to be among the first to celebrate peace and honor transatlantic ties. That gratitude was expressed in an advertorial, published in the *Mayflower Mail* just prior to launch, that referenced the Blue Riband, an unofficial accolade given to the fastest passenger liner crossing the Atlantic in any given period. After a long reign by the Cunard Line's *Mauretania* and a brief one by the ill-fated *Normandie*, the Riband had belonged to the *Queen Mary* for most of the preceding two decades until the *United States* knocked her off her pedestal in 1954. When Mobil put the replica in such company, it was meant as a great compliment, noting that "sailing ships have not much need of fuel and lubricants, but even a sailing ship must carry a radio today, and the radio of *Mayflower II* is supplied with current from a diesel engine. Fittingly enough, this and the diesel engine of the long boat are fueled and lubricated by Mobil." And of course, its "oils have been chosen to lubricate the engines of every Atlantic Blue Riband holder since 1920." The corporate giant wanted the British people, and the world, to know that it was sending "greetings to the company of *Mayflower II*, and joins them in saluting the memory of the Pilgrim Fathers."[10]

In less than one hundred days, previously reluctant companies agreed to provide the financial and material support Project Mayflower needed to complete the Brixham work and undertake the voyage. It was a remarkable achievement accomplished by a small group of inspired individuals, both known and unknown, who displayed courage, teamwork, and optimism in the face of adversity—the same traits exhibited by the 1620 passengers. Now all they had to do was convince a different set of companies that, despite what they may have heard from government officials, the replica would be an inspired cargo ship for transporting their products to America.

CHAPTER 11

Secret Meeting

THEN, JUST AS THE LATEST FUNDING HURDLES SEEMED SURMOUNTED, disaster struck as two hundred thousand shipyard workers announced plans to strike on March 16, shutting down every shipbuilder in the United Kingdom. It was the first such national work stoppage in thirty years, and an additional 2.5 million workers were poised to join the fight. Any hope that *Mayflower II* would sail in April as planned seemed doomed. Warwick Charlton quickly appealed directly to the labor union, requesting that it grant a special exception for the wooden boat. His pleas fell on surprisingly receptive ears, helped along by a letter that Charlton, through a New York contact, arranged to have sent to the London shipwrights' union by the Seafarers International Union requesting that, "in view of the special nature of the project and its importance for Anglo-American relations,"[1] an exception be made for the craft. The day before the strike began, Upham's men were told they could return to work while all other worksites remained silent.[2] Dissent from shop stewards in other Devon shipyards arose, but that too was countered.

Hidden forces may have been at work, however, as suggested in the American group's use of the words "Anglo-American relations." The stoppage happened simultaneously with preparations for the Bermuda Conference, a summit meeting between President Eisenhower and Prime Minister Harold Macmillan that hoped to mark a fresh start for the troubled alliance. If the ship had any diplomatic role to play in renewing that bond, it had to depart on schedule, and the strikers needed to make an exception for Brixham. But who could sway them to change their minds?

Figure 21. Striking workers among two hundred thousand shipwrights idled in March 1957. *(ChronicleLive)*

Ideally, it would be someone who understood leverage and saw the bigger picture—a person who had deep ties on both sides of the Atlantic, knew how unions bargained, and could convince opposing parties to agree. While the identity of this secret agent remains hidden to this day, there are only a handful of individuals who met the criteria. By coincidence, the previous month, John L. Lewis, head of the United Mine Workers of America and considered the most powerful person in organized labor, traveled with Winthrop Aldrich for four days aboard the USS *United States* from Southampton to New York as the work stoppage looming in London was echoed by a warning in America that "it is high time for the public in the Port of New York to realize the ugly imminence of another longshoremen's strike and to ponder how it still might be avoided."[3]

The charismatic union chief was a lifelong Republican, even though he crossed party lines in 1932 and 1936 to support Roosevelt before switching back to the GOP when FDR sought a third term. He was ostensibly studying "the United States mutual-aid program,"[4] but with dockworkers poised to walk off their jobs, an act that would have required careful planning and coordination well before the publicly announced action date, it would be illogical to think that strike strategies were not discussed, at least privately, with an American renowned for his skills navigating labor management disputes with national security implications. Publicly, Lewis made no comment about "other topics" when questioned by reporters about events unfolding in England, but their journalistic instincts sensed deception.[5] While silent on these undisclosed events, Warwick Charlton's personal records indicate that shortly after organizing Project Mayflower, he was introduced to the US ambassador during an unscheduled meeting at the House of Commons. He told the diplomat about his plans and later recorded that Aldrich was not only impressed but "offered to help in any way he could."[6] Perhaps he had a chat with Lewis.

Once back in New York as a private citizen, Washington's former envoy spoke publicly at the Council on Foreign Relations as the ship made final voyage preparations: "I am convinced that the complete reestablishment of the close relations which formerly existed between the United States and Great Britain is essential to the welfare and security of the Western World and I believe that this will be brought about in the near future with the exercise of patience, understanding and steadfastness of purpose on the part of the people of both countries."[7]

In February, John Hay Whitney, one of the richest men in America, became the new ambassador to the Court of Saint James's at the same time he was acquiring the *New York Herald Tribune*. Ike saw no conflict, and the new diplomat had a journalist's instinct for good storylines that could capture a reader's imagination.

While he could not openly show support for *Mayflower II*, Whitney understood the impact it would have on public attitudes and its usefulness in repairing the "special relationship." Not surprisingly, his newspaper applauded the venture. His superiors in Washington, however, could say nothing publicly even though they quietly might have interest. If they did, how would he find out and when?

Word came during the Bermuda Conference, held March 20–24, 1957, to coordinate British and American foreign policies, discuss common defense, and improve Anglo-American ties. The *New York Times* reported that the talks ended with the United States and Britain achieving "a measure of success well beyond anything envisaged when the meeting was arranged,"[8] and the two nations promised to work closely on future policies related to the Mediterranean and the Middle East.

The president and the prime minister met twice in private during the conference, and "neither the United States nor British briefing officers . . . would comment on the topics discussed."[9] Their second session took place on the afternoon of March 22 and included Secretary of State Dulles, Ambassador Whitney, British foreign secretary Selwyn Lloyd, British ambassador Harold Caccia, and other senior officials. The US State Department stamped records of the meeting RESTRICTED, and the subjects discussed remained hidden for decades—but, once declassified, shed new light on the importance of Project Mayflower. The leaders reviewed strategic defense, NATO, and a third topic:

Figure 22. Prime Minister Macmillan and President Eisenhower at the Bermuda Conference. *(Crown Copyright/Public Domain)*

The President said it was important to maintain the special relationship now existing between the US, Canada and Britain.

Selwyn Lloyd said the UK wished to proceed in this field as far as the US will permit, adding that this program would of course not include any nuclear matter. What the British want from the US now is its general blessing on this scheme, in view of the large political dividend which might be expected.[10]

Repairing the damage caused by Suez was a national security priority that had to be addressed quickly, publicly, and in a manner that would send a clear message to Moscow and the world that the two nations stood as one. They needed a display of unity that would capture the world's attention and demonstrate the enduring strength of the special relationship. In other words, they needed *Mayflower II*. Any Foreign Office misgivings about the project would be put aside for the greater good of the alliance, and while overt support was out of the question, a nod of approval was definitely in order, should it be required.

Coincidently with events in Bermuda, on March 21 Charlton's wartime friend Sir Francis de Guingand wrote to Eisenhower about Project Mayflower in a letter that awaited the president when he returned to Washington:

> Through the initiative of Mr. Warwick Charlton, who was a member of the old British Eighth Army in the desert, the scheme has now reached fruition, and the *Mayflower II* sails from Plymouth in the second week of April for Plymouth, Mass.
>
> It is hoped that there will be considerable surplus revenue available for an endowment to further Anglo-American relations, and I have agreed to become a trustee of this fund. I thought you might be interested in this development.[11]

The convergence of these events made it clear that the seventeenth-century replica being built in Brixham had a role to play in modern diplomatic history that no one could have imagined when the project was conceived.

CHAPTER 12

Finishing Touches

As Europe's trade doors with England began to close, *May-flower II* was in her final stages of construction. Since before the keel laying, Stuart Upham had spent nearly every spare moment researching ropes because they held up the masts and operated the sails. He calculated that 350 separate hemp lines would be needed, and to produce them he turned to a company his family had worked with for generations: the Gourock Ropeworks Company, one of the oldest groups in the United Kingdom, renowned for devotion to superior craftsmanship. The Scottish enterprise researched records dating back to 1736 to rediscover the secrets of making highly durable lines that would not falter under the stress of heavy seas. Most of these, the running rigging, "ran" through deadeyes and controlled and maneuvered the vessel, as distinct from the standing rigging holding up the masts. Each piece of cordage had its own purpose, many had "names . . . long . . . out of use, such as jeers, catharpins, knavelines, and the like," and some were so large they "lay upon the deck like sleek and docile boa constrictors, each 30 feet long."[1]

Upham felt very good about Gourock's involvement, but he knew installing the cordage correctly was critical to success. Every rope and block had to be positioned meticulously to prevent chafing that could damage both the lines and the sails. Failure to do so could spell disaster at sea, and Stuart Upham was not going to let that happen. As he examined mountains of historical materials to find the best way to rig the replica, the most helpful turned out to be only thirty miles away in South Devon, at Buckland Abbey. The one time home of Sir Francis Drake had an

exacting scale model of the *Golden Hind*, the ship he used to circumnav-
igate the globe between 1577 and 1580. Using that as a guide, Upham
rigged a larger likeness of *Mayflower* he kept at the shipyard. It was often
seen in photographs, including one with him and Warwick Charlton.

To start, he used small-gauge wire to rig the miniature just as he
knew he would have to do with the 180-ton vessel. Satisfied with that
step, he repeated the process using a lightweight cord. He then made a
third pass, again with cord, this time adding a full set of tiny handcrafted
blocks and miniature flax sails.[2] This intricate rope scheme, reviewed by
shipyard peers and scholars including Baker, became the guide for workers when they connected eight tons of Gourock rope to the masts and
sails. One could not find a better example of the shipbuilder's ingenuity
and problem-solving abilities than this rigging guide.

All water-exposed surfaces were sealed with Stockholm tar, similar
to that used centuries before to minimize leakage under all conditions.
The ship was then "painted from keel to topmast" with Interlux marine
paints to protect it from the harsh ocean conditions expected on the
voyage.[3] William Baker—in consultation with the curator of Sweden's
National Maritime Museum in Stockholm, Captain Sam Svensson—
chose *Mayflower II*'s color scheme. It was decided that the hull should be
painted with equal measures of raw sienna and umber pigments mixed
together. The rest of the ship reflected seventeenth-century practices,
which meant yellow ochre, earth-toned red, green, blue, oyster white,
and black. Of course, how the original *Mayflower* was actually decorated
would have depended on what was available at the time, but Baker felt
these hues were correct for the period and the ship he designed.[4]

The architect consulted with Upham throughout construction, and
together they achieved a faithful re-creation of a seventeenth-century
carrack. She had an overall length from tip to stern of 106 feet and architectural dimensions as follows:[5]

Length of keel: 58 feet 0 inches

Breadth to inside of plank: 25 feet 0 inches

Depth—top of keel to the breadth: 12 feet 8 inches

Burden by Rule of 1582: 181 tons

There were three masts. The mainmast was located with the advice of seventeenth-century texts and drawings that stated it "must stand in the middle of the keel." Next, the foremast's position was considered "in relation to the forecastle, the short prow deck, and the bowsprit." It was thus "stepped a little less than half way out on the stem with the beakhead bulkhead located just before it." As for the mizzenmast, "your judgement must be better there, than about any mast: because there is no just Rule to be given but only your eye must be your best Rule." For William Baker, this resulted in the mizzenmast being located at about a third of the distance from the mainmast to the stern.[6]

A seventeenth-century formula was used to calculate the height of each mast based on keel dimensions. The mainmast and foremast were twice the length of their tops. The nearly sixty-eight-foot mainmast had a roughly thirty-four-foot topmast above, and the nearly fifty-eight-foot foremast had a twenty-nine-foot topmast. The mizzenmast was just shy of forty-two feet, and the bowsprit, which sloped at roughly forty-five degrees down to the foremast's base, was the length of the foremast, a few inches short of fifty-eight feet.[7]

Stretching out from each mast, as a man might extend his arms, were the ship's own sail-bearing arms, its yards. As with the masts, their lengths were determined in relation to the keel. The main yard was a fifty-four-foot spar just below the mainmast's lookout platform, or main-top, and the main topsail yard was nearly twenty-two feet long. Toward the prow, the foreyard stretched over forty feet, and the fore topsail yard measured just over sixteen feet. At the stern, the mizzen yard holding the triangular lateen sail was identical in length to the foreyard and intersected the mizzenmast above its midpoint at an angle of roughly forty-five degrees, so the two looked like an open pair of scissors. Finally, from the ship's beak the spritsail yard crossed partway out the bowsprit and was just over thirty feet in length.[8]

As a finishing touch, government authorities allowed a May-blooming hawthorn flower to be painted on the stern instead of the ship's name and home port. William Baker's creation would only need five white petals surrounding a yellow floral disc flanked by two green leaves to identify her. Warwick Charlton's wish that his medium (the ship) be the message (democracy)—a symbol that required no words—was thus granted.[9]

In the captain's quarters, inkwells were added for additional authenticity. The ship's bronze bell, given by the people of Brixham, proudly told everyone that "Miles Graye Made Me in 1638." Historic words cast around its top. Graye was part of a dynastic Essex family that created more than 415 bells in the seventeenth century, many of which were still ringing clear and true three hundred years later. Remarkably, it is very possible that departing Pilgrims may have enjoyed the sound of his chimes, and family members who stayed behind could have heard this

Figure 23. On the stern, instead of the ship's name and home port, a painted mayflower. *(Travel Film Archives/Global ImageWorks)*

very one. If voyagers from 1620 suddenly appeared from the afterlife, they would have felt right at home on the new craft; she was that historically correct.

The angels would have smiled at what they saw, provided the replica stayed afloat. The possibility that she might not raced into the heads of onlookers on April 4 when the boat was pulled out of drydock into the harbor and nearly keeled over. British newspapers immediately seized on the image and mockingly dubbed Baker's creation the "Rock-and-Roll" ship, prompting the architect to note that "a few more gray hairs appeared that night among the few still left on my head."[10] Villiers was also a bit snarky and said his future ship "hung there, somewhat drunkenly, at an angle of between fifteen and twenty degrees—listed heavily, but did not capsize." The problem was quickly solved when 130 tons of railroad iron and lead, held in place with cement,[11] were put in her hold as ballast. Had that been added while she was in the protected work dock, she would have drawn too much water to be floated out. That was the official explanation, but Villiers thought "in truth the critical state of her stability had not been foreseen."[12] The team could only hope that was the last surprise.

It wasn't. British authorities refused to register the new *Mayflower* as a ship, instead calling her a "yacht." While this classification prohibited the transport of passengers, she was cleared to "carry a hold full of 'Treasure Chests' containing high quality goods of British manufacture for exhibition in the United States."[13]

The *Mayflower Mail* "sailing edition" published a list of fifty companies that bought one or more Treasure Chests, and another 115 companies and groups that bought shares in a Treasure Chest. They all wanted their names directly associated with the great seafaring adventure that was about to begin. Together, they represented Made-in-Britain products that corporate executives thought American consumers would be eager to buy. Such revenue gains could offset any losses that might be suffered by British companies should the new EEC impose tariffs on those goods. Many of the brands carried in the replica's hold were destined to become household names in the former colony: Guinness Exports, the Hudson's Bay Company, J. Florsheim, and others.

Figure 24. Treasure Chest inspected by Lord Mayor of Plymouth and others. *(Lee Israel/Mayflower Studios)*

The British Automobile News Bureau proudly told its readers that "a famous Coventry Climax engine . . . [was] included in the cargo of *Mayflower II*."[14] The motor was produced in the city bearing its name, home to a cathedral dating back to 1095. In 1950 Britain's Ministry of Defence requested bids for a new portable engine that would double the amount of water a fire pump could deliver, and Coventry Climax won with an innovative, lightweight, and powerful motor. Soon its application was expanded to auto racing, and a nimble British Lotus powered by the Climax had just won the prestigious 24 Hours of Le Mans. Because the United States was in love with driving, entering the market as part of the

Mayflower II story was good news for a British industry eager to raise its profile by showcasing technology discussed in nearly every home in America: the automobile.

The French were also interested in the adventure now, and the popular newsweekly *Paris Match* approached Warwick about putting one of its photographers on board—just as *Life* had contracted. Unfortunately, the American magazine had exclusive rights, having purchased them more than a year earlier when the project was in desperate financial straits. So the marketing maestro came up with a bold proposal. He offered the publisher the desired right to go aboard with a photographer but only prior to departure, saying, "If you are careful with your camera angles no-one will know that *Mayflower II* is not on the high seas."[15] What audacity! And the price? The French magazine agreed to pay £10,000 for a two-hour photo shoot, ten times what *Life* paid for the entire voyage. It was tangible evidence of just how firmly the pending voyage held the world's imagination.

Not to be left out, Harry Hornblower flew to England to witness final preparations and take part in departure ceremonies. Along with tourists, local residents, and others, he watched history unfold before his eyes. For the millions who could not attend, Pathé Television recorded it all, then distributed a short film called *Mayflower Sails for America*.[16] Viewers could see small craft ferry cargo boxes from dockside to the ship and watch as each was hoisted aboard and then lowered into the hold. Three lines of information boldly marked each unit. The first identified it as a MAYFLOWER TREASURE CHEST. The next two called out the recipient and destination. For example, one was for F R LAZARUS / COLUMBUS, OHIO. Another was for B FORMAN CO. / ROCHESTER, NEW YORK. Not shown on screen were those for CARSON PIRIE SCOTT CO. / CHICAGO, ILL.; HUTZLER BROS. / BALTIMORE; DAYTON CO. / MINNESOTA; and other nationally recognized retailers.

A crowd of about ten thousand watched men dressed in Pilgrim attire give speeches and pontificate. They were flanked by noncostumed dignitaries including the Lord Mayor of Plymouth, civic leaders, and representatives from America: James Frazier, chairman of the Board of Selectmen of Plymouth, Massachusetts; Harry Hornblower; and Arthur

Figure 25. *Mayflower II* Treasure Chests being loaded for all the world to see.
(© British Pathé)

Pyle. A Plantation "governor," George Olsson, was also there. He led
a worker-owned cooperative that sold products associated with a fruit
unknown to European palates until the seventeenth century—the cranberry. Not surprisingly, many of his growers were Mayflower descendants.

A short time later, a photographer captured the image of two people shaking hands aboard the replica. One was "a lean man of medium
height,"[17] wearing glasses, a conventional business suit, white shirt with
tie, and a double-breasted overcoat. A fedora—the "trademark of many
New England brokers and bankers[18]—was held in his lowered left hand.
That person was looking up at a taller fellow wearing a Pilgrim's outfit
featuring a crisp, pointed collar and a lace cuff protruding from a dark
coat sleeve, an outer vest with eight brass buttons, a wide light-colored
belt, knee breeches, knitted stockings, buckled shoes, and a tall black hat
cocked ever so slightly to the side. The two men stood on the replica's
main deck in front of a mast as others relaxed nonchalantly in the background. The businessman was Harry Hornblower, who would soon return
home to Boston to prepare for *Mayflower II*'s arrival. The Pilgrim was
Warwick Charlton.

Figure 26. Harry Hornblower and Warwick Charlton on the deck of *Mayflower II*. *(Courtesy Plimoth Patuxet Museums)*

Despite their incongruities of appearance and personality, they seemed to work cordially together, and each promised to honor his side of their bargain, starting with the Englishman. Warwick Charlton enjoyed witnessing history as it flowed forward, interpreting events as they emerged, sometimes to the sounds of conflict, sometimes to silence. He liked being present at the creation. Indeed a fighting editor who was bold and daring, he often seemed impervious to attacks by the high and mighty. In contrast, Harry Hornblower was controlled, competent, and correct—perfect traits for both his Wall Street occupation and his archaeological avocation. Unlike Charlton, Hornblower was drawn to ancient events that appeared to have been well studied but still offered revelations of fact and interpretation that captured his mind. Standing together on the deck of the second *Mayflower*, each man was fortified by a dream: for Charlton, resurrecting a maritime adventure that inspired a nation; for Hornblower, replicating life in a 1627 English colony called Plimoth Plantation. Their dual initiatives were dependent on each other and intertwined, just like their hands that April afternoon.

The Bostonian knew Charlton had pushed for delivery despite pleas from John Lowe and Felix Fenston to delay the journey and stage an exhibition in London. He was undoubtedly thinking about what would come next and knew Charlton's decision to deliver *Mayflower II* as originally promised meant the ship would arrive with debts. Given the situation, Harry may have felt Fenston was better qualified than the marketing impresario to deal with unpaid bills because he was a masterful and aggressive businessman accustomed to working with other people's money. Harry knew Felix was Project Mayflower's largest backer, and to drive that point home, the speculator wrote a £10,000 check just prior to departure so there would be no doubt about his monetary clout.[19] Harry the Wall Streeter liked that kind of bravado, and with any luck his counterpart Charlton would be out of the picture in a few months.

As for Stuart Upham, he was "under heavy fire" from his financial advisors, who regarded his decision to build the tribute without the usual financial guarantees as reckless. "In spite of this I had no doubt of the final success of the undertaking," he later wrote, because the replica "would bring its own reward."[20] He firmly believed that Project Mayflower was an homage to principle, honor, and history—not profit.

As onlookers were distracted by the freight loading and the international press corps posed for a group photo, Villiers gave an unseen nod to a nearby diver, who lowered himself into the water from a boat and swam below *Mayflower II*. The ship's smallest cargo—gold watches with a legend on the reverse side of each claiming it to be "shockproof, waterproof, and anti-magnetic"—was then "wantonly fastened here and there" under the ship.[21] Virtually no one would know about them until another diver retrieved the timepieces in America. Why the mystery? It turned out that Alan Villiers was a silent promoter for a certain Swiss manufacturer, the Enicar Watch Company of La Chaux-de-Fonds, Switzerland. This "variation on the treasure chest idea" was intended to make the company's name "sufficiently publicized" to give it a competitive advantage in the New World. Because the Australian was offering his services to Project Mayflower at no charge,[22] such personal marketing made sense, and hopefully some dollars too.

Now on to America!

Figure 27. International press corps posed with *Mayflower II* in background. *(Lee Israel/Mayflower Studios)*

CHAPTER 13

Bon Voyage

GOOD SPIRITS WERE JOINED BY FINE WEATHER, AND AROUND FIVE ON Saturday afternoon, April 20, 1957, *Mayflower II* slipped from her moorings and glided forward, politely holding a rope offered by the tugboat *Tactful*. Easterly winds that had freshened the harbor for the past several weeks were gone. Not even a breath remained. Thus an offer of assistance was gladly accepted, and for ten miles ancient wood and modern steel moved as one until the pair reached the famous Eddystone Light, well into the English Channel. After that, the ship was on her own, leaving behind a flotilla of sixty-seven yachts, dinghies, launches, and rowboats cheering her departure.[1]

Captain Villiers later told his global audience of *National Geographic* readers that he was concerned about stowaways hiding among the huge crates—so much so that he had his two sons, Kit and Peter, crawl around belowdecks to see if they could find anyone hiding there, although "I had searched the cargo hold rigorously before leaving. It was jammed full of heavy treasure chests, each bulging with British goods for exhibition and trade promotion in America. Any of those chests was quite large enough to house a stowaway, male or female, but they had been examined and each was documented and manifested."[2] That was true, but the irrepressible promoter Warwick Charlton found a way around those safeguards and snuck a man named Bob Lewis aboard during prelaunch distractions. He planned to have the stowaway appear once the voyage began, but his plans were thwarted when a final inspection was made. "The first mate had gone down to the lower hold and put his questing hand against a human head in back of a barrel. The man was hauled out, hustled up the companionway and over the side into the escort boat, which had been called along-side. Two buckets of swill from the galley cascaded down on him while we hooted and jeered."[3] It was all very annoying to Villiers, who addressed the crew shortly thereafter from the quarterdeck. "Now, lads, the bull and publicity are behind us! We have to get down to the job of delivering this ship to America."[4]

From now on it would be Alan Villiers's show, and he looked forward to entertaining the world with talents learned on the last giant windjammers in the 1920s and 1930s. Those skills were then refined further on the *Joseph Conrad* when he sailed her around the world, a total of fifty-seven thousand miles, before the outbreak of World War II.[5] Standing with him on deck as they sailed toward the Bay of Biscay were his senior officers, men born out of their time when square-riggers were being driven from the sea by steam. They were "the kind of shipmates he'd always hoped for."[6]

Villiers contacted Godfrey Wicksteed, who would serve as first mate, as soon as he got his job offer from Project Mayflower. The two had sailed together thirty years earlier on the four-masted barque *Ballands* from Western Australia around Cape Horn to Britain with a belly full of wheat for English buyers. That craft also fed Wicksteed's desire to learn as much as he could about old sailing techniques, and when he had to climb masts that could be as tall as a fifteen-story building and work in every kind of weather from velvet to volcanic, it became the perfect classroom. With that knowledge, plus a sturdy temperament, he was asked by Villiers in 1934 to take command of the *Conrad* and sail her from Copenhagen to London as his stand-in. Then came war, followed by peace, and Wicksteed went ashore to pursue a career as a schoolmaster. Now fifty-seven, he was a respected academic looking forward to retirement, yet there was still seawater in his veins. The lure of becoming *Mayflower II*'s second in command was irresistible—provided, of course, that he could get permission from the Cambridge Education Committee and his wife. How could they say no? Alan's first key hire was confirmed. Before leaving for the voyage, however, the chief mate went to nearly three hundred schools to tell them about the original *Mayflower*, describe his upcoming adventure, and commit to writing a lengthy letter to each one of them from the high seas. Aboard the ship, his teacherly ways would continue. The incoming freshmen—mariners who were unaccustomed to working before the mast—quickly discovered that Wicksteed had forgotten more about square-rigged sailing than they might ever learn.[7] He was an inspiration.

Of equal competence was Adrian Small, who left England at age sixteen to apprentice under the renowned Finnish sea captain Gustaf Erikson on big four-masted windjammers that served Australia and the world. Small spent several years on the Erikson ship *Passat* as it circled the globe delivering agricultural products to eager buyers, and he was aboard on its penultimate grain race from Australia to the United Kingdom, as a way of life for generations of mariners came to an end. Coincidently, Villiers wrote about that era in his 1933 book *Grain Race*, and the two men could talk for hours about their common love of the sea. Small subsequently worked as Villiers's second mate aboard the *Pequod* during the *Moby Dick* movie project, and today he stood beside the captain in that same capacity. At age twenty-eight, the mariner with a bright red beard was an excellent role model for novice crewmen.

The *Joseph Conrad* was then tapped again, this time for the third mate, Danish captain Jan Junker, a forty-year-old Inuit-speaking ice pilot who had been working Greenland routes since the end of World War II. During that conflict, Junker spent a year in the hell of a Nazi concentration camp. Trained as a saboteur, he had parachuted behind enemy lines from an RAF bomber, his mission to teach those dark arts to resistance fighters. Unfortunately, the Germans arrested him along with ten others, nine of whom were shot before Junker was imprisoned. After the war he returned to the sea, and this voyage looked too exciting to pass up. Alan considered him "a steadfast and supremely competent sailing-ship seaman both before the mast and abaft it, and I regarded his presence aboard as a major asset to the vessel."[8] The crew agreed, particularly when Junker gave salty sage advice to some of the younger men. Just prior to leaving Plymouth he told them that everyone was destined to get seasick at least once during the voyage, and some more often than others. His recommendation? "In bad weather, always eat apricots—they taste the same coming up or going down."[9]

Mayflower's boatswain, generally shortened to bos'n, was Alan's most important all-purpose sailor, who oversaw the crew and the ship's equipment. For this daunting and essential position, another North Sea *Pequod* veteran was chosen, Isaac "Ike" Marsh. The skillful Welshman had been working at the Barry Docks near Cardiff most recently, and he had deep knowledge and experience of mariners and materials—plus he was a fast and fearless ratline climber, a human spider who could race about the ship's hemp webs in any kind of weather, day or night. He was perfect for the job, and he told Alan, "I've looked forward to an experience like this all my life."[10]

These four men gave the man from Down Under great confidence and eased his task of assembling the rest of his crew in accordance with the rules. While the first *Mayflower* sailed under the watchful eye of God alone, its namesake was required to go forth under the glaring gaze of

Figure 28. *Mayflower II* sailing tall and proud as she heads to America. (© *British Pathé*)

bespectacled bureaucrats at the Ministry of Transport and Civil Aviation. Lifesaving gear was required for sixty-six men, twice the size of the actual crew, plus five inflatable life rafts that could each hold twelve sailors, just in case they had to abandon ship. A two-way radio was also mandated. However, no special rules were issued for the ship's cook, carpenter, and doctor, which was fine with the captain because he knew what he needed.

Alan Villiers had lived at sea for much of his life, and he knew that the old expression "The way to a man's heart is through his stomach" applied to men on shipboard as well as those targeted in romantic pursuits. He also knew that there would be no refrigeration, that the galley would be primitive, and that thirty-three men required the delivery of ninety-nine meals a day. *Mayflower II* needed an old-timer, not a rookie. Although there was no shortage of volunteers, the right man didn't appear until less-than-robust fifty-four-year-old Walter Godfrey of the General Steam Navigation Company walked through Alan's door. Wally was "wiry, resolute, and competent, with a lifetime of experience at sea dating well back to the days before refrigeration." An apparent perfect fit, as long as his London employer would give him time off, which it did. The crew was the beneficiary and his meals were pronounced "first class with plenty of variety and reasonable quantities, though jam and butter are rationed rather severely."[11]

For ship's carpenter, one of the lead workers from Upham's shipyard signed on. Edgar Mugridge knew *Mayflower II* from the keel up and continued the long maritime tradition of selecting the carpenter from the shipbuilder's yard. It would have been impossible to find someone more skilled and knowledgeable. While all ships, including those with hulls of steel, will moan and make creaking sounds, this vessel might literally snap, crackle, and pop when put to the test, which could cause leaks that would need to be plugged and then caulked. Also having Stuart Upham on board gave both Villiers and his crew confidence in the replica's construction and durability, at least on paper.

John Stevens, the executive officer on a Royal Navy submarine during the war, who finished his service aboard the South African training ship *General Botha*, was well known to the captain. He had changed his mind about a life at sea after getting out of uniform and gone to medical school.

Now a successful doctor in Ipswich, where he lived with his wife and family, he gladly put all on hold for a chance to be *Mayflower II*'s onboard physician because in his spare time "I do a bit of sailing."[12] Stevens was a fifth-generation South African but had no stomach for the country's apartheid policy, so rather than compromise his principles, he left his homeland for a new life in England, just as the Pilgrims had sought fresh starts in the New World. It added special meaning to his presence aboard because being able to express your beliefs without fearing government reprisal was a powerful force that had changed little since 1620. This, of course, is not what attracted Villiers's interest. The doc knew how to put injured men back together and take full advantage of the medicines provided by the leading pharmaceutical companies supporting the voyage. Like the others chosen, he was just right for the job, and he also brought a good sense of humor and a quick wit.

Dawn arrived on their first day at sea with Plymouth still in sight. No wind that Easter morning as the captain began a Sunday ritual that would last the voyage: a brief religious service followed by a history lesson. Today it featured an overview of Bradford's *Of Plimoth Plantation*. Breezes finally arrived late in the day, allowing the sails to fill and giving the masts and bowsprit a chance to show their initial character, which caught the captain's attention. "The fore topmast looked little better than a knotty broomstick and the main topmast was not much stouter, nor was there anything like an adequate supply of spare spars aboard if the ship were even partially demasted." For a mariner with decades of experience on square-riggers, a closer examination was demanded, so he went to the very back of the ship to stand on the poop deck, look forward, and get a better understanding of what was happening. "I could see the mainmast-head move laterally a foot or so with each roll of the ship" as the heavy mainyard jumped and the "foremast seemed to stumble and jerk violently at its supporting rigging with every pitch, like a hard-mouthed steeplechaser jerking at the reins as it came close to a fence." The Australian mariner soon "wondered how long the topmasts might stay with us."[13]

As for the bowsprit, it "waved like a wand when a strain came on it from the big spritsail," and that sheet could not be secured by itself because of Baker's commitment to architectural accuracy. "There was not a reefpoint in a single sail aboard, for there were none in 1620 and we had to be historically correct," which meant the replica could be in danger if the bowsprit was put to the test. Villiers shared his concerns with his senior officers, and they agreed that the threat was real because no one knew "how well her rigging might stand up to a succession of gales." These anxious calculations were racing through Alan's head and his voyage had barely begun as he realized the "short and chunky ship" could be in real danger on an unpredictable angry sea. "These problems might not have worried the good Captain Christopher Jones of the first *Mayflower*, 337 years before, but they worried us."[14] While Jones's crew had great experience on a carrack such as this, Alan's had virtually none because his craft's sea trials lasted only "a couple of hours" in Tor Bay just beyond the Brixham Harbor's breakwater in the days before sailing. On top of that, more than half the men were new to square-riggers. The voyage itself would have to be their trial, a kind of pass-fail test, because the maritime weather service was warning of possible storms on their planned course at latitude 40° north that included drifting ice, a hazard the service now tracked in an effort to avoid catastrophes such as the *Titanic*.[15]

Considering all the facts at his disposal, Villiers chose not to tempt fate and, five days out, decided to disregard historical correctness and his own careful prevoyage planning, turn south toward the Canary Islands, drop just below the Tropic of Cancer, catch the trade winds at latitude 25° north, and follow the path of Columbus. Seventeenth-century mariners traveling to British colonies in Virginia and the Carolinas also took such a course, and it was a wiser way to go. While that redirection would lengthen the journey to about 5,500 nautical miles instead of the planned 3,500, they had sufficient provisions for the extension. On such an ambitious journey, it was simply better to be safe than sorry. Villiers reported the change to Portishead, England, and South Chatham, Massachusetts, using the shipboard radio, and they in turn told the world, as armchair admirals, adventure lovers, and regular people who loved the story eagerly tracked the second *Mayflower*.

That change also let Villiers enjoy something totally unexpected, as he wrote in his diary the next day: "I never imagined that some day

I would be sailing a 'treasure' galleon toward the Spanish Main!"[16] Yet here he was, doing exactly that, as captain of a seventeenth-century ship bearing chests filled with bounty, including one he inspected on a daily basis with a crewmember to make certain the customs seal remained unmolested. He placed it conspicuously in the 'tween decks in full view of everyone because it contained gold from Great Britain and silver from Holland.[17] Prior to departure, it had been on public display at Garrard, the crown jewelers on Regent Street in London, and even honored at a special reception at the House of Commons. There were silver *Mayflower* earrings, gold charms depicting the Pilgrim Fathers and the Indians who greeted them, and sterling silver flatware featuring Elizabethan-era patterns. Most magnificent was a fourteen-inch-long sterling silver likeness of the *Mayflower* cast from a scale model of the craft provided by Plimoth Plantation, which seldom if ever mentioned it.[18]

Figure 29. Captain Alan Villiers inspects his most treasured cargo prior to departure. *(Lee Israel/Mayflower Studios)*

Unlike the smooth-sailing windjammers that were well known to Villiers and his senior officers, the replica "was like a wild little bronco constantly taking an uneven series of high fences and rolling and all but falling over as she came to each one." Upham's craft was sturdy but heavy, which meant slow, so the ten-knot speed originally estimated was reduced to seven owing to the weight of the railway iron and old furnace bars that provided ballast, plus another "17 tons of heavy chests on top of that." When not bucking like a stallion, the small ship "rolled violently like the pendulum of a clock" in a good breeze,[19] and while the crew had confidence in her strength, maritime correspondent Stanley Bonnett of the *Daily Mail* belittled the craft prior to departure and gave her no more than "an even chance" of completing the transit while also making a dismissive comment about her namesake: "The only thing really sweet about her 1620 predecessor was the wine in the bilges which seeped there from days in the Bordeaux wine trade."[20] Oh yeah? Not realizing the resentment his critique generated with the crew, he returned the next day for a follow-up, only to be manhandled as a bag was put over his head and his body bound to a stanchion. Moments later he was doused with frigid seawater and the possibility of throwing him overboard was audibly debated. Then a cheer went up and he was released unharmed, though now well informed of the men's pride in their vessel. Perhaps not surprisingly, a complimentary article appeared in his paper the following day.[21] As for Doc Stevens, he was not about to accept that sort of journalistic mockery and countered it by organizing a 50/50 Club "for sailors who risk their lives on *Mayflower II*."[22]

The reporter's comments, while belittling, did not annoy Villiers as much as his sleeping accommodations. The captain bunked in the charthouse high above the water, which he found most challenging. "That ruddy cabin! The worst in the flamin' ship. If you get out of your bunk you either break your head or bust your shoulder, and if you stay in, you fall out and break your ruddy neck! Never saw such a ship for things fallin' everywhere!"[23] Charlton's and Upham's cabins were at the back of the main deck beneath the quarterdeck along with the officers'. In the 'tween decks, the crew tucked away each night in cubicles measuring nine by five feet, with an open space in the middle for cargo. These sleeping areas were equipped with iron bunk beds and partitioned off from neighbors by hardboard. A total of twenty-three men could be accommodated there, and two more could sleep in the forecastle, which also served as a carpenter's shop, bos'n's storeroom, and lamp room.[24] Some of the men might add that their accommodations could double as a sound studio because carpenter Mugridge could snore as loudly as shipyard saws, the steering block could scream like a cow in agony, and the boat itself could groan like Magellan's ship rounding Cape Horn.[25] For those in the forward bunks, the waves felt like "ragged thunder rolls followed by hisses, gurgles, chuckles."[26] Depending on where you were standing, there was six to seven feet of headroom, which was greater than the original because a man's "average height has increased noticeably during the past three centuries." Back then sailors had to accustom themselves to "scrambling around a restrictive 4-foot 'tween-deck space."[27]

Because this was Charlton's inaugural experience on a sailing ship, his first task was to learn the bells. He quickly discovered that the ship's bell is used to mark half-hour intervals. A four-hour watch would have eight bells marking its beginning or end. At noon, eight bells would be heard, then one bell at twelve-thirty, two at one o'clock, three at one-thirty, and so on until eight bells were struck again at four o'clock. To ring the bell, the best technique was to get a firm grip on the clanger rope, center it, then quickly smack it to the side with a flip of the wrist. Luckily for the venture, all the other men knew this before walking aboard.

Each of the three officers—First Mate Wicksteed, Second Mate Small, and Third Mate Junker—had a team of six men who would work a four-hour shift twice a day: a watch. Thus, every hour of the day found a crewman standing at the ship's wheel as others in his detail might tend to the sails, scrub the deck, or paint. That accounted for twenty-one men. Generally excluded were the others on board: two cooks, two cabin boys, four voyage chroniclers, the radio operator, the ship's carpenter, Charlton, and of course Villiers. Everyone knew that an ancient square-rigger challenging the high seas had endless needs, and these thirty-three adventurers were on call night or day, fair weather or foul.

Feeding the crew had been carefully planned, and just as the tools used to build the ship met seventeenth-century standards, that era was

Figure 30. Captain Villiers briefed the entire crew about the voyage ahead. *(Lee Israel/Mayflower Studios)*

also the starting point for nutrition. Because there was no refrigeration on board, the historic sailors' staples of hardtack and salt pork became regular menu items. Sea biscuits, as mariners nicknamed hardtack, were no longer produced commercially, so Huntley & Palmer of England called upon recipes dating back three centuries to find just the right measures of salt, water, and wheat flour to produce these cakes, which then had every last ounce of moisture removed. The resulting product could last for weeks, months, or even years before being soaked in tea, coffee, beer, or any other liquid to make them edible. Alternatively, they could be crushed and boiled into a porridge, fried in a pan, or just sucked on during a long night's watch.

A few weeks into the voyage another ancient delicacy was literally rolled out for the crew when two barrels appeared on deck covered with burlap. They had been stored in a cool spot belowdecks and doused frequently with seawater to keep them as cold as possible. One was soon opened and revealed culinary antiquity: salt beef. Villiers quickly inspected the product, sampled it, and announced: "Mostly lean. No flamin' fat to speak of. No blue mold. No *green* mold. Not even a *taste* of green mold—not much, anyway."[28] Younger crew members soon developed their own reactions to the meat, but none of them got sick from the baconlike strips that followed twice a week and were chewed with gusto—except by Doc Stevens, a vegetarian, who grew watercress and mustard greens from seed in a portable garden he created with wet cotton balls. Once the plants achieved a certain height, he would take a pair of medical scissors and harvest a small salad!

In a nod to modern times, fresh bread was baked three times a week in the galley's oil-fired oven, which had burners on top for cooking with pots and pans to produce nourishing meals three times a day.[29] There was also a small kerosene stove for emergency use and night watch snacks. It was a far cry from the galley sandbox used to build small fires on the original voyage, a system that was of no use during bad weather because loose embers could cause an onboard fire. Back then, stewing food in pots was all they could do.

The ship carried a large supply of preserved foods in tin cans, twentieth-century versions of the glass or porcelain jars used on voyages as far back as Sir Francis Drake.[30] Nearly ten tons of fresh water was stored in two large iron tanks in the main hold that fed a thirty-gallon container over the galley for daily dispensing. It was inspected regularly by Doc Stevens to ensure purity and was used only for cooking and drinking. Bathing and clothes washing were done with seawater unless rain from a passing squall could be collected for the job. There were also a hundred cases of Truman's Pale Ale, "brewed and matured at Burton on Trent," then "Bottled for the Mayflower" with a commemorative label featuring an image of the ship with the years 1620 and 1957 on either side.[31] Although manufactured in the heart of England in Staffordshire, it was well suited for the southern route. Each man had an allotment, and while the older crew consumed their daily issue on the spot, some of the younger men saved theirs for their parents as a special souvenir.[32]

The Great Cabin was the mess hall for the officers. It had a handsome oak table that was made by boys at the Kitwood Secondary Modern School of Boston, Lincolnshire, to William Baker's specifications and then artificially aged to make it look like a rare antique.[33] Three picturesque windows provided light, solid ceiling beams offered coverage, and camera equipment, the ship's radio gear, and a box of books by Winston Churchill meant as gifts upon arrival littered the space. Eating there were Villiers, Charlton, Upham, and the ship's officers: Wicksteed, Small, Junker, and Marsh, plus Mugridge and Stevens. They were joined by *Pequod* veteran Joe Lacey, who was a bos'n's mate under Marsh, and the ship's radio operator Jim Horrocks, called by the traditional nickname Sparks. Rounding out their dining group were four chroniclers: Project Mayflower movie cameraman Julian Lugrin, Mayflower Studios photographer Lee Israel, and two men on the payroll of *Life* magazine, reporter Maitland Edey and lensman Gordon Tenney. These latter two produced "A Mayflower Sails into Today,"[34] whose coverage began with a photo taken from atop the mizzenmast at the stern of the ship looking down and forward as foam burst from the bow and a sail was unfurled. Readers were thrilled when the same issue, in a touch of irony, devoted twenty-two pages to "the impressive survival of European monarchs in a democratic era"[35] because the editors knew America was fascinated with both its Pilgrim past and the pageantry surrounding the European royalty it rejected in 1776. A reader in West Hartford, Connecticut, later wrote the editors and captured the importance of the voyage: "*Mayflower II* is a fine gift that should remind all Americans, regardless of national origin, that their heritage is nonconformity, the courage to stand and be counted for a principle."[36]

Tending to the officers' needs were the two cabin boys, Britisher Graham Nunn and American Joe Meany, the captain's gofers, who would bus the Great Cabin but could offer little comfort from the violent rocking motions that often plagued the space because of its height above the water. Graham also had an additional soul to look after, a tiny black kitten with white boots and bib that "some old lady" in Plymouth had given him just prior to departure. The nameless, barely weaned feline, who fit easily into the palm of a hand, was soon christened Felix, and his little meows quickly became pleasing to all ears on board.

Villiers and a few others were skeptical about the kitten's chances of survival because he could barely walk and looked oh-so-fragile. But Graham ignored their concerns and kept him belowdecks with the help of pro-Felix sailors until they were well out to sea. Having a feline shipmate added a further touch of authenticity to the voyage because cats were almost certainly on board in 1620. Indeed, they were such a common presence in that era that they were generally not mentioned. They helped control mice and rats that could gnaw at wood, chew through the lines holding the ship together, and eat irreplaceable food.[37] That was not a concern on this voyage, but having Felix continued a tradition that even Winston Churchill embraced, literally, when he was pictured in 1941 petting ship's cat Blackie of HMS *Prince of Wales*.[38]

Mayflower II had an official mascot!

While the captain and his officers ate in the swaying Great Cabin, the rest of the crew were fed in the tiller flat below them, which was one of the smoother-riding places and comfortable, but not without issues. Specifically, lacking the likes of Graham and Joe, "the meals were a forest of hands grabbing across the mess table and greasy dishes passed around for everyone to help themselves—three courses on the same plate to save washing up."[39]

Figure 31. Graham Nunn reading to the ship's mascot, Felix. *(Gordon Tenney/ Black Star)*

The ship's seasoned cook, Wally Godfrey, had a younger assistant who knew the culinary arts and operated a successful London restaurant called the Wig and Pen Club near Fleet Street, the hub of British journalism. His name was Dick Brennan. During the war he and Warwick Charlton were buddies, and afterward they remained close—so much so that Warwick used Dick's club as his office when meeting with people who could have a positive impact on Project Mayflower, such as sponsorship prospects, media executives, and Harry Hornblower. The Plimoth man liked the club owner and seemed to find his way there whenever he was in London during the prelaunch years. Charlton also fabricated a picturesque history for Dick's place, claiming it was not harmed in the Great Fire of London, which would have been remarkable, and wasn't a complete falsehood, because the building did not exist in 1666.[40] In exchange for Brennan's courtesy and support, Warwick promised him the position of ship's cook before he realized it was not his decision to make. Alan was initially skeptical about having two cooks in the kitchen, but after considering the size of the task and the importance of caloric intake at sea, and after meeting the pub owner, he changed his mind, which turned out to be a good decision for everyone. Assisting them both was Jack Scarr, an Oxford schoolmaster and lifelong friend of Captain Villiers. Prior to becoming a senior academic at the St. Edward's School, Scarr was a seaman specializing in the delivery of awkward small ships to various English ports. As good as he had been at maritime efforts, the classroom was where he really excelled, and the head of his school would not let him join *Mayflower II* until a suitable substitute was found. It eventually required the employment of two people to cover his singular duties.

Another good hire was John "Jumbo" Goddard, who had been prospecting for uranium in Central Australia when he got wind of a second *Mayflower* and offered his special expertise. He had served on the Erickson grain ship *Herzogin Cecilie* for several years making runs from Australia around Cape Horn to England, so he knew what he was doing on the high seas. Additionally, the Rolls Royce Company had trained him to be an engine mechanic, which normally would have had no value on a sailing ship, but the British government was requiring the replica to have a two-way radio available throughout the voyage. While the Marconi

Company provided both the equipment and a Sparks for its operation, nothing would happen without electricity. Thus a diesel generator was required, along with an expert in engine mechanics, which Jumbo definitely was. The motor could also drive a bilge pump, which would probably have more use on a daily basis than access to radio frequencies. Jumbo had a bellowing laugh, a deep voice that could be heard from one end of the ship to the other, and was a great catch.

Nine days into the voyage, the captain's Sunday practice of dressing in Pilgrim attire and leading a brief worship service continued the routine started a week earlier on Easter, with the ringing of the ship's 1638 bell at 10:00 a.m. Although the men had been at sea for only a short time, land life seemed worlds away, and they had not seen another ship in four days. On this April 28, the earthly message was about the history of the first *Mayflower* and how the decision to take a northerly route was based in part on the risk of running into Spanish galleons that controlled the seas further south. The Australian was a natural storyteller, and the tale of the 1620 passengers fleeing England to seek religious freedom and commercial fortune in the New World captivated the crew. Hearing about that moment in history while standing under fat-bellied sails surrounded by the vast ocean was thrilling to all on board. Each of them could imagine they were reincarnations of those sailors centuries earlier as their own ship approached the coast of Morocco.

Also enjoying the thrill of an unfolding adventure was mascot Felix, who discovered his sea legs and enjoyed climbing the ropes, or just lying on them, as his home swayed in the sea. At the end of a day of activity and exploration, he visited the bunks and offered a fluffy cuddle in exchange for a warm nest. His diet had expanded from evaporated milk and now included any table scraps the crew might give him, including Villiers, who treated him to the same liquid supplement offered everyone else on board. In an effort to prevent scurvy, British authorities had mandated the consumption of limes or their juice for centuries, giving rise to the nickname for Her Majesty's sailors: Limeys. By the mid-1950s the citrus drink had evolved from vile to tasty, and even Felix was willing to give it a try.[41]

Figure 32. Mascot Felix the Cat exploring the ship's ropes. *(Gordon Tenney/ Black Star)*

Villiers sent status updates on a weekly basis, and news outlets on every continent reported the ship's progress as it captured the world's imagination in the tradition of the *Kon-Tiki* and Mount Everest quests. Little or no mention was made of Plimoth Plantation, which may have annoyed its founder because he wrote a letter to the *Berkshire Eagle* in Pittsfield, Massachusetts, printed on May 2, 1957. Harry Hornblower told readers he wanted to "clear up a point or two in connection with the voyage of *Mayflower II*, her destination and permanent resting place." First, the ship was coming to his new colonial history center under the command of Captain Villiers, and after a short stay would travel to New York City for its Summer Festival before being "turned over by her English builders to Plimoth Plantation." Next, a portion of the revenue collected from tourists would be used "to establish an exchange scholarship fund for American and English students" because the boat itself was "a gift of the people of England." Finally, construction costs were being covered by an "English group" that "raised the necessary funds through free will gifts of small amounts"—which Harry knew was not entirely true because of Herbert Boynton's reports and the loading of Treasure

Chests he had personally witnessed a few weeks earlier. But if he said the construction was paid for by ordinary Britons, then perhaps everyday Americans would help pay for *his* undertaking. Hornblower then asked readers to send money to "Post Office Box 1620 in Plymouth, Massachusetts," applying a tactic he used when soliciting funds from his Harvard classmates in advance of reunions. It worked along the banks of the Charles River and was certainly worth a try on the shores of Cape Cod Bay. Warwick Charlton and Project Mayflower were not mentioned.[42]

Back in London, Hornblower's letter caused consternation and prompted financier Fenston to issue a statement to the Reuters news service "as a result of a request to clarify plans" for the ship. He confirmed that *Mayflower II* would indeed arrive in Massachusetts and then spend the summer in New York City, the de facto financial capital of the world, before being handed over to "the people of the United States as a gift from the people of Britain."[43] The transaction would take place in November as a nation-to-nation gift, not a trophy to be claimed by a private group backed by wealthy individuals. While Fenston's statement alluded to Hornblower and his enterprise, there was no mention of the American or Plimoth Plantation.

As for supporting students with a portion of visitor revenues, the British and American groups had agreed two years earlier when they joined forces to use some of the income generated from public exhibitions "to provide academic and cultural exchange and scholarship facilities to study in the United Kingdom and to further research, publications and reconstructions."[44] It was a compromise that honored both organizations' noncommercial pursuits: the Americans could use their portion to advance the study of colonial times and expand the museum, while the British could use their proceeds to strengthen Anglo-American unity and celebrate the two nations' "special relationship" by emulating the Fulbright and Marshall scholarship programs, though with only a few recipients annually. That initiative might even eclipse the museum and replica as a pillar for upholding the democratic aspirations expressed in the Mayflower Compact. Such noble efforts from both groups could support people who had an interest in a wide range of academic subjects, including anthropology and archaeology, two of Harry's favorites. While his teenage dream was influenced by the success of other institutions that featured historical settings and costumed docents, the scholarship and education programs were original, high minded, and forward looking.

In weather news, Boston was enjoying a warmer than normal spring with temperatures in the seventies, London was still in the sixties, and *Mayflower II* experienced beautifully warm days and chilly nights as she sailed less than a hundred miles off La Palma in the Canary Islands on May 2. As usual for him, Warwick Charlton was on deck early, fretting about the ship's progress and soft winds, while Peter Padfield was capturing pencil images of the lovely curved sails blooming above them. The writer liked what he saw and told the artist they were contours now lost in the modern world. "The same people who would admire the shape of the sails in that drawing would condemn them as pointless and meaningless if they saw them in the abstract without the ship and the tangle of masts and shrouds to hold them in and make them seem real objects. I mean—just take the sculpture of Barbara Hepworth."[45] Years later Padfield would use that rendering as cover art for a diary he eventually published about the voyage.

Warwick also put pencil to paper that day, writing:

This morning at about 8:30 we sighted a ship on the port quarter and ran up our ensign, but they ignored us and continued on their way. We tried to find explanations for this indifference, a hurt to our vanity, and Alan suggested that everyone must have been working in the hold so that the watch dare not disturb them even to admire us. . . .

Mayflower never fails to demand some service of us; we are her acolytes, and today we were busy as usual making chafing gear, oiling the topmast yard and shortening the mainstay. This is the stay that comes from the mainmast and keeps it from going aft.[46]

In the afternoon of the next day, Tenerife's 3,360-foot Cruz de Taborno could be seen portside sticking its head out of a collar of white clouds, as La Palma continued to sit to starboard. At the same time, a photo was taken stateside showing Hornblower sitting atop a giant bulldozer, dressed in a business suit and looking down at a man and woman wearing Pilgrim outfits.[47] It was the groundbreaking ceremony for Plimoth's new home on the property he had shown Warwick Charlton nine months earlier. Unaware of that sidebar, Villiers, Charlton, and Upham were well on their way to America, and *Mayflower II* had just found the trade winds. Warwick wrote in his journal that "the Captain was openly pleased with life,"[48] for it was "a beautiful day of northerly wind . . . the north-east trade."[49] Upham knew this too and expressed the joy on board: "At last came the day when the rising sun streamed in the Great Cabin windows, indicating we had turned west, and that night the sun set over our bowsprit. We had found the northeast trades which were to take us across the Atlantic."[50]

As the sun sank below the horizon, Villiers gave the archaic order to "splice the mainbrace," summoning all men on deck to celebrate the moment with an issue of lime juice spiked "with two bottles of rum."[51] It was a milestone well deserving a toast. Cheers to all!

Figure 33. "Splice the mainbrace!" We've reached the northeast trades! *(Lee Israel/Mayflower Studios)*

CHAPTER 14

Appreciated

WITH THAT GOAL REACHED, IT WAS NOW TIME FOR THE CREW "REALLY to know something about the *Mayflower* story, not the *Mayflower* myth."[1] As the men came topside wearing their Pilgrim costumes and the captain prepared for his Sunday sermon, Charlton's mind went back centuries, and he reflected that most people nowadays had the wrong idea about what was worn back then. Rather than being dull and drab, clothing could in fact be quite colorful. Men were not confined to the stiff hats seen in children's books, and women often "dipped their materials in saffron to get a bright orange colour, or in indigo for rich blue shades,"[2] while their necklines could be quite low, contrary to the modesty often assumed for their clothing choices. Men and women of sufficient means could be seen in big beaver-felt hats, while woolen Monmouth caps offered both style and comfort for all. As for the sea's spectrum, it was bold and dramatic, changing quickly with passing clouds, light from the sun and stars, the wind, and its own watery nature.

The crew saw its first ship in days when an unidentified tanker smudged the horizon with black smoke, altered course for a better look at the replica, and then continued on its way—most likely to the West Indies. After that sighting, the men felt in high spirits and composed a song for the occasion, to the tune of "Worried Man Blues" with its repeated line "It takes a worried man to sing a worried song" and the refrain "I'm worried now, but I won't be worried long":

Oh, blow ye nor'east Trades, now blow the *Mayflower* on,
Oh, blow ye nor'east Trades, now blow the *Mayflower* on,
Oh, blow ye nor'east Trades, now blow the *Mayflower* on,
At seven knots we won't be sailing long.
We're bound for Massachusetts, that's in the Yewesay,
And when we get there, Lord, we will bless the day.[3]

Their chorus was rewarded in the coming days with fair winds and good progress as the ship averaged over 160 miles from noon to noon for most of the week, which prompted Villiers to have Sparks send a message to the world: "Beautiful blue sea, more often marked by golden sargassum weed than by the whitecaps of breaking water. Pilgrim Fathers should have come this way instead of by the boisterous and ice-littered northern route."[4]

Aboard the replica, the message was less effusive, and the Aussie reminded his crew that such good fortune should not be expected to last the entire voyage. Sure enough, on Wednesday night into Thursday "the ship crept over the ocean like a heavy wooden monster, waddling, oh so slowly, heaving wearily from side to side with her sails flapping like broken wings."[5] Or perhaps a drying shirt being blown aimlessly on a clothesline in the backyard. A breeze came back in the morning, but at a slower pace than before, so only 116 miles were logged that day, and 95 the next.

The weather was becoming noticeably milder, and under light clouds the following afternoon the captain gathered all the men on deck for a "bottle drop" ceremony that was organized by Doc Stevens and David Cauvin, a fellow South African. Cauvin was on leave from the Blue Funnel Line of British merchant ships and had gained special sailing experience by serving on a replica of South Africa's famous three-masted *Drommedaris*—a craft that, much to Alan's delight, had the same general appearance as his. Multiple letters were typed stating, "This document was dropped overboard in a sealed bottle from the barque MAYFLOWER II during her maiden voyage, which was from Plymouth England towards Plymouth Massachusetts. The bottle was dropped overboard on the Ninth day of the month of May, Nineteen fifty seven, when the vessel's

Noon Position was Latitude 25 22 N Longitude 30 05 W." Each copy was signed by the entire crew, including Felix, who dipped his right paw in ink and placed it on the paper at a size that would have pleased John Hancock. In the upper right corner a commemorative cancellation mark was stamped to confirm that it came from the replica's maiden voyage. After that, the papers were rolled tight, put in empty cider bottles, corked, sealed with candlewax, and tossed overboard, where they would be entrusted to the wills and wiles of the Atlantic.

Figure 34. Felix joining the *Mayflower II* crew in signing the letter. *(Lee Israel/ Mayflower Studios)*

But wait! The captain calculated that they still had another 1,900 miles to go on their current course, and at least another thousand after that before landfall.[6] Throwing all the bottles overboard at once would lessen the chance of any single one being found, so it was decided to save some until they were closer to Bermuda, which would increase their chances of being discovered.[7] Whoever found one was instructed to return it to Richard Brennan Esq., The Wig and Pen Club, 230 The Strand, London, W.O.2, England, and claim a reward.

The first pair was dropped when they were northwest of the Cape Verde archipelago. It would be four years before one turned up on the coast of Norway in 1961. When the finder contacted him, Dick paid his fare to London, gathered crew members to toast the Scandinavian, and "entertained him royally."[8]

Another four years then passed until the sloop *Sea Danthy* sailed from Pompano Beach, Florida, to Abaco Island, Bahamas, with passengers eager to beachcomb for hidden treasure. No Spanish doubloons were found, but what they did discover was an old wax-corked cider bottle that contained a second letter. It too had an invitation to visit the Wig and Pen, but the offer was ignored. The finders held on to their mysterious prize until selling it at a flea market. Luckily the new owners recognized what it was and contacted Plimoth Plantation and Joe Meany, who easily confirmed its authenticity because his own signature was there along with a clear paw print. It quickly went on display for all to see, but were there more to be found? A museum scholar thought yes, that two or more were still out there, but where? Only Neptune knew.

The fourth Sunday arrived, and following his now-traditional talk the skipper got on the ship's dinghy (called a pram) to take photographs of the craft from the sea's vantage point. Nothing unusual, except that when he was getting back on board, he stumbled, lost his balance, and nearly fell into the drink. With swells turning his sightseeing craft into a carnival ride that rose fifteen feet and then dropped suddenly, the step forward had to be perfectly timed. The men watching thought for a moment they would have to dive in to save him, but he recovered himself while admirably keeping hold of all his equipment. Villiers had mastered such acts out of necessity because when it came to swimming, as he later confessed,

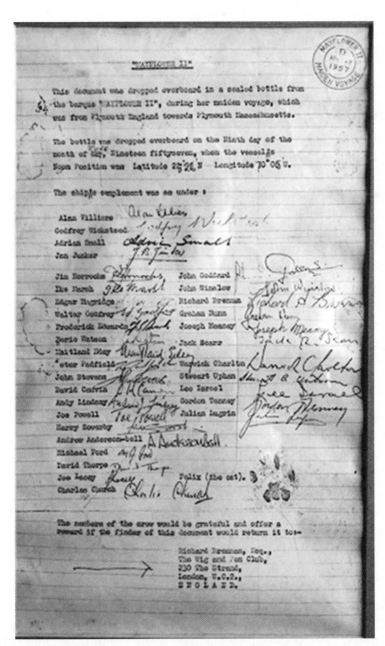

Figure 35. Felix's right paw clearly printed on the replica's May 9 letter to the world. *(Courtesy Plimoth Patuxet Museums)*

"I cannot."[9] The crew would have been amazed—but not bos'n Marsh, who couldn't swim either.

Then the ship just seemed to stop. For days, as the oily ocean lay still, she moved only with the westward flow of the current under an intense sun and cloudless sky that made the deck nearly impossible to walk barefooted. With no sails to tend, Peter Padfield was ordered to start performing a duty assigned to him in Brixham prior to departure, that of mail officer. More than a year earlier the lad was sipping gin, relaxing in the wardroom of the P&O liner and Royal Mail Ship *Strathmore*, and browsing through magazines when he saw an article about *Mayflower II*. At twenty-three he wasn't sure what he wanted to do with his life, but it was most likely not sitting high above the sea in a steel container. He had always had an interest in sailing ships, and this sounded like a great adventure, so he quickly wrote a letter addressed simply to "Commander Alan Villiers, *Mayflower II*, London," and had it sent from his next port of call. The request hit the bull's eye, the two men met, and Peter was welcomed to the crew.[10] His experience aboard a postal ship also caused an idea to pop into Alan's head: I've found my letter man.

The task was herculean and involved organizing crewmen to put postal cancellation stamps on 140,000 pieces of mail Project Mayflower had sold before the voyage as special souvenir items. In a touch of mockery, the workers were forced to look at an image of the ship in full sail traveling below huge cumulus clouds at a time when the replica sat virtually dead in the water. The etching was printed in deep red ink with the caption "*Mayflower* Ship's Mail" and British postage bearing Queen Elizabeth II's image. The cancellation stamp was uniquely designed for onetime use with the words "*Mayflower II* Maiden Voyage" circled around the date "APR–JLY 1957." Many were preaddressed for delivery to recipients in the United Kingdom, while others were to be sold to stamp collectors.

For more than a week practically every man spent about two hours a day stamping and franking either on deck or below. It was tedium but filled the hours when there was little else to do. Soon there was a production line of specialists: one tearing the stamp sheets into strips, the next reaching into a box and passing a card to another mate, who

Figure 36. *Mayflower II* becalmed on a glassy sea. *(Lee Israel/Mayflower Studios)*

would affix the postage and pass it to the canceller. Before long a rhythm developed that prompted Stuart Upham and Lee Israel to challenge Warwick Charlton and Julian Lugrin to a race. Stamping thuds soon became a drum cadence with an accelerating beat of tick-tock, tick-tock, thud-thud, thud-thud that kept increasing faster and faster until— ouch! Julian franked his thumb so hard it started to bleed, smearing an unwanted red on the passing papers and prompting the competition to be declared a draw. Villiers later reported: "My crewmen included no ex-mailmen and no stamp-lickers or cancelers, but all got manfully on with the job," although it was a "chore we could have done without."[11]

In contrast to that annoyance, the captain was quite glad to have two *Mayflower* descendants on board. The first was Chief Petty Officer Charles Church of the Royal Canadian Navy, whose forebear was Mayflower Compact signer Richard Warren. Nicknamed "Canada," Church had heard about *Mayflower II* from the chief of the Royal Canadian Naval Staff in Ottawa, Admiral de Wolfe, and signed on as a seaman for one shilling a month. He often worked as an assistant to Jumbo, fixing everything that needed repair, from a galley stove that wouldn't light to a wireless aerial that had fouled the rigging. When not doing those chores, he knew how to be a shipwright, a skilled helmsman, and always a first-rate mariner.

British aircraft carrier pilot John Winslow was a namesake of an early colonial governor and a nephew of the Kenelm Winslow who drove the ceremonial first nail into the ship's keel. On this twentieth-century transit, the airman quickly became a valued member of the crew and an expert in the art of scampering across topsail yards in rolling seas. He was also a skilled diver who joined Joe Meany for a spontaneous "high-diving competition from the ratlines."[12] The event, which could only take place in a totally calm sea, was not to be missed. Each man in turn would climb up to a yard, race out to the end, and spring off to perform with excellence. The two were clearly star aquatic acrobats and left less talented mates merely to don swimsuits, or nothing, for a dip in the sea while Charlton and others stood watch for sharks.

The vessel continued to drift slowly with the current as it sat idle in the middle of a sea that remained flat, glassy, and calm. Men on watch could see forever, but nothing moved under nature's domed cathedral. They were alone. The days were spent caulking cracks in the deck where the baking sun had caused planking to separate or plugging leaks in the hull's side by lowering Stuart Upham overboard with a rope around his waist and a container of sealing compound. These were mindless but necessary chores that filled the hours while everyone waited for the wind to return.

A few days later Charlton was on deck before dawn and looking east when "a brilliant display of color . . . slanted over the edge of the world," first frosted blue, then red and orange, then after "a fraction of time . . . a green flash of such depth and purity of color it seemed as though we were witnessing Genesis,"[13] as the sun's head broke the horizon and he understood those ancient words, "And God said, Let there be light: and there was light."

Unfortunately, such biblical thoughts did not bring the wind, so old superstitions had to be invoked. Looking up to the still sky, Adrian Small remembered a belief that sticking a knife in the mainmast might bring wind, so out came his ten-inch blade and he stabbed the beam, leaving it there for all to see. Nothing happened. Another theory held that whistling would cause the sea to respond by sending its own breath through the rigging, so men who could transform their lips into a musical instrument did so, and surely amused those who could not. Stuart Upham even put his ear to the mainmast beam to listen for movement, just as someone might put an ear to a railroad track and hear a faint sound well before the train came into sight. Again, failure. A third effort saw David Cauvin climb out to the forestay and tie one of his seaboots there. Miraculously, it worked, and within minutes they seemed to be moving again.[14] Praise be to the sea gods!

The next Sunday, May 19, Villiers used his weekly assembly to tell the crew that he expected to cover the last two thousand miles of the journey in twenty days. He then spoke about "that nut Columbus," and because he was a "very amusing, bluff, studiedly sailor-like speaker,"[15] everyone listened attentively. Columbus was not the first to cross the Atlantic, Villiers told them, contrary to what many believed. Leif Erikson and his kinsmen had done it many times via a northern route because, he said, they were not looking for some new map, they were just "tough guys . . . only interested in loot and women—tangible merchandise . . . quite right too." The Aussie might have also added that those Nordic explorers shared their ships with Felix's ancestors, Viking cats who put their paws on the New World well before the word *Mayflower* was even spoken.[16] Just imagine their little guy donning a horned Norse helmet![17]

The following days were breezy, and the sails were generally balanced, as every member of the deck crew had his turn at the wheel in thirty- or sixty-minute shifts during his assigned watch. This was where the ship's true nature might be revealed, much as a car's character can only be experienced in the driver's seat. When the wind was in the right direction, the replica would nearly steer herself. When it was more temperamental, however, the helmsman would have to spin the wheel rapidly from side to side in an effort to straighten her out. And if the wind came head-on, Villiers would remind the mate to steer "full and bye," which meant sailing close-hauled, holding as much as possible to the charted course, but not overly so, because the ship might be "caught aback" with gusts coming on the wrong side of the sails, forcing her into the opposite direction. The circle would then have to be completed in order to regain a proper heading. If that happened, the helmsman would be forced to join the 360-degree club, whose membership was to be avoided.[18]

On uneventful days, the men enjoyed learning a bit more about each other. Charlton once remarked to the third mate, now respectfully addressed by everyone as Captain Junker, that he was surprised to be feeling boredom, and the Dane responded that anything can get monotonous, including torture by the Nazis and viewing executions. "Even waiting for death can become boring. Would you believe that? It is so. The Germans used to make me stand in the cold while they hanged my friends, the men who had been captured with me. Such a sight they thought would move me, make me talk." He didn't. "Do you think I felt pity? Do you think I felt my time was nearer? I tell you I had seen so much, felt so much, I was bored and only wanted them to get it over and done with."[19] Still, this magnificent voyage was anything but torturous, and Junker's real-life experience made others realize how lucky they were just to be on deck.

One fine day a school of frolicking dolphins appeared "just under the surface of the water . . . for the best part of an hour, swimming up and down around the ship trying to make out what sort of queer fish had come into their midst," buoying everyone's spirits as they continued onward, about five hundred miles east of Barbados.[20] On other occasions, a torpedo-shaped creature would fly onto *Mayflower*'s deck to the amazement of Felix, who wasn't quite sure how to react. Was it an aquatic mouse? A bird? He had no idea, but was not about to stop eating the delicious canned seafood Wally and Dick Brennan offered him.

Figure 37. Felix playing with a flying fish that landed on deck. *(Gordon Tenney/Black Star)*

Sunsets were so consistently beautiful that days were now ending with spontaneous gatherings of men staring west as vivid pastels painted the horizon or white cumulus castles were set ablaze by distant lightning. Occasionally the famous green flash would streak across the horizon at the last moment, merging north with south in the west. Wondrous moments between a fine day and a heavenly night filled with stars.

Another lift to the crew's spirits was offered by Warwick Charlton and physician John Stevens. Prior to the voyage the two men cooked up a prank when they discussed how much the practice of medicine had advanced since Pilgrim times. Back then, a ship's surgeon would often bring a bottleful of leeches that could be used to suck bad blood from a sick sailor, whose body would then produce fresh noninfected corpuscles. This was of course nonsense, but in an effort to make every aspect of the transit historically accurate, and to inject a little levity, Doc Stevens agreed to perform a leeching on deck. As the men held Warwick down, three hungry carnivorous worms named Apollonius, Fred, and Warwick were placed on his stomach. "As they arched their slimy bodies I felt three nips and they began to feed amidst shouts of encouragement from the ship's company." The critters continued munching until salt was poured on them and the show ended.[21] Years later Jack Scarr recalled the entertainment but thought the leeches were called Faith, Hope, and Charity, even though he seemed to recall one of them also being named Warwick in honor of the PR man.[22]

On the serious side, the physician mainly dealt with cases of seasickness plus aches, pains, and sprains—except for the time David Cauvin nearly broke Felix's right front leg, the one used to sign the letter in a bottle. It was David's turn on watch, and in the darkness he heard a shriek before looking down to see Felix under his foot. Sweeping the little cat up, he immediately went to find Doc Stevens, who reassured David that cat bones were quite resilient. The medic nonetheless wrapped a small bandage around the paw and recommended cabin rest, which meant Graham's bunk. As for the humans, no major illness or injury was reported during the voyage, although Stevens did have to pull one of Jumbo's back teeth without the aid of painkillers. *Life* photographer Gordon Tenney got wind of it and had the two men reenact the procedure so he could take photos, but only after they agreed to stage the event on deck and "pull" a front tooth because it would be a better photo.

The magazine's readers also might have enjoyed learning about Joe Powell, another *Pequod* alumnus, who regularly worked as a movie stuntman, playing such roles as a Roman legionary spear fighter. Perhaps unsurprisingly, Joe was missing his two front teeth, and because he needed a good smile, he had a beautiful bridge made in pre-*Pequod* days. Early in the current voyage he appeared on deck looking like a hockey player with no front teeth, and someone asked what happened. "I lost them on a set when I was filming on *Moby Dick*. Don't want to take a chance with my new set, so I've stowed them for the voyage."[23]

A passing rain could quickly transform the main deck into a large shower stall, as naked men raced to be under God's freshwater spigot holding a bar of soap. Villiers later wrote, "They are the cleanest lot of mariners I ever saw, and their high standards would have amazed Captain Jones' crew. To them, even a piece of decent soap was a luxury. Here we have it by the case, and detergents as well."[24] Felix was not fond of the rain, however, and as the men raced topside, he would go below looking for a dry place to hide.

The ship's lavatory was found at its beak adjacent to the bowsprit, its traditional location for centuries. It could be a precarious spot in rough weather when waves might suddenly splash across the deck. The "head" itself consisted of a hole in the timber floor portside of the bowsprit. A polite sign adjacent to it read: "Officers are requested to adjust their dress before leaving."[25]

After six weeks at sea *Mayflower II* at last reached its target of latitude 25° north, longitude 65° west,[26] and turned toward Bermuda across the Sargasso Sea. While Captain Christopher Jones had been alone in the vast ocean during the original voyage, the modern replica's crossing required close monitoring for the presence of other ships. Large windjammers, which might be undetectable by modern radar, would shine powerful floodlights on their sails at night. Because Villiers did not have that luxury, he set a strict twenty-four-hour lookout. Once the Columbus path was reached, *Mayflower II* attracted the attention of all passersby regardless of size, and many went out of their way for a glimpse of the

Figure 38. Passing rain could transform the deck into a large shower stall. *(Lee Israel/Mayflower Studios)*

seventeenth-century wooden marvel. For the crew, having another ship alter course for a closer look was greatly appreciated, affording a break in the loneliness and monotony of the open sea.

When not occupied by the constant demands of managing sails that could be overflowing with wind or just hanging listlessly, the crew would fight the corrosive nature of seawater on decks, masts, and lines with seemingly endless swabbing, maintenance, painting, and caulking. Looking up intermittently from these tasks, it was easy for them to lift their voices in conversation or just let their minds wander. For instance, what was it like to be aboard in 1620? They knew every effort had been

Figure 39. Ships came close to see *Mayflower II. (Lee Israel/Mayflower Studios)*

made to make their voyage as historically accurate as possible, from the ship's design and construction to the food they ate in the absence of refrigeration. But shipboard life was impossible to replicate. There had been an additional 102 people aboard the original vessel, including women and children. On top of that, these modern men were all healthy, thanks to pharmaceutical groups that provided supplies, unlike the original passengers, half of whom did not survive their first year on land. The twentieth-century shipmates were in warm southern waters versus the cold North Atlantic of late autumn, and they had some lighting belowdecks thanks to a diesel generator. The original travelers were mostly in the dark, save for a lantern, for more than half the transit after sunset, and no one was sunbathing or diving from the masts. In those moments of reflection, everyone knew how extraordinary the 1620 group had been. Once disembarked in the New World, the Pilgrims left indelible marks on an emerging democratic landscape, while Captain Jones and his crewmen merely returned to the Old World with no inkling of the essential role they played in changing the course of nations. In contrast, each member of the modern *Mayflower* knew exactly what he was doing: returning a piece of lost history to the American people.

Just like the original, the replica at times leaked like a sieve. Cold seawater belowdecks centuries earlier was a major factor in destroying health, and the crew wondered "just how it must have been for the Pilgrim families to keep warm, or dry, or even clean in a ship like this, and how hellish her cold and much more constant leakiness must have been for them."[27] On the modern version it was merely a persistent annoyance that made the replica "far too historically accurate," according to Villiers. "Even a sixteenth century ship surely could keep the rain out," he lamented, but not his. The water came in from open planking on the quarterdeck into the captain's quarters, and from the main deck into the 'tween deck, and who knows where else. It might also come through any of the replica's ten closed and sealed gunports that mirrored those found on merchant vessels of the time: four on each side plus two on the stern. Back then, only two per side would have been used because of the known scarcity of ordnance and the crowded conditions with the Pilgrims aboard, leaving six permanently closed. The cannons themselves were probably minions or falcons that could fire five-pound or one-pound round shots and would have moved on swivels attached to rails.[28] In any event, chief carpenter Edgar Mugridge was "constantly rushing everywhere to deal with freshly reported small leaks." The only dry place belowdecks seemed to be Upham's bunk, which suffered from stale air, no ventilation, near total darkness when the door was closed, and dual occupancy, because Jumbo also bunked there. Although there was never more than twenty inches of seawater at the lowest level, it was a problem that required constant monitoring and regular use of the diesel bilge pump.[29]

Like carpentry, cooking was an endless task, and the man in charge, affectionately known as Wally, was not a youngster. He felt a special responsibility for the crew because he knew his meals sustained them, relieved monotony, and generally kept spirits up. Each day, Godfrey would carefully plan what was to be served and then post it in his Menu Book. He would also note the condition of the sea and sky, such as "soft sea, heavy with swell, brilliant sunshine" or "soft sea, slight swell, bright and

Figure 40. Crew endlessly swabbing the deck. *(Lee Israel/Mayflower Studios)*

sunny." This was important because the ship's movement could have as much effect on men's stomachs as what they put in them. Breakfast often consisted of cereal, bacon and eggs, perhaps tomatoes, served with bread and tea or coffee. Dinner, which for them was the midday meal, would find plates filled with beef or chicken, potatoes, peas or beans, some preserved fruit, bread and butter, cheese, and coffee or tea. The great British tradition of tea, on this voyage the equivalent of the evening meal, was also thoroughly planned and executed. In Wally's galley, that could mean cold meats or seafood, salad, perhaps served with an omelet, plus bread, butter, fruit preserves, and coffee or tea. At the bottom of each page describing these productions, Wally would sign: W Godfrey, Steward.[30]

It was a tiring job, and at the end of a long day he could be seen standing "in the doorway to the galley, a thin little man in white apron, hands and arms dusted with flour and streaked with perspiration, his heavy eyelids dropping with fatigue, looking in the thin yellow light a tired old tortoise of a man." One night his shipmate Beric Watson found him "at two in the morning, sitting on the edge of his bunk 'tween decks, fast asleep. Beric gently lifted up the legs of our little cook and made him comfortable."[31] This loving act would have been happily performed by any member of the crew, as demonstrated on one of those hot and sticky days of aimless drifting.

Seeing the younger men diving into the water for a swim, Wally could not resist joining them. But his timing was not good. Just as he lowered his frail body into the sea from the ship's ladder, a breeze made the craft leap forward, leaving him in its wake, clawing frantically and calling out for help. Graham Nunn immediately dove in as a line was thrown their way. He managed to grab the rope with one hand and Wally with the other, and both men were quickly pulled back on deck. It was a dramatic scene that conjured memories of John Howland being saved in 1620, an event retold by generations of *Mayflower* descendants. As for Wally, it was his last adventure in the water.[32]

Singing was often heard in the evenings as Beric Watson, Graham Nunn, and John Winslow strummed their guitars, and Andrew "Scotty" Anderson-Bell pounded an overturned bucket that became a makeshift drum for his thimbled fingers. The "Worried Man Blues" standby was now sung with ever-evolving improvised lyrics, topical or bawdy or both. Beric was from Leeds and had little interest in joining his family's printing business, so he had learned to sail and joined a small crew that delivered an ancient yacht called *Catalina* from Liverpool around to the English Channel. They hit bad weather during the voyage, and the ship's first mate told Villiers how well the young man had handled himself, a reference that made the Aussie glad to accept Beric on board when he applied for crew membership.[33] Needing no accompaniment was Irish tenor Joe Lacey, who could often be heard serenading the stars as he looked skyward through the swaying masts.[34]

Scotty Anderson-Bell had been working in Addis Ababa as the Ethiopian emperor's personal architect when he read about Project Mayflower. It sounded like a much better adventure than the one he was planning to Peru, so he set out for London, arrived minus his luggage, and found Alan Villiers, who was put off by his unkempt appearance. Undeterred, Scotty then made contact with Warwick Charlton, arrived well scrubbed, and told Charlton that he had been a merchant navy officer before Africa, was quite a ladies' man, and needed to get to the States so "he could find a rich American girl to marry, which appealed to Warwick's love of mischief but honest purpose."[35] Needless to say, Charlton was sold and took his enthusiasm to the ship's captain, who

Figure 41. Jumping from yardarms into the sea. *(Lee Israel/Mayflower Studios)*

changed his mind and signed Scotty as the last member of his *Mayflower* team.[36] Years later Warwick remembered him fondly as someone who "had an early love affair with himself and never fell out of love."[37] Scotty was a spirited and popular member of *Mayflower II*'s crew.

Away from the music, chess was played by *Life*'s Maitland Edey, Joe Powell, Peter Padfield, and perhaps Fred Edwards, another Blue Funnel Line recruit. Powell and Joe Lacey had both been members of Villiers's *Pequod* crew when it was used in the filming of *Moby Dick*, and they were among his first hires. Leaping about the ratlines and rigging was a natural delight to them both, as it was for *Joseph Conrad* veteran Harry Sowerby. A man of independent means, Sowerby chose the sea because it gave him an adventurous life that money alone could not buy. He was not a man for small talk, and when he made a rare excursion into conversation, it usually focused on the sea and sailing ships, such as his time on the world's oldest and largest square-rigged four-master, *Moshulu*, one of Erikson's most famous windjammers.

Charlton, Brennan, Winslow, and Israel often played bridge in the evening, but only after agreeing to abide by two simple rules set by Warwick: "first that we do not play for money and second that cheating is compulsory" and "consists of winks, nods, and inflections of voice when you are bidding and, just to make sure, an occasional look at your opponents' cards."[38] Books were also opened regularly for mental escape, and even Felix enjoyed a good story read by Graham. Observing Jumbo avidly reading, one curious crewmate glanced over his shoulder and discovered he was not engrossed in an exciting novel but rather in a book on investment strategy, which suggested the big man was looking forward to writing his own personal narrative once the voyage ended.[39] Others were also thinking of their postvoyage lives, including two crewmen selected from the Oxford University Yacht Club: Mike Ford and David Thorpe, "both yachtsmen of international status and the right spirit."[40]

Padfield was familiar with long days at sea, and on this voyage he developed an interest in writing and drawing that changed his life. He crafted lengthy letters to his mother describing life on board and included pencil drawings of the ship and men. The art caught the attention of Maitland Edey, who offered to take them to his publisher once

Figure 42. Felix playing hide and seek. *(Lee Israel/Mayflower Studios)*

they got to America, and Peter's creative abilities led him to a career in naval history and scholarship that eventually earned him the prestigious Mountbatten Maritime Prize. His first book, *The Sea Is a Magic Carpet*, described the crossing, and his final one was a compilation of his letters home, *Mayflower II Diary—Sketches from a Lost Age*. In between, twenty-four histories and four novels were published for global audiences.

The first mate was also crafting epistles—hundreds of them, for schools, as he had promised before departure. A typical one read, "To all the Children, the Teachers, and other Staff at Dedworth Green County Primary School, Windsor." It was about three pages long and drafted inside his "very small cabin" as he sat "on a paint drum as there is no chair.

In the old days, it would have been a barrel." He told them the captain was taking a different route than the original skipper, and "even though it is thousands of miles longer it may still be quicker," as the winds were "in the right direction." He then added, "I have just been looking at your [pictures] and reading your accounts of visits and sports, and your nice poems," which were clearly lifting his spirits. "Please keep thinking of us. Best wishes to all of you, Yours sincerely, Godfrey Wicksteed."[41]

Apart from the *Life* magazine duo, the lone American on board was cabin boy Joe Meany, who earned his passage by winning a national competition organized by the Boys Clubs of America. The selection committee was even headed by former president Herbert Hoover. Because Joe's high school graduation was scheduled for the second of June, a special ceremony was held on deck in front of the entire crew, who witnessed the captain giving him an ornate and archaically worded diploma as everyone shouted congratulations—including two other Americans who are seldom mentioned because they weren't supposed to be there.

Andy Lindsay of Biddeford, Maine, turned up unannounced in Devon with a seabag on his shoulder and asked to join the crew. When Villiers sailed the *Joseph Conrad* prior to the war, some of his best sailors were young Americans, and one of them was Lindsay. The captain knew him as a first-rate seaman and remembered him well, but unfortunately there was the matter of his nationality. Hold on! Andy was not going to be pushed aside because of some technicality, so he offered to join for free in exchange for a berth. Again Villiers was stumped because he would have to report the man, who might be forced to leave. But . . . if he was a "pierhead jump"—someone who leapt aboard the ship just as she was pulling out to sea—the other men would not toss him overboard, and he could work as an able-bodied seaman for a shilling a month. Done! (Just don't tell anyone.)[42]

Lee Israel's background was starkly different. Lee was originally from Butte, Montana, where guys "usually are able to ride before they learn how to walk."[43] That skill set eventually led the westerner to the US Army's mounted cavalry, where he was stationed in the South of England as an officer during World War II. While there, he fell in love with his future wife, whom he took back to Butte when peace arrived.

Unfortunately, business opportunities were scarce, so he returned to England in search of a better future. That's when he fell in love again, this time with photography. In 1950 he opened the Mayflower Studios in London with Howard Bryne, also American. When Warwick Charlton came up with his grand idea several years later, he found Lee's studio and introduced himself. The American Brit soon became Project Mayflower's official photo chronicler. He accepted the idea of ending his coverage when the ship sailed—no high seas adventure for him. But then financier Fenston informed Alan Villiers that he had pressing matters in London that would prevent him from sailing as expected. To fill the vacancy, the Australian invited the likeable American to take his place. Serendipity had struck again.

During these weeks on the open sea, Felix the Kitten matured into Felix the Cat, a feisty playmate who might swipe his paws playfully at a cork dangled at the end of a string or just have adventures. One day when Fred Edwards and others began unfurling a sail and gave it a mighty pull,

Figure 43. Jan Junker checking Felix's life jacket for proper fit. *(Gordon Tenney/ Black Star)*

they watched helplessly as their mascot was shot into the air from his napping spot. The startled acrobat was quickly swept up by the mate and inspected closely to be sure he was all right. He was, to everyone's relief.[44]

On another occasion, an unexpected wave splashed onto the main deck and nearly washed him into the sea before Dick Brennan pulled him back to safety. If that had happened, a rescue mission would have been launched immediately because, like the captain, Felix could not swim. The inventive Jan Junker decided their mascot needed what all the other men had, a life jacket, so he fashioned a tiny vest just in case Felix really did fall into the drink. It was sewn from fabric and stuffed with kapok, a moisture-resistant, quick-drying fiber that is buoyant. Having him participate in safety drills requiring special attire was a joy to all.

News of his antics and personality traveled faster than the ship, and upon landfall Felix quickly became a celebrity appearing in *National Geographic*, *Yankee*, and *Life* magazines, as well as postvoyage events.

CHAPTER 15

Company of Ships

WARWICK CHARLTON FIT IN RATHER ODDLY ON A CRAFT WHERE EVERY man had specific daily tasks to perform and routines were never broken. Even Upham bore a title, caulker, that made him responsible for keeping the ship watertight. But Charlton was unassigned, a bit of a puzzle, and "an interesting talker on most subjects, though he looks rather pale, unkempt and nightclubby."[1] When the crew thought about it, the only job he seemed to have was worrying, which might have him appearing on deck at all hours of the night. Would the wind blow tomorrow? How many more days at sea? Was the world still interested in *Mayflower II*? Of course, there was nothing he could do about those things, so he often joined with others in song or conversation. In the early hours of a June night, he entertained a small group with stories of his wartime experiences. They were amazing and, as it turned out, true. For those gathered, he lifted a veil of mystery about the voyage's origins and purpose, as they realized "what a remarkable man Warwick was." Before then, they had no idea that "he was credited with changing Montgomery's image with the troops from distant and austere fanatic to the approachable 'Monty' dressed in sweater and Tank Corps beret instead of peaked cap." As the heavens lit the sea, it became apparent to those listening that "all his considerable powers of imagination and persuasion were needed after the war to convert his idea into reality." One of his young shipmates later wrote about that night, saying that "against the odds, he succeeded—as one result of which I was now enjoying a life-changing experience."[2]

Others were also altering course, literally. A multinational array of ships were going out of their way for a better view: the French liners *Colombie* and *Antilles*; the *Tennyson* out of London, the tankers *Olna*, *Tide Austral*, and *Border Sentinel*; plus the *Belgian Pride* from Antwerp, which dropped a parcel containing "a dozen cigars, some packets of cigarettes, thirty-six bars of chocolate, a bottle of Belgian cognac and a bottle of Eau de Cologne" for the crew to enjoy.[3] While lifting spirits, it gave Chief Mate Wicksteed an important task that, if successful, would go unnoticed: he would take "some great pains to see that our diesel generator was shut off in case they photographed the exhaust and overflow." His boss Captain Villiers was not about to have any photographer—amateur or professional, friend or foe—capture an image that could be used to suggest his ship was propelled by anything other than the wind.[4]

The Italian liner *Lucania* appeared one day "out of the blue," circled at full speed, and then came "very close before steaming rapidly away."[5] Those actions were not, however, what caught the attention of Charlton and the crew. Like other ships, its captain came as near as safety would permit, but among the passengers on deck was one who stood out. A young lady wearing a red sweater stretched as far as she could over the deck railing for a better look at the square-rigger and no one on *Mayflower II* missed her beautiful adulations. That evening Charlton asked Fred Edwards, "Did you see that girl in the red sweater aft? . . . it may interest you to know that she was looking and waving straight at me!" "Poor Warwick," his buddy quickly responded in a consoling tone, "I'm sorry, but it was pretty obvious that she was waving straight at *me*!" Charlton soon discovered that every man was suffering from the same delusion. Except of course for Villiers, who seemed to be above such fantasy, but no one dared to ask.[6] *Viva l'Italia!*

The skipper had been quite emphatic prior to departure about the distraction fair ladies could be to men at sea and publicly announced that there would be no women aboard his ship during the transit. Yet there were daily tasks that everyone wished could be performed by a person traditionally called Peggy. Because no Peggy was aboard, one unlucky crewman would play the role. In fact it was not named after a bonnie lass but rather, as *Life* correspondent Mait Edey reported, after an old salt.

"In British ships a peggy is a waiter, cleaner-upper and dishwasher and is supposed to have got his name from the fact that disabled mariners (i.e., one-legged or peg-legged ones) were given these jobs in the old days."[7] On *Mayflower II* this meant serve the food, clean up afterward, scrub the stairs, sweep the 'tween deck, and wash the rags. And don't complain about the lack of lighting or the diesel oil fumes hanging over the generator. Each man dreaded the days when he would be required to do the "peggying." At such times he might spare a wistful thought for the modern appliances on the contemporary ships that the carrack was encountering.

Most impressive were the mighty men-of-war heading in the same direction for an International Naval Review honoring James-town later that month. They would dip their flags to the unofficial seventeenth-century merchant carrier, blast celebratory alarm horns, and occasionally send out a small boat offering good cheer and fresh fruit. Four destroyers from the US Navy passed and sent greetings, but not before the USS *Ault* dispatched a launch "by order from Washington" to fetch photos from the *Life* magazine team that were to be used to promote the voyage. Later that day Villiers wrote a note to himself "wondering how it is that a magazine may be granted such privileges."[8] Is it possible that someone at the State Department was following up on the Bermuda Conference and the desire Eisenhower expressed in his private meeting with Macmillan to strengthen the special relationship? Perhaps directing the US Navy to intercept the replica mid-ocean and leverage the reenactment for diplomatic purposes? The captain did not know, but it struck him as highly unusual, and he said so in his diary.

Two cruisers from the Italian navy, *San Giorgio* and *San Marco*, altered their course because the commander of the Second Naval Division wanted to give a personal salute on behalf of his nation to the replica and its captain.[9] The Italians delivered wine and fruit along with a letter from their admiral praising the Australian skipper and his mighty little ship.

The newest aircraft carrier in the British fleet, HMS *Ark Royal*, named after the galleon built for Sir Walter Raleigh, and two accompanying destroyers, *Diamond* and *Duchess*, also crossed their path. Were

Figure 44. HMS *Ark Royal* crossing paths with *Mayflower II* as both head to America. *(© British Pathé)*

he not on the replica, Sub-Lieutenant John Winslow would have been with his squadron on the flight deck. Although seven months earlier *Diamond* had taken part in the Suez Canal assault that caused the crisis that nearly scuttled construction of *Mayflower II*, on this day each craft sailed smoothly and peacefully. Warwick Charlton captured the dramatic moment when Her Majesty's magnificent seafaring airport pulled away: "Our sails were filled and we were making about seven knots, nearly our top speed. The *Ark Royal* had grace of line despite her size, but our sturdy wooden ship, her masts webbed with rigging, her sails curving with the wind, had a breathtaking beauty of her own."[10] Spectacular footage was taken during multiple flyovers and would soon be shared with the world.[11] But as the carrier departed, it blocked the wind and left the replica temporarily becalmed.

One morning a few weeks earlier, Villiers decided he had had enough just sitting motionless and adrift. So he ordered the men to uncover the small motorboat carried on deck, lower it into the water, and attach a tow line. If God could not get the ship to move, then by golly the Aussie

Figure 45. *Mayflower II* was a sight to behold for the crews of passing ships. (© *British Pathé*)

would! Jumbo and three others manned the minnow, then headed forward to pull the whale *Mayflower II* out of her doldrums. Of course they failed, but rather than being hoisted back up, the boat circled the beauty for sea-level photos. For hours all the men interested in taking a ride were given the opportunity. None of them had seen the ship from this angle, and it was a thrilling sight. "Even with the furled and flapping sails she looked very impressive against the fleecy white cumulus clouds and the long, curved swell," Peter Padfield later recalled, while also lamenting that it was "one of the ironies of being her crew that we never saw her at her best, flying along before a strong wind as so many other crews were to see her" from passing ships.[12]

On other occasions when there was sufficient wind, a set of extra canvas strips called "bonnets" could be laced to the bottoms of the fore, main, and lateen sails. These were roughly a third of the depth of the sail above. A bonnet might also be added to the spritsail at the bow. The devices were conceived in the seventeenth century to enhance wind-catching ability.[13] Unfortunately, the short sheets blocked the helmsman's view so he couldn't see where the ship was heading. As a result, and wisely, they were seldom used on Villiers's craft. Studding sails, also called stuns'ls, were a different matter. The crew would add them outside the square sails on both sides of the ship with a boom. They could be quite effective on calm days and help the boat gain speed with just a breath of wind.

Although these devices did not come into use until a century after the 1620 voyage, the captain liked adding them when conditions were ripe.

Unlike members of the modern armada she encountered, the replica relied on ancient navigation instruments such as a cross-staff and a traverse board, which is a flat piece of wood covered in holes forming expanding concentric circles from a center point. Think archery target with a bullseye. Little pegs are then put in the holes and form a line or curve that tracks the ship's direction and distance traveled. To people who play parlor games, it looks like a cribbage board. The cross-staff, a

Figure 46. Crew adding stuns'ls to catch more wind. *(Lee Israel/Mayflower Studios)*

forerunner of the sextant, consists of a three-foot stick and four move-able crosspieces of increasing length, roughly six, twelve, eighteen, and twenty-four inches. A navigator would hold the device near his eye, with the smallest appendage nearest, and point it at an object such as the sun or a star, perhaps Polaris at the start of the Big Dipper's handle. The angle of the target from sea level would be noted, and then using trigonometry the ship's location between the equator and the North Pole could be calculated. Those outdated items are generally found only in museums, so Villiers also brought a Kelvin & Hughes sextant[14] and modern charts.

Two binnacle pedestals that held compasses were fitted for the voyage in accordance with William Baker's specifications. The first stood tall, immediately in front of the wheel, and had a modern instrument visible under a glass-domed top.[15] The second was an old-fashioned "panelled wooden box lashed to the deck" that contained "a candle lantern and a specially made dry-card compass copied from one believed to have been made a little after the original *Mayflower* sailed."[16]

The skipper also brought a modern chronometer. That maritime clock gave the Australian a distinct advantage over his *Mayflower* predecessor Christopher Jones because it allowed him to calculate longitude, something that sailors in 1620 could not do. The original ship's passage has been retold in many ways, and while sacrifice, bravery, courage, and endurance are terms often used, longitude is never mentioned.

Latitude, or position relative to the equator (expressed in degrees, with the whole distance from the equator to the North or South Pole being ninety degrees), has been calculated pretty much since sailing began. But longitude, or position in an easterly or westerly direction, had no fixed starting point and no agreed method of calculation. This lack may have played a role when the ship *Sea Venture* was blown off course and wrecked in 1609. Such catastrophes were not uncommon, and as transoceanic travel became more important in expanding English commerce, so did the need for accurate and reliable navigation. The problem became so acute that in 1714, nearly a century after the *Mayflower* set sail for the New World, the British government established the Commissioners for the Discovery of the Longitude at Sea, more popularly called the Board of Longitude. As a spur to invention, it offered large cash prizes to anyone who could figure out how to determine the east-west component of location while at sea. The rewards were worth millions of dollars in today's currency, and they accelerated the search for a solution. A Yorkshireman named John Harrison devised a new kind of marine clock that met the challenge.[17] Because he now lived near the borough of Greenwich, London's storied maritime center, the starting point for the reckoning of time became known as Greenwich Mean Time. Today, wherever you are on earth, the local time is plus or minus GMT, and longitude is expressed (in degrees, like latitude) as distance from a vertical line on the globe passing through Greenwich. Although possession of a chronometer was not historically accurate to the original voyage, the anachronism was overlooked in navigating the second *Mayflower* so Villiers could accurately calculate her true location.

By the fiftieth day, June 8, *Mayflower II* was well into the Gulf Stream, with the water now 76°F. Before long the mighty current began living up to its reputation for treachery as the wind strengthened and shifted erratically over "a lumpy, confused, . . . irksome and ill-tempered sea" about two hundred miles off Bermuda.[18] It was something new for the crew, who for the past forty-nine days had been enjoying "little more than a pleasant cruise in the sun, albeit in extremely primitive conditions."[19] Recognizing the impending danger, the captain at three o'clock ordered the topsails, which had been dropped twice since morning, hauled up again—the weather was changing that fast—and had them secured with gaskets, small specially braided ropes used to tie the canvas. Toward the stern, the mizzenmast's lateen sail was also lowered and furled as blinding rain driven by winds over forty miles an hour lashed the ship. Lookouts were posted, and the hand-cranked foghorn began to sound its mournful cry.

Lifelines now surrounded the deck to keep lives on board as the ocean's anger continued to intensify. Everyone was ordered to don a life jacket, except Felix, who now stayed below in the least unsettling spot he could find. The hatch was securely battened. All the men knew it was the start of a long night, as Warwick Charlton later wrote:

Mayflower started to pitch heavily, and every time she thudded into the sea the bowsprit whipped in and out like a giant fishing pole. The hum of the wind in the rigging, the pounding of the seas against the ship's sides, the splash of rain across the decks, was the voice of the gale blowing with increasing fury from the east. . . .

By six o'clock there was no doubt whatsoever that we had been hit by a storm and were going to have to make a fight of it to bring the ship through intact.[20]

Villiers meanwhile, pondering how to handle such a craft in dangerously high seas, reminded himself that thousands of similar vessels "found themselves in the same state down the centuries and lived through many a gale of wind." Should he "lie a'hull, as the old ships did? With bare poles and the helm down, hove-to virtually under the windage of the big aftercastle? It would be interesting to try."[21]

An hour later, as the oddly colored light of day faded and Peter Padfield took the wheel, Villiers called all hands on deck with three peeps of a mariner's whistle that cut through now gale-force winds. Wicksteed's port watch was ordered to furl the big spritsail, where two inadequate buntlines failed to gather the canvas in and the yard refused to be hauled down. Four men leaped forward—Adrian Small, Joe Lacey, Beric Watson, and Andy Lindsay—"struggling almost uphill up the steep steeve of the waving bowsprit to fight a way on to the rolling, pitching, gyrating yard, with all the sea boiling furiously with anger under the bows."[22] Stuart Upham, watching anxiously, was not a ratliner, but he knew what thirty-eight degree rolls felt like, and they were now rocking his creation.[23] A few more degrees and she'd be over, spiraling down to the ocean's floor. Villiers knew it too, and as he watched the four sailors on the yard, "which was swooping up and down almost meeting the water at times like some fairground thrill-making machine,"[24] he was worrying "in case the bowsprit went and they all fetched up in the sea. What could I do for them then? What use are life-jackets? The ship would run over them, with her bluff bows, and keel-haul them, without the small advantage of a line to pull the bodies back from beneath the stern. They would rise again far back in the long boiling wake, perhaps a cable astern or more—if they rose again at all."[25]

But the men remained focused as they pulled the spritsail in and secured it. "See what I mean about sailing ships and character?" shouted Villiers to Charlton, pointing to the ship's beak. "This is what makes men, and you don't get it in steam."[26] Padfield, watching it all play out from his vantage point at the wheel, called it "the most spontaneously brave action by these four that I have ever seen. Anyone who had fallen would have been lost under the hull."[27]

Now there were only the main and fore courses to contend with, and the two watches under Small (fresh off the bowsprit battle) and Junker proceeded to haul them up and furl them with dispatch. As Mike Ford and Scotty put gaskets around the mainsail, Stuart and Jumbo scrambled below to check for leaks and confirm that the bilge pumps were working (which they were). Villiers then ordered Padfield to hold the wheel hard down, meaning full to starboard, as the wind howled at forty knots, gale force 8. Lie a-hull. It's what you do "when things get so bad that sailing becomes a matter of survival."[28] The result was modest forward motion in the absence of sail, replicating what thousands of similar vessels had done in mid-ocean crises over the centuries and lived to tell about it. *Mayflower II's* wheel was lashed in place.

With the primary danger passed, the captain poured each man a generous portion of Old Navy rum, honoring a tradition as old as ships and storms. Then he had Sparks send a message to the insurance companies: "Had to heave-to in stinking gale. Will get going again whenever possible. All well. Regards. Alan Villiers."[29]

Charlton, finding his berth awash, "retreated to the haven of the Great Cabin. Before I could stretch out there, I had to move Felix, who had found the driest and most comfortable place in the ship."[30] Others caught some sleep where they could. "We stayed like that all night, very snug and secure while the gale howled in the rigging and beat up against the solid Devon timbers," Padfield later recalled,[31] echoing First Mate Wicksteed's sentiment that he had "never felt so safe in a ship in a gale of wind before."[32] As for the captain's personal thoughts, "All night the gale howled and I was glad I had her under bare poles. It seems to me that I

Figure 47. *Mayflower* lying a-hull, depicted in *The Seas Were So High*, by Mike Haywood, acrylic on canvas, 2005. *(Courtesy Mike Haywood Art UK)*

was only just in time. Instead of easing, the gale worsened and blew hard even after daylight the following morning."[33]

The sea was still high and harsh at sunrise. At ten o'clock they sighted a freighter, its bow buried in the sea. As Charlton and Villiers watched the pounding the modern vessel was taking, the Englishman commented that *Mayflower* probably had an easier ride than they, and the Australian master concurred: "A steamship fights the sea, but not us. Not a sailing ship. We go with the sea. We don't fight, we're part of it."[34]

An hour later a US Coast Guard aircraft appeared and circled low around them about ten times before leaving. It had been sent out to find the voyagers because the storm had blown them far off course and radio communications had failed. A few more hours passed before they could safely get under sail again. While the storm probably cost them sixty miles, no lives were lost—and no one was washed overboard, as happened on the Pilgrims' voyage to John Howland when a similarly intense storm threw him into the sea before he managed to grab a loose halyard and get pulled back on board.

Perhaps providentially, it was now Sunday, a day of rest and certainly the last one to be spent at sea. No lengthy service with scriptures that day. While Villiers's men were deeply thankful, they had done enough praying during the storm. If there had been any doubts about the seaworthiness of the 1957 replica compared to the 1620 original, the mighty tempest laid them all to rest.

The experience also validated the decision to avoid the original voyagers' northern route, said Third Mate Jan Junker as he and Peter Padfield watched the bowsprit whip in all directions that morning, sometimes disappearing behind the foresail. Squally weather could have been a daily occurrence at higher latitudes, and an inherent flaw in early square-rigging design made it very hard to tighten the foresail and topsail, which explained "the crazy angles the topmast has been taking lately." You couldn't pull on one without impacting the other. "Once the bowsprit or topmast came down in heavy weather, it would start off a chain reaction, as the fore stay leads to the sprit and the main topmast stay leads to the fore top—and so on—a floating hulk" would be the result. The ship was solid, but this "essential weakness in the rigging" was the captain's "main reason . . . to go south."[35] That route, when traced on a map along with the Pilgrims' path, completed an outline that looked remarkably like the shape of the continental United States, where the earlier voyage represents the Canadian border and the second transit looks like a path down the Eastern Seaboard, across the Gulf of Mexico to the shores of Texas, on to California, then up the West Coast to Canada. It is no wonder some people see a reflection of America in the twin voyages.

The next morning at breakfast Jan Junker told Stuart Upham that he had had a dream about him, and it was quite vivid. "I was presenting you with a book," he said. Stuart leaned forward and asked, "And what was the title?" With a grin Jan answered, "Oh, a long title: *How to Build a Ship That Doesn't Leak.*"[36]

With the end of the adventure just a few days away, the crew began to recall highlights of their voyage: the flotilla of small craft that wished them Godspeed as the replica left England, their joy when they hit Columbus's path and the sun streamed through the main cabin to the

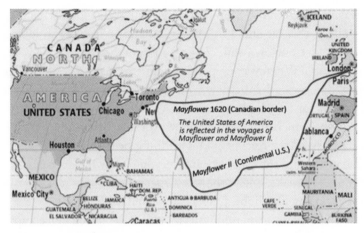

Figure 48. The two *Mayflower* voyage routes, outlining a silhouette of the United States. *(Courtesy Mayflower Event News)*

bowsprit, the starry nights, emerging dawns, and spectacular sunsets. The world they had left was nearly a dream after two months on a floating time machine, and the world they would soon reenter was no longer the undiscovered destination of the original Pilgrims, who seemed to have reincarnated themselves into the crew as if their seventeenth-century ship was inexplicably blown through a time portal into the twentieth.

Then, just as everything was going well again, their progress came to a grinding halt as the wind vanished, leaving them becalmed and adrift, only sixty miles from the Nantucket Lightship. Amid this frustration, incredibly, a periscope pierced the ocean in late morning, turned its eyepiece to the ancient wonder, and was followed to the surface by a whole submarine. It was most likely the diesel-powered USS *Bang*,[37] "a bit of a tin can,"[38] that patrolled the New England coastline and engaged in training missions. Some of the crew suggested it might be the nuclear warrior USS *Nautilus*, the same sub featured in the *Illustrated London News* when that paper announced plans for a second *Mayflower* and pictured William Baker's model. That was very unlikely. In either case, Villiers shouted out, "How about a tow?" and they shouted back, "Okay!"[39]

Not so fast! "The ignominy—after 5,000 miles sailing—of being towed in by—a submarine!" was the crew's horrified reaction. Although Villiers was "quite serious . . . and had all our towing gear ready," the crew was not with him.[40] Ship's carpenter Mugridge loudly scoffed, "We have made it this far and I don't care how long it takes so long as we get there under our own sail." *Life's* photographer quickly spoke for all hands, saying, "Whatever happens, we mustn't have a tow."[41] Charlton was torn, because authenticity was essential, but crowds might have been waiting days for the ship's arrival. The debate went on for what seemed hours, during which time a plane flew over and dropped a package that contained two dozen cans of cold, refreshing beer, so the discussion continued happily into the evening, but everyone knew the decision was only the captain's to make, unless the fates intervened.

They did. At first light, June 11 appeared with a good breeze and a slight swell. Then, in a serendipitous moment, the queen herself appeared in the form of the ocean liner bearing her name, RMS *Queen Elizabeth*, and the US Coast Guard's magnificent clipper ship *Eagle* in full sail arrived from the other direction as she began her annual midshipmen training cruise to Europe. The two vessels then converged so Captain Karl Zittel could send personal congratulations to Villiers, with whom he had sailed and whom he knew well. It was a spectacular sight. As the two craft came near, Zittel shouted the traditional greeting "What ship?" and Villiers responded: "*Mayflower*, three hundred and fifty years out of England!"[42] The American then gave his old friend the bearing and distance to the Nantucket Lightship, which *Mayflower II* reached just after noon. An armada of small ships, reminiscent of their British departure, appeared and surrounded them as the final miles to Provincetown were covered. Turning to Warwick, Alan said, "Now at last we can say we have made the crossing."[43]

They spent their first night in the New World in the same place Bradford did. The next day, June 12, the deck was awash with journalists. "For the first time," Villiers wrote, he understood how the vessel could hold so many Pilgrims, "for we had a hundred or so humans crowded on the quarter-deck alone."[44] Then he, Charlton, and Provincetown resident Harry Kemp, known locally as the Poet of the Dunes, all dressed in Pilgrim costumes, added their names to a copy of the Mayflower Compact. While the occasion was replayed with as much historical accuracy as possible, one modern convenience was allowed: Villiers used a Parker Pen ballpoint in a nod to the sponsorships that had helped pay for the voyage.

At dawn they set off in full sail across Cape Cod Bay to Plymouth Harbor, where a glorious welcome awaited by land and sea near the spot where the first *Mayflower* had anchored centuries earlier. It was to be a day of triumph for Harry Hornblower. His enterprise still consisted only of First House and two other small structures near Plymouth Rock because groundbreaking for its new home on the old Hornblower estate had started only after the replica was well out to sea. Tomorrow the nascent museum would be basking in fresh luster as the permanent custodian of *Mayflower II*. The replica somewhat nonchalantly connected to a buoy and then swung around so everyone witnessing the moment could take in the ship's full profile. At noon a cannon boomed, and Plimoth Plantation sent out a shallop it had built for the occasion, a large rowboat that could carry a small sail, to fetch the crew. Within two weeks it would be officially called "*Shallop II*, known as the launch of *Mayflower II*" on an insurance policy issued by the Old Colony Insurance Companies and described as "a replica of an old-time policy in format and terminology of the *Mayflower* days,"[45] a nod to what Warwick Charlton had creatively done with Lloyds of London. During the short ride to shore, Warwick later recalled,

> I glanced at the Captain with whom I had been so proud to sail, sitting beside me with his black Pilgrim hat in his hand, and thought how like the young Churchill he looked, with his air of imperious determination.
>
> He half-turned, and slipped a quick, almost furtive glance back to *Mayflower*, idling gracefully at her buoy, and in the second before he set his face once more I believe his mind went willingly back to the quarterdeck, with the planking beneath him and the sails set full above and the long blue horizon beyond the restless bows—and no official reception, no "flamin' publicity!"[46]

Thousands watched as a Pilgrim-clad trio of achievers—Captain Alan Villiers, Warwick Charlton, and Stuart Upham—were led up a ramp by a drummer to the Portico Over Plymouth Rock. There they were greeted by a group of dignitaries that included Ellis Brewster, the

Figure 49. *Mayflower II* anchored in Plymouth Harbor on June 13, 1957. *(AP Images/Peter J. Carroll)*

descendant of an original passenger. To applause and cheers, Brewster stretched out his hand and said, "Welcome to America."

Taking in the panoramic view offered from his vantage point above the famous rock, looking out across a beautiful sunlit harbor teeming with life, Monty's Fighting Editor felt wistful: "I remembered how we cursed *Mayflower*'s discomforts and her motion; and how we laughed at them. I remembered her inconveniences and the sheer delight and happiness she gave us, the power a sailing ship has of making you feel *really* alive; the short wild days and the long quiet ones."[47]

Upham was also thinking about their achievement, perhaps in a larger context: "*Mayflower II*, like *Mayflower*, was built entirely of vegetable fibre—oak for the hull, flax for the sails and hemp for the ropes. These humble materials were fashioned by men using the same tools their ancestors used in years long past in contrast to the monotonous, soul-destroying, switch-pressing, lever-pulling methods and count downs of this modern age."[48]

As these thoughts occupied the two voyagers, William Baker stood among the gathered multitude feeling pride in his creation and special admiration for Warwick Charlton, because "when he started his project, there were those who said that plans could not be found, but they were. Then came the statements that the ship could not be built, but she was.

Figure 50. Captain Villiers and crew of *Mayflower II*. *(Black Star Publishing Co., Inc.)*

Figure 50A. *Mayflower II* crew group photo ID number legend. *(Courtesy Mayflower Event News)*

Lastly, having to admit that the plans had been found and the ship built, the critics said that she would not sail but she did and crossed the Atlantic, weathering a fifty-knot gale with ease."[49]

Mayflower II's voyage was indeed over, but a new chapter in her story was about to begin.

1. Maitland Edey (*Life* magazine reporter)

2. Graham Nunn (British cabin boy, Corby, Northants, England)

3. Walter "Wally" Godfrey (cook, General Steam Navigation Company, London)

4. Godfrey Wicksteed (first mate, *Joseph Conrad* alumnus)

5. Adrian Small (second mate, *Pequod* alumnus)

6. Alan Villiers (captain, Australian)

7. Jan Junker (third mate, *Joseph Conrad* alumnus, Nazi prison survivor)

8. Stuart Upham (ship's builder, voyage caulker)

9. Peter Padfield (P&O officer, future author and Mountbatten Maritime Prize winner)

10. Joe Meany (American cabin boy, Waltham, Massachusetts)

11. Jim Horrocks (radio operator, Marconi Company)

12. Warwick Charlton (Project Mayflower, "the Fighting Editor")

13. John Winslow (Royal Navy pilot, *Mayflower* descendant)

14. Dick Brennan (assistant cook, Wig & Pen Club owner, London)

15. John "Jumbo" Goddard (British adventurer, *Herzogin Cecilie* alumnus)

16. Joe Lacey (boatswain's mate, *Pequod* alumnus)

17. Beric Watson (British sailor, *Catalina* alumnus)

18. Fred Edwards (British sailor, Blue Funnel Line officer)

19. Andrew "Scotty" Anderson-Bell (British sailor, city planner, adventurer)

20. Ike Marsh (boatswain, *Pequod* alumnus)

21. David Cauvin (South African sailor, Blue Funnel Line officer, *Drommedaris* alumnus)

22. Jack Scarr (British schoolmaster, St. Edwards School, Oxford)

23. Joe Powell (British sailor, stuntman, *Pequod* alumnus)

24. Charles "Canada" Church (Royal Canadian Navy, *Mayflower* descendant)

25. Harry Sowerby (London adventurer, *Joseph Conrad* alumnus)

26. Edgar Mugridge (carpenter, Upham shipyard, Brixham)

27. Dr. John Stevens (ship's doctor, Royal Navy veteran)

28. Michael Ford (Oxford University Yacht Club)

29. David Thorpe (Oxford University Yacht Club)

30. Andy Lindsay (American sailor, *Joseph Conrad* alumnus, Biddeford, Maine)

Not pictured: Gordon Tenney (*Life* magazine photographer), Lee Israel (Mayflower Studios), Julian Lugrin (Project Mayflower cameraman).

PART III

LIVING HISTORY

CHAPTER 16

Bravo!

WARWICK CHARLTON'S DREAM OF ORGANIZING A GREAT ADVENTURE that would capture the world's imagination was now a reality. It was a spectacular performance that earned applause and bravos from around the globe. *Life* magazine called the transit a "thrilling voyage that began in misgivings and ended in pride."[1] *National Geographic* went even further, saying it had just witnessed "one of the most fabulous voyages of modern times."[2] The impossible had been done: a lost seventeenth-century ship had risen from the past, ignored doubters, crossed the Atlantic, survived a storm, and captured global praise. In the halls of achievement—in which there are many pretenders but few originals—*Mayflower II* was now primal.

President Eisenhower, like millions of others, had been watching the maritime drama and spoke for the nation when he said that "the good ship *Mayflower* is dear to the hearts of all Americans" and "brings to mind our heritage of freedom and our historic ties to lands across the sea."[3] Prime Minister Macmillan echoed that sentiment with a good-work-old-chap statement: "Indeed glad to hear of successful outcome of your voyage."[4] The public's enchantment with the little craft was quickly moving her to the top shelf of the ties that bind, and both leaders knew it. The "special relationship" discussed privately in Bermuda was now back on track for all the world to see, thanks in no small measure to the success of Project Mayflower. Charlton's lack of proper diplomatic credentials was of no matter. Others stepped forward on his behalf.

Senator John F. Kennedy of Massachusetts, America's future president, gladly stood beside John Lowe and Felix Fenston at the wheel of *Mayflower II*, symbolically guiding her course. A few days later Massachusetts's senior senator Leverett Saltonstall introduced Vice President Richard Nixon to a cheering crowd. Nixon told those assembled that "no price is too great to pay for freedom," adding, "if we were a poor nation instead of the most prosperous in the history of the world, I would still say that we can afford every dollar that is truly necessary to protect our liberty and to help bring peace to the world."[5]

This chorus of congratulations was being challenged, however, by a growing number of questions about where the money came from to pay for the second *Mayflower*. One incendiary story broke the day after the ship's arrival and suggested the entire effort had been little more than an "All Sales Idea."[6] This called into question the notion that the replica

Figure 51. Felix Fenston, John Lowe, JFK, and David Thorpe on *Mayflower II*. (*Getty Images*)

had been funded primarily by "free will gifts of small amounts" from the English people, which was the basis of Harry Hornblower's request that readers of the *Berkshire Eagle* send "contributions, large or small," to help cover the "one million dollars" he needed for his new museum.[7] Did Hornblower know that corporations really paid for the replica's construction and sailing? If so, how long had he known? The *New York Times* was threatening to expose the truth and undermine his fundraising strategy— but then another story broke and, because it sounded juicy, led reporters in an entirely different direction.

When the replica spent the night in Provincetown, Warwick Charlton took the ship's log, the official daily report of events aboard "*Mayflower II*, [a] barque of London" owned by "Project Mayflower Ltd." that was traveling "from the Port of Brixham, via Dartmouth and Plymouth, towards Plymouth, Mass., commanded by Alan Villiers."[8] Every hour of the journey could be recorded, including distance traveled in nautical miles, course direction as noted on the compass, wind origin and force, barometric pressure, and the chief officer's remarks regarding ships encountered, events on board, and unusual activity. It was a legal document, an integral part of the ship—and an essential guide for crafting a book about sailing the high seas, particularly when the author had no previous personal experience to use as a reference. Without fanfare or notice, Charlton removed the handwritten document from Captain Villiers's cabin and took it to his own. Because the ship and its contents were the property of his enterprise, and he was its sole official aboard, what the maritime world calls the supercargo, it was fully in his power to do so. Charlton then asked Dick Brennan to take the journal to Little, Brown & Company in Boston to be photocopied for future use. The publisher was also to receive a draft of his new book, *The Second Mayflower Adventure*. Aiming to please, the assistant cook quietly left, traveled north, and then returned Villiers's writings to the ship.[9]

At the same time Brennan was departing, the green light was given for reporters to come aboard to interview crew members. Their newspapers were eager to print stories about the voyage. Unfortunately, Charlton had sold exclusive rights to all onboard coverage to *Life* magazine as part of its photo license, so no information was forthcoming from the men. For the news editor of the *Old Colony Memorial*, Walter Haskell, it was a bitter moment, because it also meant that the photos he had asked Joe Meany to take during the crossing could not be used. Perhaps out of frustration, Haskell focused his pen on the ship's cat, and other reporters followed his lead. (Years later, the interest in the mascot was as strong as ever and inspired Peter Arenstam to write a children's book called *Felix and His* Mayflower II *Adventures*.)

Journalists from other periodicals faced similar frustration, and one of them heard about a heated argument in which Alan Villiers accused Warwick Charlton of stealing the ship's log. Now that's a story! The accusation wasn't true, but that didn't matter. It gave the press something to write about other than who really paid for the replica. There was also a grain of truth to it, as Charlton confessed during an interview several years later:

> It has been rumoured that Villiers and I were always at loggerheads. Certainly there was a good deal of friction between us. I don't think he ever got used to the idea of a mere landlubber like myself building the *Mayflower*. But although Villiers was frankly critical of the way I sometimes publicised *Mayflower*, he was determined to hold onto his job of captain. He was usually able to smother his resentment until we were at sea. But then he could contain it no longer and we hardly spoke a civil word to each other during the fifty-four-day voyage.[10]

A few days later, during a speech Alan gave at a dinner in his honor sponsored by the Ancient and Honorable Artillery Company at Faneuil Hall in Boston, he said the log was now back on the ship and its temporary removal was "an innocent misunderstanding." The matter was closed. However, questions about the construction money persisted, and Villiers's relationship with Charlton soured to the point that, in his own book describing the *Mayflower* voyage and others, he would refer to Charlton not by name but only as "the ideas man" and would acknowledge his presence on board only glancingly as "one of the promoters."[11]

Treasure Chests were unloaded "with extreme care" at the State Pier on June 14 "as hundreds of persons were on hand for the activities." Men, women, and children were so eager to see what was going on that they "slowed the unloading" process. For anyone unable to be there, the *Boston Globe* took a photo that filled the top half of its front page later that day, headlined "Vessel Stays within Easy View." Two large crates are clearly seen being off-loaded into a service boat, with two large arrows added so no reader would miss seeing them. The text below described the Treasure Chests and said, "Many were consigned to Boston customers, including Filene's, Jordan Marsh and Shreve Crump & Low Co."[12]

A *New York Times* reporter was also there and wrote about it the next day under the headline "Mayflower Gets Down to Business."[13] The replica disgorged seventy-seven Treasure Chests, eighteen cases, eight cartons, three small boxes, one bale, a parcel, and an iron chest. The items inside were as varied as clothing, metal toys, boots and shoes, gold and silver, microscopes and scientific instruments, paintings, Scotch whiskey, textiles, and toilet brushes. Crates for corporate giants Colgate-Palmolive, Shell-Mex British Petroleum, and the Carborundum Company were also pulled out, along with the 140,000 pieces of commemorative mail that the crew had franked during the voyage "for collectors in the United States and in more than seventy foreign countries."[14]

Of special note was a Treasure Chest consigned to "H.E. Sir Harold Caccia, British Embassy, Washington." Sir Harold had served on then–General Eisenhower's staff in North Africa, participated in the secret Bermuda Conference meeting, and became England's ambassador to the United States the day after Eisenhower's reelection victory at the height of the Suez Crisis. His chest contained "animal feeding stuffs" for a "farmer of Gettysburg"—the president of the United States—and it was delivered to Ike just before Thanksgiving, along with a painting of *Mayflower II* by British artist Howard Jarvis. The president subsequently told the Associated Press that he planned to display the art in his office.[15] Ambassador Caccia fully embraced the "special relationship," understood the importance of British-American interdependence,[16] and by his actions acknowledged the diplomatic utility of Warwick Charlton and his creation.

None of this would have come as a surprise to the 131,000 readers of the *Boston Globe*, which reprinted a shipboard radio interview Captain

Villiers gave to Milton Lewis of the *New York Herald* a few days earlier on June 11, just prior to his ship's arrival in Plymouth. While the headline on the front-page story teased what Villiers and his crew wanted to eat when they stepped ashore—"Get Steaks Ready for All"—the real meat of the story was in the text. Question: "What do you have on board?" Answer: "We have a collection aboard of valuable and rare British goods. You know, like the Pilgrim fathers brought across, like clocks, good woolen clothes and gold and silver ornaments—and a present for President Eisenhower, and a few things like that." Lewis's ears immediately perked up. "What does the present for President Eisenhower consist of?" Evasive, Villiers responded, "Darned if I know, brother. It's locked up. Wait a minute while I check. I believe it's a lovely medallion watch." Of course, the Australian knew what was in the chest going to the British embassy because the contents were listed on the ship's manifest. Rather than stealing Ambassador Caccia's thunder, however, Villiers chose to leverage the query and subtly promote the goods of special interest to him: Swiss watches.

Figure 52. *Mayflower II* cargo unloaded. *(Courtesy Plimoth Patuxet Museums)*

While thousands of tourists explored the Town of Plymouth, the executives at dockside had a job to do and were not on vacation. A fleet of Mayflower Transit moving vans then executed a marketing coup when the company exchanged free delivery to any location for exclusivity, thereby linking its corporate name to the replica. To drive the association home, it put large billboards on each truck declaring: "Riding Safely inside, TREASURE CHESTS from *Mayflower II*." The deal that Charlton had cut with the mover prior to sailing, which spared his venture the cost of delivering British goods to Cleveland, Detroit, Philadelphia, and twelve other cities across the country, was further evidence of the project's inventive marketing. As for Harry and his Plimoth Plantation directors, they were happy with the big rigs' fast departure because they did not want the backside of a truck causing a stink.

Once unpacked by their recipients, the Morris chests were put into storage, discarded, and simply disappeared. Years later, one might turn up—a heavy, dark-colored oak box with a lid that dropped forward, perhaps a faded logo, but no glittering ornamentation that might signal

Figure 53. Mayflower Transit vans with billboard. *(Courtesy Plimoth Patuxet Museums)*

a collector's item, or even an embodiment of "crass commercialism"—a pleasing outcome for those who had wanted to disassociate *Mayflower II* from her cargo. Captain Alan Villiers, however, was not embarrassed and gladly lent his endorsement to the Swiss watches he had quietly hidden under the ship.

Harry and his directors had little interest in discussing Project Mayflower's financing tactics and just waited for the topic to fade from conversation. As for the Treasure Chest, the Carton, and the Small Box listed as Harry's on the ship's manifest, well, if people weren't asking, he wasn't telling. The goods contained in the chest were not "Sloe Gin" as stated on the bill of lading but rather valuable British collectibles donated by the Plymouth Gin Company of England as a gift to the museum with the expectation that they would be displayed. Unfortunately, Hornblower

Figure 54. Alan Villiers promoting the Enicar Ultrasonic Watch. *(Courtesy Enicar Watch)*

was embarrassed by the offer, and the items, rather than being honored publicly, were treated as personal tribute and given away to friends.[17]

Alan Villiers made clear to *National Geographic* readers that "the money to build the new ship has been paid by British industry" as well as by people who "paid their shillings to visit the building ship" in Brixham and by small private contributions.[18] While the average Englishman paid a fee to view the ship, that did not bring in nearly enough money for construction, which was why Treasure Chests and in-kind donations were so important, eventually generating more than 80 percent of the funds needed to build and sail the replica.

Corporate support was no secret in Britain, but the Americans made every effort to avoid mentioning it. The New Englanders happily accepted funds from the State of Massachusetts to help uphold their side of the bargain, but apparently wanted no one to know that the bulk of British revenues came from creative marketing and corporations. When a reporter asked rhetorically, "Just who are her sponsors?" the journalist was required to answer his own question by identifying Project Mayflower, a group in New York, and Harry's Plimoth Plantation, with a hint of mystery around the museum. It had apparently "raised funds for a special mooring basin and adjacent village for tourists," but that work was "not expected to be completed until next year."[19] Because the replica had already been delivered, it was clear that Harry's team needed more time to complete its now past-due construction that included $277,000 in financing from the Commonwealth of Massachusetts: taxpayers' money.[20] What was going on? The museum had been planning to build a stationary ship on a concrete slab before Charlton entered the picture, so why the mystery? Was there more to the story?

Sensing an opportunity to redirect the public conversation as well as the media's focus, Felix Fenston gathered British reporters in London and told them where the bulk of the *Mayflower* money really came from: him! He claimed he had personally put £35,000 ($98,000) into the "replica of the Pilgrim Fathers' ship," a huge sum. He then demanded that Charlton and his partner immediately hand over their interest in the venture to him. "I will gladly assume responsibilities for any outstanding debts," he boasted, "as soon as the necessary authority is in my hands.

. . . I have no financial interest in the profits of Project Mayflower Ltd., apart from certain sums advanced by me."[21] But wait. That enterprise was established as a nonprofit for the public good. Why was Fenston suddenly talking about a profit? Whatever his motives, Charlton quickly gathered his own set of reporters and told them, "I have no intention of resigning,"[22] adding that *Mayflower II* was being turned over to Plimoth Plantation by November 22. Soundly rebuffed publicly, Fenston fired back and issued a statement that, effective immediately, he "had severed all connection" with Project Mayflower, including his offer to take over its interests. *Then go!* was Warwick's angry reply. "We've done all the work. We got her over there and we are not going to be thrown out now by anyone no matter how big they are."[23] After Fenston's failed efforts to keep *Mayflower II* in London for a year to entertain Britons, generate revenue, and improve his public image, this was a stinging rebuff that left the speculator hungry for payback.

There were many ways to exact it, but manipulating the press had a particular elegance when the target was someone in love with words. Thus an unverified item ran in the London *Daily Sketch* suggesting the replica might be an embarrassment to Queen Elizabeth II. No such concern had been expressed by Buckingham Palace, of course, and the uncorroborated report from an unnamed source was pure speculation. But it was irresistible muckraking, the Associated Press picked it up, and the *New York Times* published the blurb under the subhead "London Paper Critical."[24] Felix Fenston must have purred with delight.

To most readers, it was gossip about a trip the monarch was planning to Jamestown and how the Pilgrim ship was getting more than its share of attention. The chairman of the Virginia 350th Anniversary Commission condescendingly told news outlets that his festival had "no commercial aspect" and was "completely historical and dignified." The British tabloid contended that, in contrast, the voyage reenactment was a blatant press event. Without naming Charlton directly, it was noted that the efforts "threatened to embarrass Queen Elizabeth II on her October visit" to the historic Virginia site. All in all, it was a none-too-subtle jab at the replica's future owner, Plimoth Plantation. Here's the backstory.

For several years, the State of Virginia and the US government had been planning an elaborate celebration of the colony's founding, and together invested "state and federal funds amounting to twenty-five million dollars." They even created a second Jamestown settlement on the original site. Additionally, "the British Government had done what it could to help . . . as a gesture of goodwill and real Anglo-American co-operation."[25] It was an eight-month affair that featured two signature events: the visit by Queen Elizabeth II in October and, preceding it in June, an international naval review that was to be one of the mightiest peacetime displays of sea power in history.[26] The US Postal Service even issued a special commemorative stamp titled "International Naval Review," which included the logo of the Jamestown Festival and the image of a Forrestal class aircraft carrier.[27]

The three-day event started on June 11 and involved 115 men-of-war from eighteen nations, including the British aircraft carrier HMS *Ark Royal*, which crossed paths with the replica while both were sailing to America a few weeks earlier. More than one hundred military aircraft, helicopters, and blimps filled the sky, and the US Navy's Blue Angels fighter squadron performed aerial acrobatics. Reviewing officers included the secretary of the navy, the chief of naval operations, and the Supreme Allied Commander of NATO. It was the largest exercise of its kind ever held in the United States, and the organizers had carefully planned for success. Unfortunately, they seemed to have ignored or overlooked the potential simultaneous arrival of a certain seventeenth-century wooden ship five hundred miles to the north, that "upstart *Mayflower*."[28] Adding insult to the Virginians' injury, the vice president of the United States even made a special visit to Plymouth to celebrate Project Mayflower's achievement. How dare he!

Charlton's media and marketing genius generated such buzz in the domestic and international press that the wind was taken out of Virginia's sails, to the predictable chagrin of its organizers—the State of Virginia, Washington bureaucrats, the US Navy, and social elites who included Jamestown and *Mayflower* descendants. The Foreign Office was also angered by the maverick who upstaged them, even though his efforts greatly benefited the United Kingdom and its Commonwealth.

Figure 55. Vice President Richard Nixon with *Shallop II* crew, pictured from back to front, left to right: Benjamin Brewster, Lothrop Withington Jr., Paul Withington, William Stearns Jr., Nixon, George Davis, Russell Fry Jr., Russell Coffin, Robert Briggs, and Spencer Brewster. *(Courtesy of the University Archives & Special Collections Department, Joseph P. Healey Library, University of Massachusetts Boston: "Mass. Memories Road Show Collection.")*

"Whatever the rights or wrongs . . . it [all] had an extremely bad effect,"[29] but it could not undermine or tarnish Project Mayflower's gift to America, a piece of her lost history returned.

CHAPTER 17

Meanwhile in London

ACROSS THE SEA, WHERE THE *MAYFLOWER* SAGA BEGAN CENTURIES EAR-lier, the British government was launching an investigation into Felix Fenston's property speculation tactics and practices. His plan to destroy the historic St. James's Theatre and replace it with a seven-story office building was now making headlines and causing a national outcry. The live performance venue built in 1835 was one of only two remaining Georgian architecture theaters in London. *Jane Eyre* author Charlotte Brontë had been a patron and enjoyed dramatic productions there. In the postwar years it thrived as Orson Welles, Peter Finch, Margaret Leighton, Sir Michael Redgrave, and other well-known actors performed. On top of that, since 1950 the St. James's had been managed by the actor Sir Laurence Olivier and his wife Vivien Leigh. Olivier was universally considered one of the greatest performers; his Hollywood accolades included an Oscar for Best Actor in *Hamlet,* and King George VI had honored him in 1947 with a knighthood. Comanager Leigh was the Oscar-winning star of *Gone with the Wind.* Together, they made the theater part of the city's modern cultural fabric.

Now Project Mayflower's chief financial patron was threatening that jewel, and the public relations "insurance policy" he helped underwrite was about to be tested. With any luck, *Mayflower II* would allow Fenston to portray himself as a cultural hero rather than a villain, and public scandal would be avoided. He had managed to get the cream of the New England press to refer to him as a financial "angel,"[1] and he now hoped to do the same in London. But that would require the ouster of Warwick

Charlton as head of the replica undertaking, and the Fighting Editor had made it crystal clear that he wasn't about to go anywhere.

The hearings into the "Proposed Demolition of St. James's Theatre" began on July 9,[2] and they continued in multiple public sessions until July 31. During the course of those spirited debates, it was revealed that Felix Fenston's company Viarex Property Investment purchased the St. James's Theatre on October 29, 1954, for £250,000 and gave a deposit.[3] Not mentioned was his £500 contribution around the same time to jump-start Project Mayflower. The Lords learned that "the vast majority of the hundreds of applications received each week by the London County Council [were] dealt with either by a panel of three members, or by the chairman or vice-chairman." In Fenston's case, the latter method was used, and while no improprieties were suggested, that decision process would have allowed Viarex to make a strong, direct, personal appeal to just one man whose vote was final.[4] At the time, the LCC was told that the new owners planned to "continue running the theatre," but that deception was exposed when the public learned it was soon to be demolished so an office building could be built on the property. That news came in May, as *Mayflower II* was being heralded in London and around the world. Opposition to Fenston's newly revealed scheme was quickly voiced by newspapers large and small across the country.

The public had been duped, and Parliament wanted to stop Fenston, who had the sole right to do as he wished with the property. He "could pull it down, or keep it empty, or turn it into a Turkish bath or cinema, without permission from anybody."[5] But he was a businessman, and the Lords knew what drove him: money. So they came up with a strategy to compensate him in return for abandoning his plans. The funds would come from private donors including Winston Churchill, who pledged £500, and two American millionaires, philanthropist Huntington Hartford and a Mr. Cort, plus the Piccadilly and St. James's Association, a group of larger industrialists. They were all united in their opposition to Fenston's destruction desires, his Plan A. The idea was to offer him £300,000, representing a 20 percent return on his investment, as a Plan B, renumeration for changing his mind. The speculator might be greedy, but he was also "more . . . publicly spirited than the average man," according

Figure 56. *Daily Mirror*: "'Dear Felix' and Vivien Leigh." *(Mirrorpix/Reach Publishing Services Ltd.)*

to Lord Pakenham, who asked his peers to look at Fenston's involvement "in the *Mayflower* venture."[6]

In a late-night 22-to-18 vote on July 30, the Lords voted to stop Fenston, and the next day declared that "in the opinion of this House no action should be taken to demolish or otherwise prejudice the continued use of St. James's Theatre as a theater pending a decision on the matter by both Houses of Parliament." Minister of Housing and Local Government Henry Brooke then outlined the legal position to the House of Commons and said he had spoken with Fenston but did not elaborate.[7]

While Parliament debated and anti-Fenston protesters marched in the streets, Plimoth Plantation was either unaware of or chose to ignore the news relating to *Mayflower II*'s chief financial patron. Even the *Boston Globe* seemed unaware that Fenston was behind the group at the center of the controversy because his name never appeared in multiple stories about the ongoing events. It was of no matter to Hornblower's museum, which just wanted to finalize the replica's transfer in accordance with the original offer to get it for free. Now, however, a new problem arose in an unexpected quarter.

The British government suddenly demanded that Project Mayflower change its deal with the museum and not simply give them the treasured craft. No free gift to the Americans while foreign currency reserves remained desperately low following Suez. The New Englanders would have to pay hard cash for the asset to help generate much needed foreign revenue for the Crown. Such a sale could also fill the venture's less-than-full coffers and offset the income lost when Charlton defied Fenston and Lowe, refusing to let *Mayflower II* stay in England for a year to entertain residents and tourists. The government effectively wanted the Fighting Editor to sacrifice principle for profit, and he was not about to do that. But he also knew a direct order from the government could not be ignored. Now what? He needed to think creatively to find an alternate route to finalizing the deal with Plimoth. And he did. Here's how:

Individuals traveling abroad could not take more than £100 in cash with them annually,[8] and it seemed absurd that Warwick Charlton would somehow be able to just sail away with a made-in-Britain product "that could not be valued at less than £100,000."[9] But the promoter, like his creation, was unlike anything the authorities had ever encountered.

When the official assigned to Project Mayflower's export request case turned out to be someone with a famous American surname, Warwick instinctively knew his powers of persuasion could be used to overcome a potentially major obstacle. "Penn. That's one of the most important names in the history of America. Any relatives in Pennsylvania?" he inquired politely. "Of course if you do, I know you will not allow it to cloud your judgment." Did it? Charlton never knew. But after interviewing the promoter, hearing the grand vision behind the undertaking, and perhaps considering the "special relationship" the replica was strengthening, the government agency that Mr. Penn represented notified the impresario that he would be permitted to sell the replica for a nominal sum. A buck.[10]

Harry of course agreed to the revised terms, but he would remain silent on where Warwick Charlton found the money to build and sail his museum's future star. As for the revenue opportunities not pursued in London, that was Warwick's problem, not his.

The Big Apple was about to come to Project Mayflower's rescue. The visit was carefully choreographed, and on July 1 the square-rigger was met with blue skies and a harbor filled with welcoming pleasure craft, fireboats spraying salutatory geysers, aircraft circling overhead, and a Navy blimp hovering aloft.[11] After the Bermuda Conference, Washington had authorized the airship as a gesture of respect and nod of approval for a craft that bound British and American history closely together. Cannons were fired in salute from Governors Island, and the replica responded by dipping her ensign for each shot.[12]

Mayflower II docked at Pier 81 on the Hudson River, a short walk from Times Square and Broadway via 42nd Street, and quickly became a top attraction for both tourists and residents. Near the pier, to add historical perspective, a simulated Pilgrim Village consisting of sixty log cabins with thatched roofs was constructed,[13] strikingly similar in concept to the three Plimoth Plantation structures near the famous Rock. The city additionally staged an exhibition of "twenty-seven 'treasure chests' of British merchandise brought over in the hold of *Mayflower*,"[14] capturing the public's imagination and paying tribute to the companies that made the voyage possible.

July 2 was declared Mayflower Day,[15] and "a salty-looking crew of adventurers received a cheering ticker-tape reception." They were "the deeply tanned crew of the *Mayflower II* and, in their Pilgrim garb, they looked as if they might have just stepped off a Hollywood movie set."[16] The men walked up Broadway as their captain rode in an open-air car and Felix the mascot was held proudly by Scotty Anderson-Bell. Not only could the feline melt hearts with a mere gaze, the little rascal was the only one dressed to the nines in formal wear that featured a rich black suit accented with white cuffs at the end of each arm (front paws).

Starting at noon from Battery Park at the lower tip of Manhattan and traveling up Broadway past Harry Hornblower's Wall Street and then to City Hall Plaza, they were welcomed by the mistress of ceremonies, *Mayflower* descendant Priscilla Alden Kiefer.[17] Her namesake Priscilla Mullins had traveled to the New World with her family, but within months her mother, father, and brother were all dead, leaving Priscilla to fend for herself as the only single woman of marriageable age in the colony. She eventually wed John Alden, a story immortalized in Henry Wadsworth Longfellow's 1858 poem "The Courtship of Miles Standish." Priscilla went on to raise ten children, among whose great- and great-great-grandchildren were US presidents John Adams and John Quincy Adams. Today's Priscilla, in addition to personifying the nation's early history and honoring the *Mayflower* mariners, had to greet bands from the US Army, Navy, Air Force, Coast Guard, and Merchant Marine Academy, plus the New York Fire Department and the city's mounted police. Oh, and don't forget to welcome the honored guests from the Colonial Dames of America, the Society of Mayflower Descendants, the Huguenot Society of America, Sons and Daughters of Pilgrims, Daughters of Founders and Patriots, Descendants of the Signers of the Declaration of Independence, Daughters of Colonial Wars, Colonial Daughters of the Seventeenth Century, Federation of Women's Clubs of New York, Sons of the American Revolution, and (certainly not least) Daughters of the American Revolution.[18] Project Mayflower's gift to America was clearly a big deal.

On the third day, while an estimated five thousand people waited in line to board the Pilgrim memorial, Broadway star Ethel Merman arrived to cut a ceremonial ribbon at the foot of the gangway. Visitors were rewarded with a special souvenir: a *Mayflower* Ship's Mail envelope with the Queen's stamp and cancellation mark containing a pocket-size copy of the Mayflower Compact signed by Captain Villiers. It marked the start of the replica's career as a colonial history teacher to students of all ages and all walks of life. By sundown, more than nine thousand people had boarded and explored the wooden craft. One opening day criticism was that the public could not go belowdecks, and that restriction was lifted within twenty-four hours so guests could walk topside or below and examine the ship's bunks, galley, wheel, and compass.[19] The ship's bell was an unexpected treat when visitors came close and read "Miles Graye Made Me in 1638," a mere eighteen years after the famous voyage three centuries earlier.[20] Additionally, the great cabin was heavily trafficked because this was where historians think the Mayflower Compact was signed. Questions were answered by experts and Villiers's crew, and they soon learned that one of the most popular queries related to Felix. Where is he hiding? Can we see him? What's going to become of your mascot? Paparazzi was one thing, but what if someone tried to abduct him? He was too precious to be left roaming the only home he had known, and the decision was made to let him see the world from a different perspective—land. Soon he was discovering a new life in Massachusetts while the replica spent 137 days in the metropolis and more than 500,000 tourists walked her decks after paying an entrance fee of ninety-five cents for adults and forty-five for children.[21]

Leading department stores, always on the lookout for a new sales angle, seized upon growing public interest in the voyage and put Treasure Chests on display in their huge windows throughout the city. These included fashion leaders such as B. Altman, Bloomingdales, Lord & Taylor, and Brooks Brothers. Many families also wanted to know more about Pilgrim life, and Abraham & Straus and Gimbel's responded with special events featuring colonial times. If a retailer had not been represented on

Figure 57. *Mayflower* Ship's Mail envelope and Mayflower Compact. *(Courtesy Mayflower Event News)*

the cargo manifest, it was easy to get involved by merely selling "Made in Britain" products, to the delight of the English government.

Throughout the summer and fall, greater New York's eight million residents celebrated their featured guest, and when she said farewell in November, her colors were dipped in salute as she sailed past the Statue of Liberty.[22] Lessons from the historic exhibition, including ticket pricing, were not lost on the ship's future owner, which planned to heed them once their prize dropped final anchor in the Bay State—because *Mayflower II* was now a proven moneymaker.

CHAPTER 18

Promise Kept

WARWICK CHARLTON WAS A MAN OF HIS WORD, AND HE KNEW HIS pledge to Hornblower would not be fulfilled until the replica was formally conveyed to the Americans. Now that Fenston's attempt to take over the venture had failed, the transfer process was in Warwick's hands, which was good for the enterprise because Felix was distracted with other matters, as the *Birmingham Daily Post* proclaimed on August 7, 1957, under the headline "Demolition of St. James's Deferred." For a price. The questionably benevolent financier had indeed met with the Ministry of Housing and Local Government's Mr. Brooke, heard the Plan B offer of £300,000, learned how the money was to be raised from both sides of the Atlantic, and demanded more. "It should be realized that at least £350,000 is required to . . . cancel the [destruction] agreement."[1] That would of course double his profit from the initial offer. Some might consider it an obscene counterproposal, but it was just the way Felix Fenston did business. Nothing personal. He knew he had something others wanted. If there had been any doubt about the importance of profit in Fenston's mind, his actions surrounding the London theater laid them publicly to rest. Money was the god he worshipped.

In contrast, Warwick Charlton moved forward with his pledge to deliver *Mayflower II* to Plimoth Plantation for virtually nothing, even though Harry had not yet fulfilled his side of the bargain. The Englishman firmly believed he would. He considered the American trustworthy and a man of probity. It was a blessing for Hornblower that Fenston's attempt to take over the project had failed. If the real-estate speculator had succeeded, it is easy to imagine the gift's price tag jumping to well over $100,000. Felix understood leverage and knew he had something the museum desperately needed, for it had almost certainly committed to the reproduction's delivery when state funding was secured. Failure to produce the replica as promised would have created a huge problem. Besides, if Fenston had demanded such a price, Hornblower would still be getting a bargain. They both knew it, and the Wall Streeter almost certainly would have found a way to come up with the money. Coincidentally, Harry made news about the same time underscoring his financial acumen when the *Boston Globe* ran a story headlined "Hornblower Stresses New Securities Gift Law for Minors." As governor of the Association of Stock Exchange Firms, he wanted investors to know how easy it was going to be to direct gifts of securities or money to minors. "No court proceedings are required," just simple paperwork.[2] A gift such as *Mayflower II* might be just as straightforward.

And Charlton remained at the project's helm, trustful that Hornblower would meet his promise—an attitude Fenston would have considered confirmation of the Fighting Editor's negotiating weakness. He and John Lowe then dutifully transferred ownership of their work in late August from the English entity Project Mayflower Ltd. to a new, Connecticut-based nonprofit called the Mayflower Foundation.[3] As with the British enterprise, Warwick and John were the sole owners of the new US venture. Less than a month later, the creative duo said goodbye to their fair lady and unconditionally transferred their entire interest in the ship to Plimoth Plantation for $1, a price Harry's directors still thought too good to be true. At the specific request of the museum and its attorneys, a bill of sale was signed at the US embassy in London, where a British notary public attested to its authenticity as an American official witnessed the process.[4] The document itself was quite straightforward:[5]

BILL OF SALE

To all to whom these presents may come, greeting:

Know ye, that The Mayflower Foundation, incorporated, a corporation duly organized and existing under the laws of the State of Connecticut, owner of the sailing ship called the "Mayflower II," of the burden of 260.12 tons, or thereabouts, in consideration of the sum of $1.00 to it in hand paid, the receipt whereof is hereby acknowledged, have bargained and sold, and by these presents do bargain and sell, unto Plimoth Plantation, Inc., a corporation duly organized and existing under the laws of the Commonwealth of Massachusetts, the said sailing ship, together with the mast, bowsprit, sails, boats, anchors, cables and other appurtenances thereto appertaining and belonging.

To have and to hold the said sailing ship and the appurtenances thereunto belonging unto the said Plimoth Plantation, Inc., its successors and assigns, to its and their sole and only proper user, benefit and behoof forever.

And further The Mayflower Foundation, Incorporated, does here by promise, covenant and agree for itself, its successors and assigns, that it is the sole owner of said sailing ship, that this Bill of Sale is intended to transfer unconditionally the entire interest in said ship and the appurtenances thereto belonging, and that it will warrant and defend the title to said sailing ship, and the appurtenances aforesaid, against all and every person and persons whomever.

IN WITNESS THEREOF, the said The Mayflower Foundation, Incorporated, has caused these presents to be executed and its corporate seal to be hereunder affixed by its officers thereunto duly authorized this 16th day of September, 1957.

The Mayflower Foundation Incorporated
[signed]Warwick Charlton
Title: Incorporator and Director / W. CHARLTON

[signed]John Lowe
Title: Incorporator and Director / J. LOWE

Personally appeared before me the above-named officers of The Mayflower Foundation, Incorporated, and acknowledged the foregoing Bill of Sale to be the free act and deed of said corporation.

[signed]M. Phillips
Notary Public. / NOTARY PUBLIC, LONDON, ENGLAND.
[corporate seal affixed]

At the same time, final preparations were being made for Queen Elizabeth II's inaugural visit to the United States as the second *Mayflower*'s upstaging of the Naval Review in Virginia remained a fresh memory at the Foreign Office. The queen was to be the headline attraction in the second act of the Virginia drama, and diplomats were determined to make it a success. The royal journey began on October 17 with an excursion to England's first permanent settlement in the New World, Jamestown, after which she and Prince Philip toured the College of William & Mary before spending the night at the elegant Williamsburg Inn.[6] Next on the agenda was Washington, where they met with the British ambassador and other dignitaries before being honored at a state dinner hosted by President Eisenhower, a triumphant evening that set the stage for the queen's next stop, New York City. There the monarch would address the United Nations General Assembly on October 21, 1957, and endorse the goal of "equality of justice for all before the law"—the underlying belief that had inspired Charlton to launch Project Mayflower.[7]

After speaking to world leaders, Queen Elizabeth visited the Statue of Liberty and the Empire State Building. Atop America's tallest skyscraper, she was able to see the entire city, the Hudson River, and a small wooden ship called *Mayflower II*. It was a thrilling sight, and she was delighted that she had become part of its history a few days earlier when the Order of the British Empire (OBE) was bestowed upon a man involved with its success.

A title of chivalry and one of the United Kingdom's highest honors, the OBE was established in 1917 by Elizabeth's grandfather George V to celebrate Englishmen who made great contributions to the arts, science, and the nation. Considering the benefits the replica was delivering to the Commonwealth, Queen Elizabeth called upon British diplomats to identify the person driving Project Mayflower who most certainly had earned this special recognition. But its noble creator—the man whose genius and hard work had inspired the magnificent vessel—was not someone the Foreign Office found pleasing. Quite the contrary. Since the early 1940s, Warwick Charlton had been an irritant to bureaucrats, and they had no intention of elevating his name to Her Majesty. However, they did need to offer a candidate with an association to the vessel.

Good fortune was about to shine on Ronnie Forth, a British expat who had been living near Plymouth for thirty years and was familiar to town officials and friendly with staffers at the Boston consulate. After Warwick Charlton's visit fifteen months earlier, local leaders quickly recognized that *Mayflower II* could help revive the town's declining fortunes, and the chummy Brit volunteered to head the town's reception committee.[8] His love for Albion and the White Cliffs of Dover was as strong as ever, and in 1953 he helped organize a ball in Boston to celebrate the coronation of the new queen. Other Anglo-American events and charities also colored his résumé. In short, the local man was a terrific party planner, and he had done a splendid job preparing the town for the arrival of the 1620 lookalike, the world press, and future prosperity. Ronnie was congenial, detail oriented, and a godsend to the British staffers who had provided little support for the historic voyage—and it was he they singled out for special praise during the queen's inaugural visit to the USA.

Accordingly, on the day before traveling to New York City, the queen presided over a special investiture ceremony at Britain's Washington embassy and bestowed the title of Honorary Officer of the Most Excellent Order of the British Empire on "the organizer of the *Mayflower II* welcome in the United States."[9] As for the Englishman who actually earned the honor, denying him recognition was sweet revenge for those who had spent years waiting for the right moment to teach him a lesson about the risks of challenging long-held British mores. Although their knives were out, officials did not make him suffer the fate of Sir Walter Raleigh, the seafaring legend who was a favorite of the first Elizabeth but beheaded for treason by her successor, James I, just two years before the Pilgrims made history. Warwick Charlton's body would remain intact, but his good name was effectively tossed overboard.

CHAPTER 19

My Rules

HARRY HORNBLOWER HAD PLENTY TO BE THANKFUL FOR, THAT Thanksgiving week of 1957. On Sunday the replica was towed into her home port as three thousand watched from the shore.[1] This was well below June's crowd of more than twenty-five thousand. To counter any potential drop in public enthusiasm, his institution announced plans for a special tourist package of $1 for adults and $0.50 for children (a 5 percent increase over New York City prices for grownups and an 11 percent jump for kids) to inspect its three primitive buildings near the state pier and then board the beautiful new attraction. Only Harry and a few others knew that the first adult to buy a ticket would reimburse the museum for the dollar it paid for the icon. Now it was Plimoth's time to make money and, said the *New York Times*, to raise the $800,000 needed to augment the $200,000 it already had in hand to finish the long-discussed colonial village.[2]

The paper then touched on missteps made by Project Mayflower. There were two big ones. The first was not exhibiting the ship in London "where fees from the British public had been counted on to complete most of the financing." John Lowe's strategy could have resulted in *Mayflower II* arriving on American shores debt free, but his partner objected because Hornblower had been pressuring him for delivery and Charlton had given his word that the vessel would arrive before the start of summer. A London exhibition might also have tempered some of Fenston's aggressive behavior toward Charlton after the ship landed on American shores and the speculator tried to oust him. The second mistake occurred when the replica arrived in Massachusetts at the same time as the mighty naval review celebrating the 350th anniversary of Jamestown. "*Mayflower II* was bombarded editorially at long range for having made landfall at the tip of Cape Cod during the height of the Virginia observances," the *Times* said.[3] Without intending to ruffle mighty feathers, that is exactly what happened—and when it was time to issue punishment, Charlton would find himself an easy target.

On Wednesday, November 27, an official ceremony was held to applaud the transfer of ownership. Harry's special guests included Alan Villiers, Massachusetts governor Foster Furcolo, and other important local officials—but not Charlton or Lowe, who conspicuously had not been invited.[4] The next day was Thanksgiving, and the NBC *Today Show* went to Plymouth so host Dave Garroway could interview Hornblower on live television.[5] Harry first thanked Felix Fenston, then Warwick Charlton—in a slap faintly reminiscent of British diplomats' dismissive retribution. Just weeks before Harry's praise of the moneyman, Sir Laurence Olivier told reporters in London that those seeking to save the St. James's Theatre felt they had "been a little bit played with in rather a skittish manner" by Fenston and his tactics.[6] Nonetheless, he got top billing on Harry's thank-you roster.

Fenston would have been pleased, not surprised, to hear that praise because the two men spoke the same financial language. It was recognition of the future value the London land speculator might represent for the museum founder. Harry had privately encouraged Felix's failed takeover attempt and "believed the millionaire businessman could continue to be a good friend of Plimoth Plantation,"[7] of which Harry was chairman and founder. If the museum succeeded, then Harry Hornblower succeeded. Had there been any viewers of the NBC program in England, however, such admiration would have been hard to find because Felix Fenston thumbed his nose at public demands and government efforts to save the irreplaceable St. James's Theatre and was about to demolish it despite national opposition. His offer of reprieve had been a mere ploy to buy time, and within weeks a London icon that had survived the Blitz and entertained patrons for 122 years was demolished. While Harry was sentimental about his new historic prize, the London businessman had little time for emotion when it came to expanding his financial holdings.

Harry then directed his second thank-you to Monty's Fighting Editor and read a telegram Warwick had sent him: "Today I hand over *Mayflower Two* to your safe keeping. May she be a reminder to the people of our two countries that although the Atlantic Ocean may separate us it can never keep us apart."[8]

The transfer ran as front-page news in the *Boston Globe* under the headline "*Mayflower II* Returns, Docks at Plymouth," and readers learned the ship would soon be heading to "various southern ports as part of the attempt to pay off heavy debts clinging like barnacles to the craft." As for Harry's own land-based American undertaking, "Plimoth Plantation has $200,000 in cash and pledges toward its $1 million" goal. Harry then appealed to readers to send contributions for his still unfinished ship berth. "The mailing address is easy to remember," he said. "It is Plimoth Plantation, P.O. Box 1620, Plymouth, Mass."[9] Further south, the *New York Times* reported the change of ownership that day by writing, "*Mayflower* Saga Ends; Ship Is Officially Turned Over to Plymouth."[10] The short article appeared at the bottom of the Obituaries page.

Alan Villiers too was wrapping up the experience by writing a candid personal letter to *National Geographic*'s Mel Grosvenor: "Charlton and Lowe, the London promoters, were really a pretty terrible pair of fellows—their trouble, I suppose, was (at any rate in part) that it took crazy people to make such an idea work, anyway. At least they produced the ship, and we sailed her, and Plimoth Plantation are very glad to have her. Those are the important things."[11] Bottom line, the Australian and his crew had been given the chance to experience something no other mariners had known for centuries, and he knew it.

The following week, as a wrecking ball struck the St. James's Theatre, Sir John Gielgud led the Royal Shakespeare Company in a new production of *The Tempest* at the Theatre Royal, Drury Lane. For those who knew that the character Stephano was based in part on the real-life exploits of Mayflower Compact signer Stephen Hopkins, it was an ironic moment because the man who helped finance the second Pilgrim ship was the same person whose greed led to the loss of a performance venue so many had fought to save.

Now down to business. The third group identified by the *Times* on June 14 under the headline "Aide Denies Ship Is All-Sales Idea" was Mayflower Ltd., "a group of New York insurance and real estate men and others, who put up funds to finish construction of the ship. In return they received permission to exhibit the ship at a West Fortieth Street pier until Thanksgiving as part of the New York *Mayflower II* Exposition, a commercial venture."[12] As soon as the replica was firmly in Hornblower's hands, his executives moved quickly to take control of that company and sever all ties with the two Englishmen who brought the gift to life and ensured her safe delivery.[13] They also revalued their $1 acquisition at $300,000 for insurance purposes.[14]

The museum honored the group's original pledge to have the replica spend the winter in Florida but demanded updated deal terms. The new Mayflower Ltd. of New York and Plimoth Plantation each agreed to contribute $25,000 to pay for delivering the attraction to Miami, plus the expenses associated with a three-month visit. Revenues generated from ticket sales would then be split evenly until each side recovered its initial investment, after which 80 percent would go to the Plantation, leaving 20 percent for the New York group.[15] Nothing was offered to Project Mayflower, even as a gesture of thanks in the way that successful gamblers might tip the croupier. Building on the Summer Festival success, it was estimated that an additional 220,000 people walked aboard the ship that winter and the following spring,[16] making the southern tour very lucrative for Harry's group and proving that America's interest in its early history extended far beyond New England. Visitors were given copies of the Mayflower Compact and learned about the vessel's conception, construction, and crossing, supplemented with news articles written in English and Spanish by the *Miami Herald*, *Miami News*, and *Diario Las Americas*.

After leaving the Caribbean gateway, she sailed north, arriving in Washington on April 16 sporting a new coat of paint and an onboard team that included "two girl crew members,"[17] according to news reports that would have brought a smile to Priscilla Mullins. The Potomac River

Figure 58. *Mayflower II* wintering in Miami. *(Charles Trainor/Miami News)*

became the setting for ceremonies, and Mayor Robert McLaughlin honored *Mayflower II*'s captain with a bronze key to the city.[18] With the Washington Monument rising in the background, a band played and speeches were given.[19] It was another pairing of American icons, echoing the scene in New York Harbor, when the tribute shared the spotlight with Lady Liberty. Before the summer solstice, Plimoth's star was back in Massachusetts,[20] ready to entertain Independence Day crowds.

As for the British impresario, he spent 1958 laboring as a guest speaker for Mayflower Transit and trying to make ends meet because the nonprofit he founded with John Lowe had given away its only asset. In other words, he was out of a job. The marketing maestro entertained crowds in thirty-three states with tales of the great adventure and a full-color film called *The Voyage of* Mayflower II. It became so popular that Modern Talking Pictures was brought in to manage distribution,[21] and by year's end more than fifteen million people were estimated to have seen the show on television and at nontheatrical venues such as schools, churches, and clubs.

Figure 59. *Mayflower II* in Washington, DC. *(© British Pathé)*

And Harry Hornblower? He remained a partner in the family business bearing his name, Hornblower & Weeks, as it celebrated its seventieth anniversary "serving as manager or major participant in underwritings of corporations and tax-exempt securities" via "more than 750 employees in 16 offices located in 14 cities."[22] Away from investment banking duties, his "chief outside interest" continued to be Plimoth Plantation, and he proudly told friends, "*Mayflower II* is one of our prize exhibits."[23]

CHAPTER 20

Living History

PROJECT MAYFLOWER'S GIFT TO AMERICA QUICKLY BECAME PART OF the nation's living history. Warwick Charlton's team had successfully raised some £154,000 ($432,000) for construction and sailing,[1] but the craft still arrived owing $190,000 in outstanding debts.[2] Of that amount $56,000 was due Fenston, who had already stated publicly that he was willing to forgive this. That left $134,000 due "100 other British creditors" who were offered and accepted "$.50 on the dollar," which reduced the balance to $67,000. Additionally, creditors had "agreed to be patient."[3] The bulk of the revised net arrival debt was then covered when more than 730,000 tourists paid an admission fee to board her in New York, Miami, and Washington and bought souvenirs. The replica would eventually generate more than $830,000 in gross revenue.[4] Once *Mayflower II* was firmly in Plimoth Plantation's grip, memberships grew by 50 percent,[5] and by 1960 the vessel earned more than $140,000 for the museum.[6] Harry Hornblower's pocket change decision had proved its worth by making him "the proud possessor of a beautiful ship, built to our own specifications from designs of our own naval architect, William A. Baker," which "could not possibly be replaced for less than 300,000 dollars."[7]

America clearly loved *Mayflower II*, but would the romance last? As 1957 came to an end, the attention of America and the world shifted from the past to the future when Russia launched the first man-made object into earth orbit on October 4: *Sputnik*. It was about the size of a beach ball and weighed less than 190 pounds, yet it marked the start of a new era of scientific discovery. Yes, the 180-ton wooden ship had captured the public's imagination sailing the Atlantic, but now what? Would the inspiring words that motivated Warwick Charlton—"just and equal laws for the general good"—be heard by future generations? More important, could William Baker's ship endure Mother Nature and maintain the public's attention?

It quickly became apparent that the gift of lost American history floating in Plymouth Harbor had a role to play as a teacher, and before long busloads of elementary, middle, and high school students were coming to see her as part of organized field trips. So much so that making the walk up her gangway became an informal rite of passage for youngsters throughout New England. The replica also became a symbol of national heritage as the country grappled with the civil rights movement, Vietnam War protests, and Native American history. Coming to terms with the way indigenous peoples had been treated after the arrival of the Pilgrim ship was not an easy subject. Where should it begin, and how could it be made relevant when so many pundits were focused on a foreign conflict and the remnants of slavery? Let's start with an eye-popping headline: "Native Americans Invade *Mayflower II*."[8]

It had been 350 years since the English voyagers arrived, and by the fall of 1970 it was clear to Wampanoag elder Frank "Wamsutta" James that powerful ideas and nonviolent protest could be more effective than confrontation and conflict when addressing grievances. For example, How should he respond to those who had suppressed a speech he had been asked to give at the start of Massachusetts's eighteen-month celebration marking the 1620 landing? Officials had asked to see the remarks in advance of delivery, ostensibly to make copies for public distribution, but were shocked by the words. Frank was summarily disinvited. So two months later, the Wampanoag statesman scheduled a protest that would coincide with Thanksgiving, sent the word out to tribes everywhere, and used William Baker's replica as a backdrop. On the morning of the big day, about two hundred people gathered on Cole's Hill near the statue of Massasoit, the great Wampanoag leader from colonial times. They had come in response to James's planned announcement of a new way to approach the nation's past, and among those present were representatives from twenty-five indigenous nations, including Penobscots, Cherokees, Navajos, Passamaquoddies, Cheyennes, and Narragansetts, as well as their Wampanoag hosts. Firebrand activist Russell Means of the American Indian Movement also came with his message of confrontation but was no match for the powerful nonviolent approach advocated by the event's organizers.

James had a simple idea: connect all Americans through the concept of shared mourning for the loss of loved ones. It was what brought people together at funerals, wakes, and memorial services. Why not start a new tradition that would honor the lives of countless indigenous people lost over hundreds of years? If it were held simultaneously with Thanksgiving celebrations, it could become an annual event that would "set the table," so to speak, for conversation and reflection when the nation sat down as one for its late November meal of unity.

As protesters waited for Frank's oratory, their eyes gazed out upon Plymouth Harbor and then began to focus on a Doric-columned monument and the famous geologic formation below it. Someone shouted out, "That damn rock! I'd like to blow it up. It was the start of everything bad that has happened to the American Indian."[9] Then a tidal wave seemed to rise as more than one hundred men, women, and children flowed to the spot where Villiers, Charlton, and Upham had been greeted after *Mayflower II*'s transatlantic crossing. Several people jumped over the railing around the Rock, landed on the earth below, and began to douse the stone with handfuls of sand, symbolizing their disdain, as onlookers and news groups watched safely from above.

Then it was "on to the *Mayflower*," where about two dozen trespassers walked onboard, climbed her hemp ratlines, shimmied up the Canadian pine mainmast, and captured a Union Jack flag. Others explored the ship, found a mannequin portraying the captain, and threw him overboard, where he was left to float like a buoy.

Then, just as quickly as it began, the occupation ended when local police walked up the gangway and asked the miscreants to leave. They did—peacefully and immediately—as some lifted their arms to the sky in a gesture of victory. It was all very calm, and after leaving the ship, the crowd went back up the hill, reassembled around Massasoit, and waited

Figure 60. Russell Means speaking in front of Massasoit statue. *(© The Patriot Ledger—USA TODAY NETWORK)*

Figure 61. Native American protesters on *Mayflower II*, November 25, 1970. *(AP Archives)*

to hear Frank James. He spoke clearly, thoughtfully, and honestly, ending his address with this admonition:[10]

> What has happened cannot be changed, but today we must work towards a more humane America, a more Indian America, where men and nature once again are important; where the Indian values of honor, truth, and brotherhood prevail.
>
> You the white man are celebrating an anniversary. We the Wampanoags will help you celebrate in the concept of a beginning. It was the beginning of a new life for the Pilgrims. Now, 350 years later it

is a beginning of a new determination for the original American: the American Indian.

The leader hoped his idea for a National Day of Mourning, articulated in sight of Project Mayflower's gift to America, would gradually gain acceptance. At the very least, he had put down a marker.

In coming years, the replica would entertain tens of millions of visitors in what Harry Hornblower proudly called "one of the top outdoor museums in the country," as the nation charted a course through remarkable and often unsettling events while it continued to write its history, and Harry remained "a concerned optimist in these very uncertain times."[11] By 1997 more than ten million people had walked through his Pilgrim Village and 30 percent more—13 million—stepped aboard Charlton's replica. This naturally had "a tremendous impact on the region," according to Brooks Kelly, executive director of the Plymouth County Development Council, who credited the Hornblower complex with "about $53 million being pumped into the local economy" annually.[12]

In 1997 President Bill Clinton wrote a letter to those celebrating the ship's creation in Britain and reminded them that it was still "as important as ever to celebrate the continuing friendship between our two countries":

The White House
Washington
June 13, 1997

Warm greetings to everyone gathered in Plymouth, England, to mark the 40th anniversary of the sailing of Mayflower II to America.

In June of 1957, Mayflower II arrived in Provincetown, Massachusetts, after a transatlantic voyage that captured the attention of American and British citizens alike. The brainchild of Warwick Charlton, Project Mayflower highlighted not only the courageous voyage made by the Pilgrims in 1620, but also the strong ties still enjoyed between the United States and Great Britain.

Four decades after Mayflower II docked at Provincetown, it is as important as ever to celebrate the continuing friendship between our two countries. I am delighted to join you in observing the 40th anniversary of the Mayflower II project and in applauding the important role it has played in teaching millions of Americans about our rich past. Hillary joins me in saluting the members of the original crew of Mayflower II, and we extend best wishes to all for a truly memorable anniversary celebration.

BILL CLINTON

No mention was made of Harry Hornblower, who had died twelve years earlier and was remembered by the *New York Times* as "a Boston stockbroker, history buff and the founder of the Plimoth Plantation living history museum," which is basically how the *Boston Globe* reported his passing.[13] Peter Gomes, minister of Harvard's Memorial Church, added more when he spoke at Harry's memorial service:

Few are the men who live to see their dreams and visions come to fruition. Harry Hornblower was one of those fortunate few. . . . The wonder of Harry Hornblower to me is that he would appear to be an unlikely dreamer. He was born to cold-roast Boston and destined from the womb to the necessary, but unromantic, work of making money for himself and others. . . . [This] would have been the fate of Harry Hornblower (to the great loss of all of us) had he not been inspired by an idea and pursued a dream.

The Plantation was a dream for Harry, a project, a scheme, for whom he could never do enough or too much. From a hobby, a sideline, it moved increasingly toward the center of his life. . . . There was to Harry Hornblower, despite his impeccable Boston breeding, Harvard training, and Federal Street obligations, something of the visionary and rebel.[14]

Gomes later offered a more nuanced description of his parishioner: Harry "took no advanced degree, wrote no books, and was not paid to do what he did. He was an amateur in the 18th-century sense of that term, a learned gentleman for whom leisure was an opportunity to pursue what others pursued for a living." While it was tempting "to suggest that at the heart of Henry Hornblower's achievement at Plimoth Plantation was his money," the clergyman said that the real philanthropy consisted in "Harry's lavish investment of himself in all its wonderful and generous complexity."[15] Sinclair Hitchings, a close friend and keeper of prints at the Boston Public Library, said the man he knew "was an incurable enthusiast, with an unquenchable enthusiasm for books, maps, travel, archeology and history in general."[16] It was Hornblower's passion for discovering America's earliest artifacts that prompted the museum's annual budget to grow from a meager $2,000 to almost $3 million as others caught the colonial history bug. Those who knew Harry well understood that while he was married to the family business, his true love was archaeology and discovery.

"I got to know him well in the 1970s and 1980s," said James W. "Jim" Baker, Plimoth's senior historian and director of research for twenty-six years. "I found him to be a sincere, generous, idealistic and ingenuous individual." Harry was "full of enthusiastic if often impractical projects (every bit the 'dreamer' like Charlton but without the other man's cunning), cherished but patronized by the Plantation staff who thought of him as an admirable anachronistic figure from the past." Although Harry had his name on the masthead of Hornblower & Weeks, he was not the active driver of that enterprise. His father, Ralph, held those reins. Baker went on to say that from his perspective the museum founder "had been obliged by his father to join the family investment banking firm rather than follow his true ambition of an academic career in archaeology. He was never truly happy with this, but having a dogged rather than combative nature," he complied as a dutiful son. Looking back on those years, which often included archiving Harry's "latest cache of correspondence and publications," the historian reflected: "I enjoyed listening to him and never underestimated him."

When Warwick Charlton passed away in 2002, he was remembered as a "dreamer" and "the man who got the idea that the world needed an exact replica of the *Mayflower* and made it happen." His life had been consumed with "a grand vision . . . to thank the United States for its help in World War II by presenting a life-size facsimile of the *Mayflower* to Americans." The *Times* reporter told readers that Charlton "had no money of his own, but raised what would today be the equivalent of several million dollars. He fought on despite angry creditors, striking shipyard workers, jealous keepers of the Pilgrims' torch in Massachusetts and ingrates who suggested his motives were less than pure—meaning commercial. He loved the whole glorious mess." In short, Warwick's time on earth was a "triumph."[17]

Some at Plimoth Plantation, however, might have disagreed with this assessment, particularly in the 1980s following Hornblower's death. According to Jim Baker, "When Warwick Charlton stopped by in 1986, no one else wanted to meet him due to the influence of both the [museum's] archival records and the testimony of his shipmates." The animus was so great that the executive assigned to meet with the Englishman "didn't [even] offer him coffee." Years later that staffer said, "I now regret I hadn't been more forthcoming, as in the final analysis, for all of his shenanigans and fiscal trickery, he did deliver as he said he would." Baker then added, "No one without Warwick Charlton's temperament and character could have succeeded in delivering *Mayflower II*." Her Majesty's ex-soldier deserved—and had indeed earned—more respect than a cold shoulder and an empty cup.

As for *Mayflower II*'s life and health, she was diagnosed with a life-threatening condition—what mariners call wood rot—when she turned fifty-six. The news was shocking because the signs of decay had been hidden behind good cosmetics: paint and a wide copper band nailed just above her waistline to protect the oak hull from ice damage in the winter.[18] During the warm months when docked, her harbor-facing side was changed regularly in a process similar to rotating the tires on a car to maintain even wear. Then every other winter, the craft would be hauled out of the water, put on stilts, and inspected by the US Coast Guard to certify she was safe to carry passengers.[19] The sad news was discovered at the Fairhaven Shipyard in Massachusetts during her routine biannual checkup in early 2013.

Technicians found some odd exterior skin discoloration and soon diagnosed it as wood rot. To confirm that finding, her metal girdle was peeled off, revealing putrefied exterior planks and interior framing ribs.[20] More inspections followed, and it was determined that the decay had metastasized. Without expert care, she could be dead in a few years. Plimoth's management team was then thoroughly advised of the problem, and because "ninety percent of the plantation's annual budget of $8.5 million is derived from gate receipts and gift shop sales,"[21] a metric from 1997 that was still valid, the museum knew what it had to do: a full renovation. The broader importance of that decision was then underscored by the Plantation's deputy director, who told a local newspaper that "when the ship was away" for repairs in Fairhaven, Massachusetts, "waterfront businesses reported they were down 36 percent."[22]

While Harry had been able to acquire the revenue engine for virtually nothing, keeping her alive would be expensive. It was estimated that millions of dollars were needed to repair and maintain Plimoth's star attraction—a figure far exceeding financial reserves. Consequently, a plan to save *Mayflower II* was developed, with three key elements. First, ask the state for money, based on the revenue the ship generated for the Commonwealth and the credibility it would give the project. It was the tactic Harry had used more than fifty years earlier when he needed a mooring site and Massachusetts responded with cash plus harbor dredging. This new request was also granted, and in July 2014 Governor Deval Patrick signed a 2015 fiscal budget that included $2 million in funding for *Mayflower II*.[23] Next, the museum started the application process to have the replica named a National Historic Place. It was a five-year task that began when the Massachusetts Historical Commission acknowledged receipt of the museum's proposal on July 8, 2015. If all went according to schedule, the US Department of the Interior's National Park Service would announce this special status in 2020, coinciding with the 400th anniversary of the Pilgrims' landing in Plymouth. Third, the Plantation joined forces with the Henry B. duPont Preservation Shipyard at the Mystic Seaport Museum to develop a collaborative program to save the treasured ship while adhering to the Secretary of the Interior's Standards for Vessel Preservation Projects.[24] This final part was confirmed in December 2014,[25] along with a reminder that major funding was coming from taxpayers via state government.

The shipyard at Mystic was the nation's leader in historic ship restoration and had a skill set equivalent to Stuart Upham's yard. No one knew wooden ships better. Before the Pilgrim craft, it had gained renown for saving the *Charles W. Morgan*, an American whaler built in 1841 that is now the oldest US vessel still afloat, apart from the USS *Constitution*.[26] Although the Plantation's carrack was relatively new, her materials and design were seventeenth century. The first *Mayflower* returned to England in the spring of 1621 and three years later was declared "in ruins," scrap valued at 128 pounds, 8 shillings, 4 pence.[27] That fate was not going to befall *Mayflower II*. After nearly sixty years, many people considered the replica a national treasure similar to the Statue of Liberty because they both honored the nation's immigrant past. She was discussed in schools across the country every year, which Plimoth Plantation considered very important, for it suggested that any investments made to bring the gift back to first-launch condition could be recovered if the replica was freshly and vigorously promoted to the public. Because the colonial park operated as a nonprofit entity without a large endowment, a special $20 million capital campaign was organized,[28] both to finance the current work, which cost $11.2 million,[29] and to fund future upkeep.

Restoration requires expertise and a special temperament, as anyone who has remodeled a house or brought an old car back to life knows well. In the case of *Mayflower II*, there were three primary areas of focus: hull, sails, and rigging. Starting with the wood, nearly 70 percent of it had to be replaced, excluding the keel, which remained as laid in 1955.[30] Workers would effectively have to replicate the replica. The Seaport's first challenge mirrored that of the British sixty years earlier: finding tons of the right wood. While Upham had an ancient forest within reasonable proximity, the replacement timber came from a variety of locations including Belle Chase, Louisiana, where twelve live oak trees were harvested and transported nearly fifteen hundred miles to the shipyard in Connecticut.[31] Other sources included Pass Christian (Mississippi), Charleston (South Carolina), Berea College (Kentucky), New Orleans, various locations in Rhode Island, and the shipyard's own holdings. From Scandinavia, the Royal Danish Forestry Service harvested centuries-old trees that were transformed into "20,000 board feet of white oak" timbers that were "38 to 40 feet long, 3 inches thick, and 24 to 30 inches wide, without knots or defects."[32]

As Mystic began to remove the hanging and lodging knees that held the main deck and core elements of the ship, it discovered that the iron bolts securing beams had rusted internally. This created an expanding coat of ferrous oxide that pushed outward and caused previously unseen damage. Marine scientists studied the chemical reaction and recommended replacing the original metal type with bronze alloy bolts, which are more fatigue resistant than brass and more corrosion resistant than stainless steel. They are also beautiful to the eye. Not stopping below-decks, Stuart Upham's inventive cider barrel treenails used for decking and siding were replaced with long bronze trunnels. Old-time tricks were no longer sufficient in the new millennium, and the new thin spikes were just as inventive in the twenty-first century as Upham's spears in the last.

Once the hull was remade, workers turned to the spars. The original Oregon pine mainmast and foremast were replaced with laminated Douglas fir,[33] which was shaped with a lathe and then hand finished.[34] A far cry from Stuart Upham's choice, but predicted to be stronger and longer lasting than a single massive tree.[35] Other masts and yards were taken down, refurbished, and then put back in use.

Francis Webster's canvas sails from Scotland were also updated with a fabric unknown until the mid-1990s. About that time, the USS *Constitution* was being freshened up for its 200th birthday, and Commander Michael Beck wanted to take the frigate to sea. This would require new sails, however, so a meeting was arranged with a premier manufacturer, North Sail. Engineer Brian Doyle and sail designer Nat Wilson of East Boothbay, Maine, met with Beck. After hearing the requirements and doing some calculations, they determined that the weight of the replacements would be nearly too heavy for the crew to lift in challenging conditions. Something new was needed. They came up with an innovative lightweight material that combined the longevity of modern polyester with the feel of cotton cloth. Their fabric had twice the strength and half the weight of canvas. The duo quickly filed for a patent but didn't know what to call their invention. How about Force 10, the Beaufort Scale description of a storm with high winds and destructive waves, to signify its strength? Maybe. Wilson then happened to look at the underside of a mug for Pusser's Rum, a Royal Navy favorite for generations, and saw the words "Oceanus Atlanticus, Oceanus Pacificus" on its bottom. That's it! thought the designer. We'll call our fabric Oceanus! Before they knew it, sheets with that name adorned not only Old Ironsides but also the *Eagle*, the *Pride of Baltimore II*, and *Mayflower II*.[36]

Cordage had also changed greatly since the Gourock Ropeworks Company made the original rigging sixty years earlier. High-grade hemp was now almost impossible to source and had been replaced with new superlight materials such as Dyneema, which had a strength fifteen times greater than steel by weight.[37] Mystic's chief rigger then supervised its installation with a wealth of knowledge gained during decades of work on ships such as the *Golden Hind*, the *Kalmar Nyckel*, and the *Amistad*. On top of that, he studied the writings and works of both R. C. Anderson and William Baker to gain a full understanding of how they envisioned rigging on the original *Mayflower* and her progeny.

These sail and rope innovations reduced the replica's weight above deck by a third that of 1957. Lighter above was complemented with improved ballasting below. The 130 long tons of rusty iron railroad ties and other material from England were replaced with almost the same weight of lead, settled compactly deep in the hull, held in place by slatted bulkheads and well ventilated.[38]

Painting came last. The colors selected had names such as Damask Gold, Pomegranate, Antiquity, and Buffett Green, and they honored William Baker's guidelines, with one exception. The 1957 signature image of a flower spreading its wings across the stern was gone. It had been exchanged in the late 1980s for an inverted triangle pinned to the back of the ship—maritime jewelry that could be removed during maintenance and then reattached, a brooch for the fair lady. Although efficient, it lacked the flight of spirit expressed in the butterfly-like flower, which might have disappointed William Baker, who in 1957 cited Dr. R. C. Anderson's belief that "triangular decoration is probably a bit old-fashioned for 1620."[39] It might have been appropriate for 1607 and the Jamestown era, but not for the Pilgrims' ship, in the architect's opinion.[40] Also missing was the 1638 ship's bell cast by Miles Graye. It now sat in Plimoth's archive, having been replaced with a new one made in 2019 by Verdin Bells of Cincinnati, Ohio.[41]

The Mystic Seaport craftsmen considered themselves maritime sculptors tasked with restoring the ship's beauty, strength, and vitality—just as artists at a museum might be called upon to bring an ancient statue back to life. All work before the relaunch was conducted in a huge outdoor tent called "the mailbox" because it looked like the postal receptacle commonly seen on rural routes. For old navy veterans, it was reminiscent of a blimp hangar that provided protection from rain, wind, snow, and all the unusual weather that brews along the New England coast. Workers were allowed to use modern tools, but only in the manner that an expert might use such instruments when restoring a seventeenth-century painting: sparingly and carefully. They did a spectacular job and attracted more than 250,000 visitors to the yard,[42] which reminded historians of the huge crowds drawn to Devon sixty years earlier. Once work on *Mayflower II* was completed in 2019, global applause lifted the Connecticut shipwrights beyond the top maritime restorationists in America to the finest in the world. They had done William Baker, Stuart Upham, and the workers of Brixham proud.

CHAPTER 21

New Beginning

PROJECT MAYFLOWER'S REVITALIZED GIFT TO AMERICA WAS LOWERED
slowly and gently into the Mystic River,[1] as a mother might do when
introducing her newborn to its first bath. An onshore crowd and small
boats in the harbor looked on, just as in 1957. No splashing into the
water with roaring thunder this time around.

Several thousand visitors witnessed the ceremony and were inspired
by the keynote speaker, Nathaniel Philbrick, the bestselling author of

Figure 62. *Mayflower II* relaunched at Mystic Seaport on September 7, 2019.
(Courtesy Plimoth Patuxet Museums and Mystic Seaport Museum)

Mayflower: *A Story of Community, Courage and War.*[2] Philbrick told the audience: "*Mayflower II* is much more than a replica of a famous ship. She is a famous ship in her own right. She is also a symbol, a source of inspiration for those in search of new beginnings and the possibility of multicultural cooperation in this nation of immigrants. She also speaks to the dark truths underlying the settlement of New England and America."[3]

Philbrick's words were music to the ears of Plimoth Plantation directors because they placed the museum's star attraction on a noble pedestal. His comments also described an unresolved paradox framed by "multicultural cooperation" and "dark truths," such as those enumerated on Plymouth's second rock, approved in 1998 by the Town of Plymouth to honor the National Day of Mourning. The monument stands adjacent to the Massasoit statue on Cole's Hill, within view of the 1620 rock and a short distance from the replica. The bronze plaque says what the relaunch orator did not, that Native Americans had endured "the genocide of millions of their people, the theft of their lands, and the relentless assault on their culture."[4] Plimoth Plantation's guest speaker said nothing more about "dark truths" than the two words themselves and left that discourse for another day.

If members of the crowd were asked what made the replica legendary beyond imagery, they likely would have cited William Baker's unprecedented achievements in maritime scholarship and ship design. Some might have recalled Stuart Upham, whose involvement put life into tons of Devon oak that became the vessel they were celebrating today. Indeed, without his shipyard's craftsmen, Baker's plan might have ended up in a museum archive and the floating history lesson could have been replaced with a waterline model of the Pilgrims' transport sitting in concrete. Ironically, attendees might have described the medium and not its message. What beautiful woodwork! Such magnificent sails! How amazing its value! These expressions were more likely than any related to diplomatic heroics, the "special relationship," project management innovations, underdogs overcoming adversity, or the Mayflower Compact's aspirational goal of "just and equal laws for the general good." For today—a magnificent September afternoon—it was all about what new role this second *Mayflower* might assume in the twenty-first century.

There was plenty more to be done. The following spring Plimoth Plantation announced it would henceforth be known as Plimoth Patuxet in honor of the Wampanoag and their homeland before the arrival of the English immigrants. It openly embraced the idea that while the past cannot be changed, it can help light the road ahead. Reinforcing that belief, the United States of America honored the replica in September 2020 by adding her to its National Register of Historic Places, saying the craft had "made a significant contribution" to the nation's history. While the organizers of Project Mayflower considered her a symbol of democracy, others often found broader meaning and inspiration related to making a new start in life, honoring freedom of speech and religion, and enjoying the fruits of collaboration and unity. The ship also reminded many of the tragic impact of English colonial expansion on the Wampanoag, other tribes, and millions of Native American lives. Given the huge

Figure 63. *Mayflower II* in Plymouth Harbor, September 2020. *(Karen Wong Photography, Duxbury, Massachusetts)*

number of people journeying to Plymouth Harbor annually since the seventeenth-century replica's arrival, she seems to be part of the nation's continually evolving destiny. Harry Hornblower would have felt great pride for his museum's achievement, as he told members of Harvard's Class of 1941 in his twenty-fifth reunion Class Report: "My business continues to consist of investments, cranberries, and land—all in the New England area, while my hobby gone wild continues to be Plimoth Plantation."[5] As for a courageous British war veteran, an American architect, a Devon shipyard owner, an Australian skipper, and a cat named Felix, there could be no higher praise. *Mayflower II*'s future was now protected, and she would continue to educate and inspire for generations to come.

Epilogue

The Town of Plymouth and Plimoth Plantation (Plimoth Patuxet Museums) honored Project Mayflower's gift to America in 2008 with a commemorative plaque "in recognition and grateful appreciation of the thirty-three bold men who sailed *Mayflower II* from Plymouth, England, to Plymouth, Massachusetts, April 20–June 13, 1957." The name of every crew member is clearly written, including Felix the mascot. It is publicly displayed adjacent to the seventeenth-century replica.

Top billing went to "Warwick Charlton, Founder, Project Mayflower Ltd."

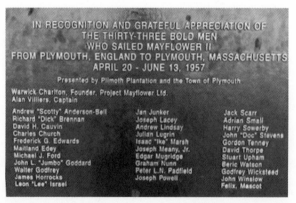

Figure 64. Plaque at Plymouth Pier honoring the "thirty-three bold men" who sailed *Mayflower II. (Courtesy Plimoth Patuxet Museums and the Town of Plymouth)*

Acknowledgments

Randal Charlton, the son of Warwick Charlton, introduced me to his father's achievement and was a mentor during the writing of *Project Mayflower*. We met by chance shortly after the relaunch of *Mayflower II* at the Mystic Seaport Museum in Connecticut. That's when I first learned about his father, the leader of Project Mayflower. Warwick's vision and determination made the construction and voyage of *Mayflower II* possible. Randal oversees the Warwick Charlton Archive, and is the author of *The Wicked Pilgrim: The True Story of the Englishman Who Gave* Mayflower II *to America*, Warwick Charlton's biography. Randal's sister Victoria Charlton was an additional resource and gave me a better understanding of her father, Warwick.

Harry's daughter Harriet "Hatzy" Hornblower witnessed many of the events as they unfolded in Plymouth with an American perspective. Indeed, her grandparents' house and property became the home of Plimoth Plantation. Harry's OSS service was a source of family pride, and Hatzy helped me understand the tension Harry felt between his love of archaeology, scholarship, and cranberry bogs, and the pressure he experienced to join the family brokerage business. Her contributions to the narrative were special and important.

Allan Israel was a remarkable resource because his father, Lee Israel, was Project Mayflower's official photographer, and Allan made Lee's large photo archive available to me. Many of these unique images are seen in the text and add a special dimension to the narrative. Indeed, they alone tell a story.

James W. "Jim" Baker, Plimoth Patuxet Museums' emeritus senior historian and director of research for twenty-six years, provided invaluable insight on the early years of Plimoth Plantation, Harry Hornblower, and Warwick Charlton. The author of two books on the museum's history, Jim is also an authority on the history of Thanksgiving and penned *Thanksgiving: The Biography of an American Holiday.*

Tom Begley, Plimoth's director of collections and special projects, was particularly helpful when scouring the museum's archives for such materials as the Letter in a Bottle and the 1638 ship's bell. Whit Perry, Plimoth Patuxet's director of maritime preservation and operations, who oversaw *Mayflower II*'s spectacular renovation in collaboration with the Mystic Seaport Museum and is her current captain, was a resource, and Rob Kluin, director of marketing and communications, provided encouragement as well as insights into Plimoth Patuxet's educational mission.

Peter Arenstam, executive director of the Howland Society and *Mayflower II*'s captain for more than twenty years, provided personal recollections of the replica. His children's books include one about the ship's mascot, *Felix and His* Mayflower II *Adventures*, and another about the original *Mayflower.*

Linda Coombs spent thirty years at Plimoth's Wampanoag Indigenous Program, including fifteen as its associate director. She was invaluable to my understanding of the 1970 Thanksgiving Day protest that featured Frank "Wamsutta" James's famous "Suppressed Speech," saw the "invasion" of *Mayflower II*, and inaugurated the National Day of Mourning. Coombs is the author of *Colonization and the Wampanoag Story.*

At the Pilgrim Hall Museum, Executive Director Donna Curtin shed light on the connection between the museum's 1926 *Mayflower* model, built by Warwick Charlton's mentor Dr. Roger Charles Anderson of London's Greenwich Museum, and the creation of *Mayflower II.*

Desiree Mobed, director of the Alden House Historic Site, provided encouragement during the book's creation and information on Priscilla Alden Kiefer, who was the mistress of ceremonies for the 1957 New York City ticker-tape parade honoring *Mayflower II* and a descendant of 1620 passengers Priscilla Mullens and her husband, John Alden.

At Lyons Press, among the many excellent and supportive individuals, one stands out: Brittany Stoner, my editor at this unit of Globe Pequot. She is terrific.

Acknowledgments

Ann Marlowe was my mentor, early editor, and fact-checker extraor-
dinaire. She has become a dear friend, and without her this book would
not exist.

Of course, none of this would have been possible without the
patience and loving support of my wife, Joan.

NOTES

CHAPTER 1

1. "Press: Monty's Fighting Editor," *Time*, May 1, 1944, 86–87.
2. Joseph J. Thorndike Jr., "The 'Monty' Legend," *Life*, May 15, 1944, 53–60.
3. Patrick Skene Catling, "Warwick Charlton: The Man Who Brought the Monty Out of Montgomery," *Guardian*, January 3, 2003, www.theguardian.com/media/2003/jan/03/all and link to "Warwick Charlton."
4. Winston Churchill, "Sinews of Peace (Iron Curtain) Speech," National Churchill Museum, www.nationalchurchillmuseum.org/sinews-of-peace-iron-curtain-speech.html.
5. Warwick Charlton, *The Voyage of* Mayflower II (London: Cassell, 1957), 4.
6. William Bradford, *Of Plymouth Plantation, 1620–1647: The Complete Text*, ed. Samuel Eliot Morison (New York: Knopf, 1952), 47 ("of burthen about 9 score"), 59 ("caught hold of the topsail halyards").
7. "Beyond the Pilgrim Story: Text of the Mayflower Compact," Pilgrim Hall Museum, www.pilgrimhall.org/mayflower_compact_text.htm.
8. James I, "James I's Speech before Parliament, March 21, 1609," in *The Penguin Book of Historic Speeches*, ed. Brian MacArthur (New York: Penguin, 1997); online at www.luminarium.org/sevenlit/james/1609speech.htm.
9. Samuel Eliot Morison, "The 66-Day Saga of *Mayflower* I," *New York Times*, April 14, 1957.

CHAPTER 2

1. "Climbing Mount Everest Is Work for Supermen," *New York Times*, March 18, 1923.
2. Lawrence C. Wroth, ed., *The Voyages of Giovanni da Verrazzano, 1524–1528* (New Haven, CT: Yale University Press, 1970), 139.
3. David J. Silverman, *This Land Is Their Land: The Wampanoag Indians, Plymouth Colony, and the Troubled History of Thanksgiving* (New York: Bloomsbury, 2019), 61–63.
4. Silverman, *This Land Is Their Land*, 66.
5. John S. Marr and John T. Cathey, "New Hypothesis for Cause of Epidemic among Native Americans, New England, 1616–1619," *Emerging Infectious Diseases*, February 2010, https://wwwnc.cdc.gov/eid/article/16/2/09-0276_article.

6. Samuel Purchas, *Hakluytus Posthumus, or, Purchas His Pilgrimes* (Glasgow: James MacLehose and Sons, 1906), 19:129.

7. "Harvard Presidential Insignia: Charter of 1650," Harvard Library Research Guides, https://guides.library.harvard.edu/c.php?g=880222&p=6323072.

8. "Digging Veritas—Students in the 17th Century—About the Indian College Students," Peabody Museum of Archaeology and Ethnology, Harvard University, 2021, https://peabody.harvard.edu/galleries/digging-veritas-students-17th-century-about -indian-college-students.

9. Eric B. Schultz and Michael J. Tougias, *King Philip's War: The History and Legacy of America's Forgotten Conflict* (New York: Countryman Press, 1999), 4–5.

10. Edward Winslow, "A Letter Sent from New-England to a Friend in These Parts," in *Mourt's Relation, or Journal of the Plantation at Plymouth*, ed. Henry Martyn Dexter (Boston: John Kimball Wiggin, 1865), 133 [61].

11. Abraham Lincoln, "Gettysburg Address," in National Park Service, www.nps.gov/ linc/learn/historyculture/gettysburgaddress.htm.

12. Abraham Lincoln, "Lincoln's Second Inaugural Address," in National Park Service, www.nps.gov/linc/learn/historyculture/lincoln-second-inaugural.htm.

13. On these organizations, see "The Pilgrims of Great Britain," Pilgrims Society, https: //pilgrimsociety.org; "Our Mission," English Speaking Union, www.esu.org/our-mission.

14. "The History of the Pilgrims of Great Britain," Pilgrims Society, https:// pilgrimsociety.org/history.php.

15. Betsy Mason, "Bomb-Damage Maps Reveal London's World War II Devastation," *National Geographic*, May 18, 2016, www.nationalgeographic.com/science/article/bomb -damage-maps-reveal-londons-world-war-ii-devastation.

16. The Bank of England set sterling-to-US-dollar parity at £1 = $2.80 in 1949. It held at that rate until 1967.

17. W. Charlton, *Voyage of* Mayflower II, 9.

18. W. Charlton, *Voyage of* Mayflower II, 11.

CHAPTER 3

1. Not to be confused with Horatio Hornblower, the fictional character who was a Royal Navy officer of the Napoleonic Wars and the protagonist of a series of novels by C. S. Forester.

2. Melissa Berry, "Mayflower Descendants: Who's Who, Part 16," Genealogy Bank, April 29, 2022, https://blog.genealogybank.com/mayflower-descendants-whos-who-part -16.html.

3. James W. Baker, *Plimoth Plantation: Fifty Years of Living History* (Plymouth, MA: Plimoth Plantation, 1997), 7.

4. "Today in Society," *Boston Globe*, June 2, 1948.

5. Irene Sege, "Old Notebooks Give New Insight into Indian Relics," *Boston Globe*, November 24, 1986; Peter J. Gomes, "Memoirs: Henry Hornblower II," *Proceedings of the Massachusetts Historical Society*, 3rd series, vol. 97 (1985): 157.

6. Harriet "Hatzy" Hornblower, written communication to the author, November 25, 2023.

7. Sege, "Old Notebooks."

8. J. Baker, *Plimoth Plantation*, 7–8.

9. J. Baker, *Plimoth Plantation*, 9; "Henry Hornblower, II," Harvard College Class of 1941 Decennial Report (Cambridge, 1951), 164, Harvard Archives.

10. "The Dames and Plymouth Rock," National Society of the Colonial Dames of America, https://nscda.org/the-dames-and-plymouth-rock.

11. "America's Museum of Pilgrim Possessions," Pilgrim Hall Museum, Plymouth, Massachusetts, www.pilgrimhall.org.

12. R. C. Anderson, "A 'Mayflower' Model," *Mariner's Mirror* 12, no. 3 (1926): 260–63, doi.org/10.1080/00253359.1926.10655374.

13. W. Charlton, *Voyage of* Mayflower II, 127.

14. William A. Baker, "The *Mayflower* Problem," *American Neptune* 14, no. 1 (1954), and "Early Seventeenth-Century Ship Design," *American Neptune* 14, no. 4 (1954), usefully summarized in W. Charlton, *Voyage of* Mayflower II, 49–71.

15. "Henry Hornblower, II," Harvard College Class of 1941, Sexennial Report (Cambridge, 1947), 145, Harvard Archives.

16. William A. Baker, *The New* Mayflower, *Her Design and Construction* (Barre, MA: Barre Gazette, 1958), vi.

17. "The Gjøa Expedition (1903–1906)," Fram—The Polar Exploration Museum, https://frammuseum.no/polar-history/expeditions/the-gjoa-expedition-1903-1906/.

18. W. Baker, *The New* Mayflower, vi.

19. Joan Feder, "Step Back: Disneyland's Chicken of the Sea Pirate Ship," *All Ears*, July 28, 2020, https://allears.net/step-back-disneylands-chicken-of-the-sea-pirate-ship.

20. R. G. Marsden, "The 'Mayflower,'" *English Historical Review* 19, no. 76 (October 1904): 671, www.jstor.org/stable/548611.

21. W. Baker, *The New* Mayflower, 76.

22. W. Baker, *The New* Mayflower, 63.

23. W. Baker, *The New* Mayflower, 27.

24. James W. Baker to author, email, December 12, 2022.

25. Randal Charlton, *The Wicked Pilgrim: The True Story of the Englishman Who Gave* Mayflower II *to America* (Delanson, NY: Three Sisters, 2019), 86.

26. James W. Baker, introduction to Mayflower II*: Plimoth Plantation* (Little Compton, RI: Fort Church, 1993), 7.

27. W. Baker, *The New* Mayflower, xiv.

28. "New *Mayflower* to Sail with Goodwill for U.S.," *New York Times*, March 20, 1955.

29. "*Mayflower* to Sail the Atlantic Again," *Dundee Courier and Advertisers*, March 21, 1955.

30. W. Baker, *The New* Mayflower, xiv.

31. R. Charlton, *The Wicked Pilgrim*, 28.

32. "Appraising a Model of the Mayflower at Plymouth, Massachusetts," *Illustrated London News*, April 16, 1955, 682.

33. W. Charlton, *Voyage of* Mayflower II, 27.

34. Stuart Upham, *The Illustrated Story of How* Mayflower II *Was Built* (Plymouth, MA: Plimoth Plantation, 1963), 6.

35. Alan Villiers, "We're Coming Over on the *Mayflower*," *National Geographic*, May 1957, 708.

36. W. Charlton, *Voyage of Mayflower II*, 28.

37. "The Hound of the Baskervilles (1939): Plot," IMdB, www.imdb.com/title/tt0031448/plotsummary.

38. Upham, *Illustrated Story*, 23.

39. Emily C. Dooley, "'Old Salts' Swap Yarns from 1957 Atlantic Voyage," *Cape Cod Times*, July 30, 2000, http://www.capecodtimes.com/story/news/2000/07/30/old-salts-swap-yarns/51018253007.

40. W. Baker, *The New* Mayflower, 125.

41. Gene Smith, "Even *Mayflower*'s Insurance Is Authentic," *New York Times*, May 19, 1957.

42. Smith, "Even *Mayflower*'s Insurance Is Authentic."

CHAPTER 4

1. W. Baker, *The New* Mayflower, 122.

2. Upham, *Illustrated Story*, 21.

3. W. Baker, *The New* Mayflower, 121.

4. R. Charlton, *The Wicked Pilgrim*, 113.

5. Bradford, *Of Plymouth Plantation*, 58.

6. D. Kenelm Winslow, Mayflower *Heritage* (New York: Funk & Wagnalls, 1957), 35.

7. W. Baker, *The New* Mayflower, 121.

8. "Britain Starts Building a New 'Mayflower,'" Warner Pathé News, July 27, 1955, www.youtube.com/watch?v=PMDQo5mKaCg.

9. "The Laying of the Keel of *Mayflower II*," *Illustrated London News*, August 6, 1955.

10. Peter D. Whitney, "New Mayflower Is Begun in England," *New York Times*, July 29, 1955.

11. Recommendation for Membership, *National Geographic Magazine*, November 1957, https://archive.nationalgeographic.com/national-geographic/1957-nov/flipbook/Ad3.

12. Quoted in Villiers, "We're Coming Over," 714.

13. Villiers, "We're Coming Over," 720.

14. Recommendation for Membership, *National Geographic*, November 1957.

15. "Villiers to Be Captain of the New *Mayflower*," *New York Times*, November 25, 1955.

16. "About Fulbright," US Department of State, Bureau of Educational and Cultural Affairs, https://eca.state.gov/files/bureau/fulbright/index.html.

17. "Marshall Scholarships," Marshall Aid Commemoration Commission, www.marshallscholarship.org.

18. Ted R. Bromund, "'This Somewhat Embarrassing Ship': The British Foreign Office and the *Mayflower II*, 1954–1957," *New England Quarterly* 72, no. 1 (March 1999): 47.

19. "Our History," English Speaking Union, www.esu.org/our-history, quoting Sir Evelyn Wrench, 1918.

20. Bromund, "This Somewhat Embarrassing Ship," 51.

Chapter 5

1. Bromund, "This Somewhat Embarrassing Ship," 52.
2. R. Charlton, *The Wicked Pilgrim*, 133.
3. R. Charlton, *The Wicked Pilgrim*, 122.
4. R. Charlton, *The Wicked Pilgrim*, 124.
5. Bromund, "This Somewhat Embarrassing Ship," 52.
6. W. Baker, *The New* Mayflower, 85–87.
7. W. Baker, *The New* Mayflower, 74–83.
8. W. Baker, *The New* Mayflower, vii.
9. Upham, *Illustrated Story*, 27.
10. W. Charlton, *Voyage of* Mayflower II, 41.
11. W. Charlton, *Voyage of* Mayflower II, 41.
12. W. Charlton, *Voyage of* Mayflower II, 41.
13. Bromund, "This Somewhat Embarrassing Ship," 50.
14. Bromund, "This Somewhat Embarrassing Ship," 47.
15. Bromund, "This Somewhat Embarrassing Ship," 48.
16. Bromund, "This Somewhat Embarrassing Ship," 51.
17. Bromund, "This Somewhat Embarrassing Ship," 44–45.
18. Bromund, "This Somewhat Embarrassing Ship," 51.
19. Bromund, "This Somewhat Embarrassing Ship," 52n34.
20. Bromund, "This Somewhat Embarrassing Ship," 53–54.

Chapter 6

1. Bromund, "This Somewhat Embarrassing Ship," 55.
2. Kennett Love, "New Mayflower Taking Shape in English Port," *New York Times*, April 14, 1956.
3. W. Charlton, *Voyage of* Mayflower II, 43.
4. "The Progress of the Second *Mayflower*: Building the Ship and Setting the Stage," *Illustrated London News*, June 23, 1956.
5. Upham, *Illustrated Story*, 26.
6. Laurence Brown, "Obituary: Paul Vincze." *Independent*, March 31, 1994, www .independent.co.uk/news/people/obituary-paul-vincze-1367203.html.
7. "'Get Steaks Ready for All,' Roars Villiers over Radio," *Boston Globe*, June 11, 1957.
8. Kate Lance, *Alan Villiers: Voyager of the Winds*, second edition (Korumburra, Australia: Seabooks, 2020), 239.
9. Bromund, "This Somewhat Embarrassing Ship," 55–56.
10. Bromund, "This Somewhat Embarrassing Ship," 54.
11. "The Progress of the Second *Mayflower*," *Illustrated London News*.
12. R. Charlton, *The Wicked Pilgrim*, 219.
13. "Plymouth Harbor Navigation Project," US Army Corps of Engineers, www.nae .usace.army.mil/Missions/Civil-Works/Navigation/Massachusetts/Plymouth-Harbor/.
14. "Henry Hornblower, II," Harvard College Class of 1941, Fifteenth Anniversary Report (Cambridge, 1956), 123–24, Harvard Archives.
15. R. Charlton, *The Wicked Pilgrim*, 170.

16. R. Charlton, *The Wicked Pilgrim*, 130.

Chapter 7

1. James W. Baker, email to author, July 14, 2023.

2. "Britain Launches New *Mayflower*," *New York Times*, September 23, 1956; "Mayflower the Second Is Launched (1956)," British Pathé, www.youtube.com/watch?v =tCCrY8QBRfw. The commentary begins: "Pouring rain can't spoil a great day at a Brixham shipyard when *Mayflower II* is to be launched. Guest of honor is Reis Leming, American hero of the Norfolk Floods of 1953, who has come from Washington to name her. The men who started it all—Warwick Charlton and John Lowe—watch the unusual christening ceremony." Charlton and Lowe are shown full screen.

3. Upham, *Illustrated Story*, 35.

4. W. Baker, *The New* Mayflower, 128.

5. R. Charlton, *The Wicked Pilgrim*, 168.

6. John Allen May, "G.I. Hero Launches New *Mayflower*," *Mayflower Mail*, December 1956, pictured at Project Mayflower, https://mayflowereventnews.com/mayflower-mail -launch/.

7. Upham, *Illustrated Story*, 43.

8. W. Baker, *The New* Mayflower, 130.

9. Bromund, "This Somewhat Embarrassing Ship," 56.

10. Bromund, "This Somewhat Embarrassing Ship," 57.

11. R. Charlton, *The Wicked Pilgrim*, 315.

Chapter 8

1. Emmet John Hughes, *The Ordeal of Power: A Political Memoir of the Eisenhower Years* (New York: Atheneum, 1963), 217.

2. Winthrop W. Aldrich, "The Suez Crisis," *Foreign Affairs* 45, no. 3 (April 1967): 547.

3. Charles Keightley, *Lessons from Suez*, extract from a report dated October 11, 1957, on Suez operations in the Eastern Mediterranean, November–December 1956, National Archives [of Britain], https://www.nationalarchives.gov.uk/education/resources/fifties -britain/lessons-suez/.

4. Dwight D. Eisenhower, "Developments in Eastern Europe and the Middle East," address to the nation, October 31, 1956, *Department of State Bulletin* 35, no. 907 (November 12, 1956): 744–45.

5. Richard Nixon, interview by Richard D. Challener, March 5, 1965, John Foster Dulles Oral History Project, Princeton University Library, 31–32, https://findingaids .princeton.edu/catalog/MC017_c0187.

6. James M. Boughton, "Was Suez in 1956 the First Financial Crisis of the Twenty-First Century?" *Finance & Development* 38, no. 3 (September 2001), www.imf .org/external/pubs/ft/fandd/2001/09/boughton.htm.

7. Ivone Kirkpatrick, *The Inner Circle: Memoirs* (London: Macmillan, 1959), 265.

8. Keightley, *Lessons from Suez*.

9. Bromund, "This Somewhat Embarrassing Ship," 57.

10. "U.S. Oil for Britain Plan," *Northern Daily Mail*, November 29, 1956.

11. Upham, *Illustrated Story*, 26–27.

12. W. Baker, *The New* Mayflower, 125.

CHAPTER 9

1. "Eisenhower Doctrine, 1957," US Department of State, Office of the Historian, https://history.state.gov/milestones/1953-1960/eisenhower-doctrine.

2. Translated from Christian Pineau, *1956, Suez* (Paris: Robert Laffont, 1976), 191: "La France et l'Angleterre ne seront plus jamais des puissances comparables aux Etats-Unis et à l'Union soviétique. L'Allemagne non plus d'ailleurs. Il leur reste donc un seul moyen de jouer dans le monde un rôle décisif, c'est de s'unir pour faire l'Europe. L'Angleterre n'est pas mÛre mais l'affaire de Suez contribuera à y préparer les esprits. Nous, nous n'avons pas de temps à perdre: l'Europe sera votre revanche."

3. Pineau, *1956, Suez*: "l'Europe . . . gagna sur tous les tableaux."

4. Bromund, "This Somewhat Embarrassing Ship," 58.

5. "*Mayflower II* Nears Completion," *Sphere*, February 16, 1957.

6. R. Charlton, *The Wicked Pilgrim*, 179.

7. Andrew Boxer, "Winthrop Aldrich, 1953–57," in *The Embassy in Grosvenor Square: American Ambassadors to the United Kingdom, 1938–2008*, ed. Alison R. Holmes and J. Simon Rofe (New York: Palgrave Macmillan, 2012), 124.

8. Will Lissner, "Winthrop Aldrich Dead; Banker and Diplomat, 88," *New York Times*, February 25, 1974.

CHAPTER 10

1. W. Charlton, *Voyage of* Mayflower II, 138.

2. R. Charlton, *Wicked Pilgrim*, 201.

3. W. Charlton, *Voyage of* Mayflower II, 137.

4. W. Charlton, *Voyage of* Mayflower II, 109.

5. W. Charlton, *Voyage of* Mayflower II, 138.

6. R. Charlton, *Wicked Pilgrim*, 203.

7. Warwick Charlton, "Equipment for the Ship," *Mayflower Mail*, sailing edition, April 1957, 19.

8. W. Charlton, "Equipment for the Ship," 19.

9. W. Charlton, "Equipment for the Ship," 19.

10. "Pioneers," *Mayflower Mail*, sailing edition, April 1957.

CHAPTER 11

1. R. Charlton, *The Wicked Pilgrim*, 192.

2. "No Strike Threat to Pilgrim Ship," *Herald Express* (Torbay, Devon), March 15, 1957.

3. "Dock Strike Warning," *New York Times*, January 18, 1957.

4. "Aldrich Sails for Home," *New York Times*, February 2, 1957.

5. Monica Furlong, "Man in a Muzzle," *Truth*, January 25, 1958, 86.

6. R. Charlton, *The Wicked Pilgrim*, 75.

7. Aldrich, "The Suez Crisis," 552.

8. Drew Middleton, "U.S. and Britain Agree on Aims If Not Means," *New York Times*, March 24, 1957.

9. Drew Middleton, "U.S.-British Talks at Bermuda End; Results Praised," *New York Times*, March 24, 1957.

10. "Memorandum of a Conversation, Mid-Ocean Club, Bermuda, March 22, 1957, 4:25 p.m." in *Foreign Relations of the United States, 1955–1957*, vol. 27, *Western Europe and Canada*, ed. John P. Glennon et al. (Washington, DC: Office of the Historian, US Department of State, 1992), document 277, www.history.state.gov/historicaldocuments/frus1955-57v27/d277.

11. R. Charlton, *The Wicked Pilgrim*, 18.

CHAPTER 12

1. Villiers, "We're Coming Over," 726, 710.

2. Upham, *Illustrated Story*, 37.

3. "1957 *Mayflower II* Ship Boat Color Photo Interlux Paint Vintage Print Ad," AValuer, https://avaluer.net/explore/27850024-1957_mayflower_ii_ship_boat_color_photo_interlux_paint_vintage_print_ad.

4. W. Baker, *The New* Mayflower, 135.

5. W. Baker, *The New* Mayflower, Plan A—Profile, Sections & Waterlines.

6. W. Baker, *The New* Mayflower, 108–9.

7. W. Baker, *The New* Mayflower, 106–7.

8. W. Baker, *The New* Mayflower, 107–8.

9. Alan Villiers, "How We Sailed the New *Mayflower* to America," *National Geographic*, November 1957, 658.

10. W. Baker, *The New* Mayflower, 138.

11. "A Steel Frame for *Mayflower II*," Mystic Seaport Museum, January 27, 2017, www.mysticseaport.org/category/mayflower-ii-restoration/.

12. Alan Villiers, *Give Me a Ship to Sail* (London: Hodder & Stoughton, 1958), 132.

13. W. Baker, *The New* Mayflower, 137.

14. Alistair Cooke, "The *Mayflower* Lands Again," *Guardian*, June 12, 1957, www.theguardian.com/theguardian/1957/jun/12/1.

15. R. Charlton, *The Wicked Pilgrim*, 214.

16. "*Mayflower* Sails for America (1957)," British Pathé News, April 20, 1957, www.youtube.com/watch?v=Heu2VCoaJuk.

17. Edgar J. Driscoll Jr., "Henry Hornblower 2d, 67, Broker, a Founder of Plimoth Plantation," *Boston Globe*, October 22, 1985.

18. Harriet "Hatzy" Hornblower, written communication to author, November 25, 2023.

19. R. Charlton, *The Wicked Pilgrim*, 216.

20. Upham, *Illustrated Story*, 59–60, 6.

21. Villiers, *Give Me a Ship*, 172.

22. Lance, *Alan Villiers*, 237.

Chapter 13

1. W. Charlton, *Voyage of* Mayflower II, 145.

2. Villiers, "How We Sailed," 630.

3. Maitland A. Edey and Gordon Tenney, "A *Mayflower* Sails into Today," *Life*, June 17, 1957, 21–22.

4. W. Charlton, *Voyage of* Mayflower II, 146.

5. Alan Villiers, "North About," *National Geographic*, February 1937, 220–50.

6. Lance, *Alan Villiers*, 240.

7. Peter Padfield, *The Sea Is a Magic Carpet* (London: Peter Davies, 1959), 37.

8. Villiers, *Give Me a Ship*, 163.

9. Peter Padfield, Mayflower II *Diary: Sketches from a Lost Age* (Decatur, GA: Casa Forte Press, 2019), 92.

10. Villiers, "We're Coming Over," 721.

11. Padfield, Mayflower II *Diary*, 30.

12. W. Charlton, *Voyage of* Mayflower II, 198.

13. Villiers, *Give Me a Ship*, 177.

14. Villiers, *Give Me a Ship*, 178–79.

15. Villiers, *Give Me a Ship*, 155–57.

16. Villiers, *Give Me a Ship*, 187.

17. "Chest of Gold and Silver Will Sail with *Mayflower II*," *Torbay Express and South Devon Echo*, March 21, 1957.

18. "Captain and the Treasure Chest," *Mayflower Mail*, sailing edition, April 1957, 15.

19. Villiers, "How We Sailed," 633–36.

20. W. Charlton, *Voyage of* Mayflower II, 119–20.

21. Padfield, *Magic Carpet*, 15.

22. R. Charlton, *The Wicked Pilgrim*, 196.

23. W. Charlton, *Voyage of* Mayflower II, 141.

24. W. Baker, *The New* Mayflower, 133.

25. Padfield, Mayflower II *Diary*, 36.

26. Edey and Tenney, "A *Mayflower* Sails into Today," 23.

27. W. Baker, *The New* Mayflower, 87.

28. Edey and Tenney, "A *Mayflower* Sails into Today," 38.

29. Villiers, "How We Sailed," 642.

30. Villiers, "We're Coming Over," 725.

31. "Ben Truman Ale Bottle—Object ID 903.006," Plimoth Patuxet Museums, Plymouth, Massachusetts, https://sites.google.com/plimoth.org/mayflower-ii-exhibition/beer-bottle.

32. Villiers, *Give Me a Ship*, 200.

33. W. Baker, *The New* Mayflower, 133–34.

34. Edey and Tenney, "A *Mayflower* Sails into Today," 19–37.

35. Lord David Cecil, "The Reigning Royalty of Europe," *Life*, June 17, 1957, 58–79.

36. B. J. Long, letter to the editors, *Life*, July 8, 1957, 6.

37. Virginia Wells and Susan B. Hall, "Were Dogs and Cats on the *Mayflower*?" Pet Place, August 10, 2015, https://www.petplace.com/article/dogs/pet-behavior-training/were-dogs-and-cats-on-the-mayflower/.

38. "Churchill Bends to Restrain 'Blackie,'" History Net, www.historynet.com/photos-of-winston-churchill-at-war/winston-churchill-as-prime-minister-1940-1945.

39. Padfield, Mayflower II *Diary*, 39.

40. Catling, "Warwick Charlton."

41. Villiers, "How We Sailed," 646.

42. R. Charlton, *The Wicked Pilgrim*, 250.

43. "*Mayflower* Plans Are Confirmed," *The Shields Evening News*, May 13, 1957.

44. W. Charlton, *Voyage of* Mayflower II, 22.

45. Padfield, *Magic Carpet*, 44.

46. W. Charlton, *Voyage of* Mayflower II, 166–67.

47. J. Baker, *Plimoth Plantation*, 13.

48. W. Charlton, *Voyage of* Mayflower II, 172.

49. Villiers, *Give Me a Ship*, 193.

50. Upham, *Illustrated Story*, 60.

51. W. Charlton, *Voyage of* Mayflower II, 172.

CHAPTER 14

1. Villiers, *Give Me a Ship*, 189.

2. W. Charlton, *Voyage of* Mayflower II, 176.

3. W. Charlton, *Voyage of* Mayflower II, 178–79; Padfield, *Magic Carpet*, 43.

4. Villiers, "How We Sailed," 656.

5. W. Charlton, *Voyage of* Mayflower II, 183.

6. Villiers, *Give Me a Ship*, 196.

7. W. Charlton, *Voyage of* Mayflower II, 186.

8. Nicole Logan, "Plimoth Plantation: Missive from *Mayflower II* Crew Finally Finds Its Way Home," *Courier-Sentinel* (Plymouth County, MA), April 25, 2012. www.wickedlocal.com/story/courier-sentinel/2012/04/25/plimoth-plantation-missive-from-mayflower/39037277007/.

9. Villiers, "How We Sailed," 646.

10. Padfield, *Magic Carpet*, 11.

11. Villiers, "How We Sailed," 646.

12. W. Charlton, *Voyage of* Mayflower II, 196.

13. W. Charlton, *Voyage of* Mayflower II, 200.

14. W. Charlton, *Voyage of* Mayflower II, 201.

15. Padfield, Mayflower II *Diary*, 61.

16. Bec Crew, "Cats Sailed with Vikings on Their Quest to Conquer the World," *Science Alert*, August 8, 2018, www.sciencealert.com/cats-sailed-with-vikings-to-conquer-world-genetic-study-reveals.

17. Padfield, *Magic Carpet*, 59.

18. Padfield, *Magic Carpet*, 41.

19. W. Charlton, *Voyage of* Mayflower II, 190–91.

20. W. Charlton, *Voyage of* Mayflower II, 213–14.

21. W. Charlton, *Voyage of* Mayflower II, 185–86.

22. Dooley, "'Old Salts' Swap Yarns."

23. W. Charlton, *Voyage of* Mayflower II, 149.

24. Villiers, *Give Me a Ship*, 214.

25. Padfield, Mayflower II *Diary*, 41.

26. Villiers, "How We Sailed," 661.

27. Villiers, *Give Me a Ship*, 203.

28. W. Baker, *The New* Mayflower, 96.

29. Villiers, *Give Me a Ship*, 187.

30. Walter Godfrey, "Menu Book," Plimoth Patuxet Museums, Plymouth, Massachusetts, https://sites.google.com/plimoth.org/mayflower-ii-exhibition/menu-book.

31. W. Charlton, *Voyage of* Mayflower II, 173, 175.

32. Padfield, *Magic Carpet*, 54.

33. Villiers, *Give Me a Ship*, 165.

34. Padfield, Mayflower *Diary*, 42.

35. R. Charlton, *The Wicked Pilgrim*, 186.

36. R. Charlton, *The Wicked Pilgrim*, 188.

37. Dooley, "'Old Salts' Swap Yarns."

38. W. Charlton, *Voyage of* Mayflower II, 164.

39. W. Charlton, *Voyage of* Mayflower II, 162.

40. Villiers, *Give Me a Ship*, 165.

41. W. Charlton, *Voyage of* Mayflower II, 230–31.

42. Villiers, *Give Me a Ship*, 164.

43. Allan Israel, email to author, August 14, 2023.

44. Ora Dodd, "Felix, the *Mayflower* Cat," *Yankee*, November 1958, 46–47.

CHAPTER 15

1. Padfield, Mayflower II *Diary*, 28.

2. Padfield, Mayflower II *Diary*, 81.

3. Villiers, *Give Me a Ship*, 210.

4. Padfield, Mayflower II *Diary*, 76.

5. Padfield, Mayflower II *Diary*, 58.

6. W. Charlton, *Voyage of* Mayflower II, 200.

7. Edey and Tenney, "A *Mayflower* Sails into Today," 36.

8. Villiers, *Give Me a Ship*, 217.

9. W. Charlton, *Voyage of* Mayflower II, 232–33.

10. W. Charlton, *Voyage of* Mayflower II, 239.

11. "Meeting of HMS Ark Royal and *Mayflower II* at Sea (1957)," British Pathé, March 13, 2014, https://youtu.be/JW7znw0U6Wg. Records suggest the footage was shot around June 7, 1957, with the Film ID 2878.24.

12. Padfield, *Magic Carpet*, 53.

13. W. Baker, *The New* Mayflower, 114.

14. "Kelvin & Hughes Sextant—Object ID 64.654," Plimoth Patuxet Museums, Plymouth, Massachusetts, https://sites.google.com/plimoth.org/mayflower-ii-exhibition/sextant.

15. "Ship's Binnacle—Object ID 95.660.3," Plimoth Patuxet Museums, Plymouth, Massachusetts, https://sites.google.com/plimoth.org/mayflower-ii-exhibition/mayflower-ii-binnacle.

16. W. Baker, *The New* Mayflower, 131.

17. The definitive account is Dava Sobel's *Longitude* (New York: Walker, 1995). See also "Longitude Found: The Story of Harrison's Clocks," Royal Museums Greenwich, www.rmg.co.uk/stories/topics/harrisons-clocks-longitude-problem.

18. Villiers, *Give Me a Ship*, 220.

19. Padfield, *Magic Carpet*, 71.

20. W. Charlton, *Voyage of* Mayflower II, 241.

21. Villiers, *Give Me a Ship*, 221.

22. Villiers, *Give Me a Ship*, 222.

23. Upham, *Illustrated Story*, 60.

24. Padfield, Mayflower II *Diary*, 96.

25. Villiers, *Give Me a Ship*, 222.

26. W. Charlton, *Voyage of* Mayflower II, 242.

27. Padfield, Mayflower II *Diary*, 96.

28. Nico Caponetto, "Heavy Weather Sailing: Lying A-Hull," *Yachting News*, www.yachtingnews.com/lying-a-hull.

29. W. Charlton, *Voyage of* Mayflower II, 243.

30. W. Charlton, *Voyage of* Mayflower II, 245.

31. Padfield, *Magic Carpet*, 72.

32. Villiers, *Give Me a Ship*, 223.

33. Villiers, "How We Sailed," 667, 670.

34. W. Charlton, *Voyage of* Mayflower II, 246.

35. Padfield, Mayflower II *Diary*, 99.

36. W. Charlton, *Voyage of* Mayflower II, 246.

37. Villiers, "How We Sailed," 671.

38. Padfield, Mayflower II *Diary*, 99.

39. W. Charlton, *Voyage of* Mayflower II, 247.

40. Padfield, Mayflower II *Diary*, 100.

41. W. Charlton, *Voyage of* Mayflower II, 248.

42. Lance, *Alan Villiers*, 241–42.

43. W. Charlton, *Voyage of* Mayflower II, 250.

44. Villiers, *Give Me a Ship*, 231.

45. "Plimoth Plantation Receives Insurance Policy on *Shallop*," *Boston Globe*, June 21, 1957.

46. W. Charlton, *Voyage of* Mayflower II, 255–56.

47. W. Charlton, *Voyage of* Mayflower II, 256.

48. Upham, *Illustrated Story*, 9.

49. W. Baker, *The New* Mayflower, 140–41.

CHAPTER 16

1. Edey and Tenney, "A *Mayflower* Sails into Today," 19.

2. Recommendation for Membership, *National Geographic Magazine*, November 1957, https://archive.nationalgeographic.com/national-geographic/1957-nov/flipbook/Ad3.

3. John H. Fenton, "*Mayflower II* Hailed at Plymouth Rock," *New York Times*, June 14, 1957.

4. Fenton, "*Mayflower II* Hailed."

5. John H. Fenton, "Nixon Cites Pilgrims in Stressing Worth of Liberty," *New York Times*, June 23, 1957.

6. John C. Devlin, "Aide Denies Ship Is All-Sales Idea," *New York Times*, June 14, 1957.

7. Hornblower, "*Mayflower's* Home Port."

8. Reproductions of pages from *Mayflower II* log, shown before title page in Warwick Charlton, *The Second* Mayflower *Adventure* (Plymouth, MA: Plimoth Plantation, 2007).

9. R. Charlton, *The Wicked Pilgrim*, 270.

10. Undated *Today* newspaper interview with Warwick Charlton, circa 1977, Papers of Alan Villiers, MS6388, series 9, Correspondence—"Mayflower" project US—box 104, National Library of Australia, quoted in Lance, *Alan Villiers*, 240.

11. Villiers, *Give Me a Ship*, 135, 138, 160, 167.

12. Frank P. Harris, "*Mayflower* Bows to Public," *Boston Globe*, June 14, 1957.

13. John H. Fenton, "*Mayflower* Gets Down to Business," *New York Times*, June 15, 1957

14. Kent B. Stiles, "News of the World of Stamps," *New York Times*, June 9, 1957.

15. "President Gets Gifts—*Mayflower II* Chest Contains Animal Feed for 'Farmer,'" *New York Times*, November 6, 1957.

16. Harold Caccia, *The British Ambassador Addresses American Newcomen at New York* (Exton, PA: Newcomen Publications, 1958), https://ia600603.us.archive.org/4/items/britishambassado00cacc/britishambassado00cacc.pdf.

17. R. Charlton, *The Wicked Pilgrim*, 284.

18. Villiers, "We're Coming Over," 726.

19. Devlin, "Aide Denies Ship Is All-Sales Idea."

20. "*Mayflower* Sure of a Big Welcome," *New York Times*, May 5, 1957.

21. "*Mayflower* Man Withdraws," *Birmingham Daily Post*, June 21, 1957.

22. "*Mayflower* Man Withdraws."

23. Thomas P. Ronan, "*Mayflower* Hits Financial Squall," *New York Times*, June 21, 1957.

24. "London Paper Critical," *New York Times*, June 14, 1957.

25. Villiers, *Give Me a Ship*, 233.

26. Hanson W. Baldwin, "Wilson to Review Ships of 18 Navies," *New York Times*, June 9, 1957.

27. Kent B. Stiles, "News of the World of Stamps," *New York Times*, April 28, 1957.

28. Villiers, *Give Me a Ship*, 233.

29. Villiers, *Give Me a Ship*, 234.

CHAPTER 17

1. James Hammond, "Plymouth Rides Out Storm, Awaits Nixon," *Boston Globe*, June 21, 1957.

2. UK Parliament, House of Lords, "Proposed Demolition of St James's Theatre," *Hansard: House of Lords*, vol. 204, July 9, 1957, https://hansard.parliament.uk/Lords/1957 -07-09/debates/0d9f0ac8-1610-45b8-b12e-3a7dbf0e214e/ProposedDemolitionOfStJa messTheatre.

3. UK Parliament, House of Lords, "The St James's Theatre," *Hansard: House of Lords*, vol. 205, July 30, 1957, https://hansard.parliament.uk/Lords/1957-07-30/debates /8e048f83-0f0b-4cf8-82f3-a1f6a5f0e391/TheStJamesSTheatre.

4. UK Parliament, House of Lords, "The St James's Theatre," *Hansard: House of Lords*, vol. 205, July 29, 1957, https://hansard.parliament.uk/Lords/1957-07-29/debates/ a99effb0-6209-4f6e-9a4e-19bee4e35e7c/TheStJamesSTheatre.

5. UK Parliament, House of Lords, "St James's Theatre," *Hansard: House of Lords*, vol. 205, July 23, 1957, https://hansard.parliament.uk/Lords/1957-07-23/debates/620e9b7b -7275-48c8-a8ec-efbb339d2f72/StJamesSTheatre.

6. UK Parliament, House of Lords, July 30, 1957.

7. UK Parliament, House of Commons, "St James's Theatre," *Hansard: House of Commons*, vol. 574, July 31, 1957, https://hansard.parliament.uk/Commons/1957-07-31/ debates/d8aa5778-6df5-45fe-bfb0-435fccf0b641/StJamesSTheatre.

8. UK Parliament, House of Commons, "Foreign Travel Allowance," *Hansard: House of Commons*, vol. 604, April 21, 1959, https://api.parliament.uk/historic-hansard/commons /1959/apr/21/foreign-travel-allowance.

9. R. Charlton, *The Wicked Pilgrim*, 186.

10. R. Charlton, *The Wicked Pilgrim*, 186.

11. The arrival may be seen in "New York Welcomes *Mayflower* (1957)," British Pathé, July 1, 1957, https://youtu.be/vcI5XnkeQZY.

12. John C. Devlin, "*Mayflower II* Will Get Escort Past Welcoming Jam in Sound," *New York Times*, June 29, 1957.

13. "60 Log Cabins to Rise as Pilgrim Village on 41st St. Pier for *Mayflower II* Visit," *New York Times*, April 12, 1957.

14. John C. Devlin, "Thousands Visit *Mayflower II*; Some Protest Fees and Delays," *New York Times*, July 4, 1957.

15. "Mayflower Day July 2," *New York Times*, June 25, 1957.

16. John C. Devlin, "*Mayflower* Crew Hailed in Parade," *New York Times*, July 3, 1957.

17. "'Priscilla' Is Chosen: Pilgrim Descendant to Greet Mayflower II on Arrival Here," *New York Times*, May 25, 1957.

18. Devlin, "*Mayflower* Crew Hailed."

19. Devlin, "Thousands Visit"; "Curbs Are Eased by *Mayflower II*," *New York Times*, July 4, 1957.

20. W. Charlton, *Voyage of* Mayflower II, 38, photograph between pages 84 and 85.

21. "Last Visitors See the *Mayflower II*," *New York Times*, November 18, 1957.

22. "*Mayflower II*, Plymouth Bound, Bids City Farewell," *New York Times*, November 24, 1957.

CHAPTER 18

1. "Demolition of St. James's Deferred," *Birmingham Daily Post*, August 7, 1957.

2. "Hornblower Stresses New Securities Gift Law for Minors," *Boston Globe*, September 26, 1957.

3. R. Charlton, *The Wicked Pilgrim*, 297.

4. R. Charlton, *The Wicked Pilgrim*, 300–301.

5. R. Charlton, *The Wicked Pilgrim*, 10.

6. "British State Visit to United States, 1957," Royal Watcher, https://royalwatcherblog.com/2022/10/21/british-state-visit-to-the-united-states-1957/.

7. British Movietone, "The Queen Begins U.S. Tour—1957," October 16, 2017, https://youtu.be/lk85oxAD5vc; John Kelly, "Elizabeth II Conquers Washington," *Washington Post*, June 16, 2012; NetworkNewsToday, "Queen Elizabeth II Address to United Nations," October 21, 1957, www.facebook.com/watch/?v=496877635102535; Elizabeth II, "Address to the U.N. General Assembly," text at http://emersonkent.com/speeches/address_to_the_un_general_assembly_elizabeth_1957.htm.

8. R. Charlton, *The Wicked Pilgrim*, 175.

9. R. Charlton, *The Wicked Pilgrim*, 310.

CHAPTER 19

1. "*Mayflower* Back in Plymouth," *New York Times*, November 25, 1957.

2. John Fenton, "*Mayflower* to Join Plymouth Thanksgiving," *New York Times*, November 24, 1957.

3. Fenton, "*Mayflower* to Join Plymouth Thanksgiving."

4. R. Charlton, *The Wicked Pilgrim*, 306.

5. "NBC Today Show November 27, 1957, Live from Plymouth, Massachusetts," TheHubToday2, https://vimeo.com/341620801.

6. "The Fate of St. James's."

7. R. Charlton, *The Wicked Pilgrim*, 290.

8. R. Charlton, *The Wicked Pilgrim*, 306.

9. James H. Hammond, "*Mayflower II* Returns, Docks at Plymouth," *Boston Globe*, November 25, 1957.

10. "*Mayflower* Saga Ends," *New York Times*, November 28, 1957.

11. Villiers to Mel Grosvenor, October 28, 1957, Papers of Alan Villiers, MS6388, series 9, Correspondence—"Mayflower" project—US, box 104, National Library of Australia, quoted in Lance, *Alan Villiers*, 245.

12. Devlin, "Aide Denies Ship Is All-Sales Idea."

13. R. Charlton, *The Wicked Pilgrim*, 308.

14. Smith, "Even *Mayflower*'s Insurance Is Authentic."

15. R. Charlton, *The Wicked Pilgrim*, 308.

16. "220,000 Visit *Mayflower II*," *Birmingham Post & Gazette*, June 27, 1958.

17. "*Mayflower II* at Capital," *New York Times*, April 17, 1958.

18. "Key to Washington D.C.—Object ID 95.662," Plimoth Patuxet Museums, https://sites.google.com/plimoth.org/mayflower-ii-exhibition/key-to-washington.

19. British Pathé, "*Mayflower II* Arrives in Washington 1958," April 16, 1958, www .britishpathe.com/video/mayflower-ii-arrives-in-washington.

20. "*Mayflower* Back in Plymouth," *New York Times*, June 29, 1958.

21. "Color Movie, 'The *Mayflower* Story' Exceeds All Popularity Expectations," *Mayflower Aerogram*, December 1958, 1.

22. "Hornblower & Weeks Celebrating Firm's 70th Anniversary," *Boston Globe*, August 12, 1958.

23. "Henry Hornblower II," Harvard College Class of 1941, Twentieth Anniversary Report (Cambridge, 1961), 124, Harvard Archives.

CHAPTER 20

1. R. Charlton, *The Wicked Pilgrim*, 337.

2. Plimoth Plantation Board of Governors records, January 3, 1958, reported by James W. Baker, email to author, July 14, 2023.

3. Hammond, "*Mayflower II* Returns."

4. R. Charlton, *The Wicked Pilgrim*, 333.

5. R. Charlton, *The Wicked Pilgrim*, 333.

6. R. Charlton, *The Wicked Pilgrim*, 334.

7. Plimoth Plantation annual report for 1957, quoted in Villiers, *Give Me a Ship*, 240.

8. Associated Press, "Native Americans Invade *Mayflower II*," AP Archive, November 26, 1970, https://youtu.be/kP0rD6UxxOE.

9. "Mourning Indians Dump Sand on Plymouth Rock," *New York Times*, November 27, 1970.

10. Frank B. James, "The Suppressed Speech of Wamsutta (Frank B.) James, Wampanoag," September 10, 1970, United American Indians of New England, www.uaine.org/suppressed_speech.htm.

11. "Henry Hornblower, II," Harvard College Class of 1941, Thirty-Fifth Anniversary Report (Cambridge, 1976), 115, Harvard Archives.

12. Davis Bushnell, "Plimoth Plantation at a Crossroads," *Boston Globe*, April 27, 1997.

13. "Henry Hornblower 2d, Founder of 'Plimoth,'" *New York Times*, October 23, 1985.

14. Gomes, "Remarks at the Memorial Service."

15. Gomes, "Memoirs: Henry Hornblower II," 159–60.

16. Driscoll, "Henry Hornblower 2d."

17. Douglas Martin, "Warwick Charlton, a Dreamer, Dies at 84," *New York Times*, December 21, 2002.

18. Peter Arenstam, "Repairing the *Mayflower II* (2013)," Boating Local.com, April 24, 2013, www.youtube.com/watch?v=urcxPFIo1Hw.

19. Don Cuddy, "*Mayflower II* in Fairhaven for Sprucing Up," *South Coast Today*, January 3, 2008, www.southcoasttoday.com/article/20080103/News/801030337.

20. Arenstam, "Repairing the *Mayflower II*."

21. Bushnell, "Plimoth Plantation at a Crossroads."

22. Joe Wojtas, "Restoration Begins on *Mayflower II* at Mystic Seaport," *New London (CT) Day*, December 23, 2014, https://www.theday.com/local-news/20141222/restoration-begins-on-mayflower-ii-at-mystic-seaport.

23. "Massachusetts State Budget Approves \$2 Million to Fund *Mayflower II* Restoration," National Maritime Historical Society, July 14, 2014, https://seahistory.org/massachusetts-state-budget-approves-2-million-fund-mayflower-ii-restoration.

24. Wojtas, "Restoration Begins."

25. "Mystic Seaport Announces Collaborative Restoration of *Mayflower II*," Mystic Seaport Museum, December 4, 2014, www.mysticseaport.org/news/mystic-seaport-announce-collaborative-restoration-of-mayflower-ii/.

26. "Charles W. Morgan," Mystic Seaport Museum, https://www.mysticseaport.org/explore/morgan/.

27. Villiers, "We're Coming Over," 726.

28. "Plimoth Plantation to Host *Mayflower II* Restoration Pennies for Planks Drive," WickedLocal.com, November 10, 2018, https://www.wickedlocal.com/story/old-colony-memorial/2018/11/10/strong-plimoth-plantation-to/8501934007/.

29. Jesse Leavenworth, "Following an \$11.2 Million Restoration in Mystic, the *Mayflower II* Sets Sail," *Hartford Courant*, July 21, 2020, www.courant.com/news/connecticut/hc-news-ct-mayflower-sets-sail-20200720-yobdr5gvxfchvbtb54sj4v2qle-story.html.

30. Tom Jackson, "*Mayflower II*'s Rebirth," *WoodenBoat*, May 2020, 74, https://www.woodenboat.com/mayflower-ii's-rebirth.

31. Mystic Seaport Museum, "*Mayflower II* Live Oaks Part of Legacy," March 22, 2017, www.mysticseaport.org/news/mayflower-ii-live-oaks-part-of-legacy/.

32. Jeff Bolster, "*Mayflower II* Restoration," *Soundings*, August 29, 2018, www.soundingsonline.com/features/mayflower-ii.

33. Jackson, "*Mayflower II*'s Rebirth," 74.

34. "*Mayflower II* Refits for 400th Anniversary of Pilgrims' Voyage," *Classic Boat*, https://www.classicboat.co.uk/news/mayflower-ii-refits-for-400th-anniversary-of-pilgrims-voyage/.

35. Jackson, "*Mayflower II*'s Rebirth," 74.

36. Joe Gelarden, "Nat Wilson: East Boothbay's Sailmaker, Part 2," *Boothbay Register*, February 2, 2022, www.boothbayregister.com/article/nat-wilson-east-boothbay-s-sailmaker-part-2/156443.

37. "Dyneema Fiber: The World's Strongest Fiber," Avient, 2023, https://www.dsm.com/dyneema/en_GB/our-products/dyneema-fiber.html.

38. Jackson, "*Mayflower II*'s Rebirth," 75.

39. Griffith Baily Coale, "Arrival of the First Permanent English Settlers off Jamestown, Virginia, 13 May 1607," *American Neptune* 10, no. 1 (1950): 9, https://archive.org/details/sim_american-neptune_1950-01_10_1/page/n15/mode/2up.

40. W. Baker, *The New* Mayflower, 135.

41. Tana Weingartner, "Verdin to Cast Bell for *Mayflower II* at Plimoth Plantation," 91.7 WVXU News NPR, August 30, 2019, www.wvxu.org/local-news/2019-08-30/verdin-to-cast-bell-for-mayflower-ii-at-plimoth-plantation.

42. Jackson, "*Mayflower II*'s Rebirth," 69.

CHAPTER 21

1. BSGT2TREKFAN88, "*Mayflower II* Back in the Water!" September 7, 2019, https://youtu.be/Q8nqyQ6IrF4.

2. Kimberly Drelich, "'A National Treasure': *Mayflower II* Relaunches," *New London (CT) Day*, September 8, 2019, www.theday.com/article/20190907/NWS01/190909536.

3. Mystic Seaport Museum, "*Mayflower II* Launch September 7, 2019," keynote speech by Nathaniel Philbrick, www.youtube.com/watch?v=qYKrHWR_XOI.

4. James W. Baker, *Thanksgiving: The Biography of an American Holiday* (Durham: University of New Hampshire Press, 2009), 193.

5. "Henry Hornblower, II," Harvard College Class of 1941, Twenty-Fifth Anniversary Report (Cambridge, 1966), 631, Harvard Archives.

Selected Bibliography

Anderson, R. C. "A 'Mayflower' Model." *Mariner's Mirror* 12, no. 3 (1926): 260–63. https: //doi.org/10.1080/00253359.1926.10655374.

Arenstam, Peter. *Felix and His Mayflower II Adventures.* Plymouth, MA: Plimoth Plantation, 2007.

———. "Repairing the *Mayflower II* (2013)." Boating Local.com, April 24, 2013. www .youtube.com/watch?v=urcxPFIo1Hw.

Baker, James W. Introduction to *Mayflower II: Plimoth Plantation.* Little Compton, RI: Fort Church, 1993.

———. *Plimoth Plantation: Fifty Years of Living History.* Plymouth, MA: Plimoth Plantation, 1997.

———. *Thanksgiving: The Biography of an American Holiday.* Durham, NH: University of New Hampshire Press, 2009.

Baker, William A. "Early Seventeenth-Century Ship Design." *American Neptune* 14, no. 4 (1954): 262–77.

———. "The *Mayflower* Problem." *American Neptune* 14, no. 1 (1954): 5–17.

———. *The New Mayflower, Her Design and Construction.* Barre, MA: Barre Gazette, 1958.

Bolster, Jeff. "*Mayflower II* Restoration." *Soundings*, August 29, 2018, www.soundingsonline .com/features/mayflower-ii.

Bradford, William. *Of Plymouth Plantation, 1620–1647: The Complete Text.* Edited by Samuel Eliot Morison. New York: Knopf, 1952.

British Pathé. "*Mayflower* Sails for America." April 20, 1957. www.youtube.com/watch ?v=Heu2VCoaJuk.

———. "*Mayflower* the Second Is Launched (1956)." www.youtube.com/watch?v =tCCrY8QBRfw.

———. "*Mayflower II* Arrives in Washington 1958." April 16, 1958. www.britishpathe .com/video/mayflower-ii-arrives-in-washington.

———. "Meeting of HMS Ark Royal and *Mayflower II* at Sea (1957)." March 13, 2014. https://youtu.be/JW7znw0U6Wg.

———. "New York Welcomes *Mayflower*." July 1, 1957. https://youtu.be/vcI5XnkeQZY.

Bromund, Ted R. "'This Somewhat Embarrassing Ship': The British Foreign Office and the *Mayflower II*, 1954–1957." *New England Quarterly* 72, no. 1 (March 1999): 42–60.

BSGT2TREKFAN88. "*Mayflower II* Back in the Water!" September 7, 2019. https://youtu.be/Q8nqyQ6IrF4.

Catling, Patrick Skene. "Warwick Charlton: The Man Who Brought the Monty Out of Montgomery." *Guardian*, January 3, 2003. www.theguardian.com/media/2003/jan/03/all and link to "Warwick Charlton."

Charlton, Randal. *The Wicked Pilgrim: The True Story of the Englishman Who Gave* Mayflower II *to America*. Delanson, NY: Three Sisters, 2019.

Charlton, Warwick. "Equipment for the Ship." *Mayflower Mail*, sailing edition, April 1957.

———. "Manifest of the *Mayflower II*." Typed document, 1957. Charlton Foundation, Grosse Pointe Farms, Michigan.

———. *The Second Mayflower Adventure*. 1957. Plymouth, MA: Plimoth Plantation, 2007.

———. *The Voyage of Mayflower II*. London: Cassell, 1957.

Classic Boat. "*Mayflower II* Refits for 400th Anniversary of Pilgrims' Voyage." https://www.classicboat.co.uk/news/mayflower-ii-refits-for-400th-anniversary-of-pilgrims-voyage/.

Dodd, Ora. "Felix, the *Mayflower* Cat." *Yankee*, November 1958, 46–47.

Dooley, Emily C. "'Old Salts' Swap Yarns from 1957 Atlantic Voyage." *Cape Cod Times*, July 30, 2000. http://www.capecodtimes.com/story/news/2000/07/30/old-salts-swap-yarns/51018253007.

Edey, Maitland A., and Gordon Tenney. "A *Mayflower* Sails into Today." *Life*, June 17, 1957, 19–37.

Gomes, Peter J. "Memoirs: Henry Hornblower II." *Proceedings of the Massachusetts Historical Society*, 3rd series, vol. 97 (1985): 157–60.

———. "Remarks at the Memorial Service of Henry Hornblower II, '41." The Memorial Church, Harvard University, October 25, 1985.

Hornblower, Henry, II. "Henry Hornblower, II." Personal notes in reunion books for Harvard College Class of 1941: *Sexennial Report* (1947), 144–45; *Decennial Report* (1951), 163–64; *Fifteenth Anniversary Report* (1956), 123–24; *Twentieth Anniversary Report* (1961), 123–24; *25th Anniversary Report* (1966), 631–32; *Thirtieth Anniversary Report* (1971), 108; *35th Anniversary Report* (1976), 115; *40th Anniversary Report* (1981), 100. Cambridge, MA: Harvard University Archives.

———. "*Mayflower's* Home Port." Letter to the editor. *Berkshire Eagle* (Pittsfield, MA), May 2, 1957.

Jackson, Tom. "*Mayflower II's* Rebirth." *WoodenBoat*, May 2020, 74. https://www.woodenboat.com/mayflower-ii's-rebirth.

Lance, Kate. *Alan Villiers: Voyager of the Winds*. Second edition. Korumburra, Australia: Seabooks Press, 2020.

Marsden, R. G. "The 'Mayflower.'" *English Historical Review* 19, no. 76 (October 1904): 669–80.

Martin, Douglas. "Warwick Charlton, a Dreamer, Dies at 84." *New York Times*, December 21, 2002.

Morison, Samuel Eliot. "The 66-Day Saga of *Mayflower* I." *New York Times*, April 14, 1957.

Mystic Seaport Museum. "*Mayflower II* Launch September 7, 2019." Keynote speech by Nathaniel Philbrick. www.youtube.com/watch?v=qYKrHWR_XOI.

———. "*Mayflower II* Live Oaks Part of Legacy." March 22, 2017. www.mysticseaport .org/news/mayflower-ii-live-oaks-part-of-legacy.

———. "Mystic Seaport Announces Collaborative Restoration of *Mayflower II*." December 4, 2014. www.mysticseaport.org/news/mystic-seaport-announce-collaborative -restoration-of-mayflower-ii.

———. "A Steel Frame for *Mayflower II*." January 27, 2017. www.mysticseaport.org/ category/mayflower-ii-restoration/.

NBC. "NBC Today Show November 27, 1957, Live from Plymouth, Massachusetts." TheHubToday2. https://vimeo.com/341620801.

Padfield, Peter. *Mayflower II Diary: Sketches from a Lost Age.* Decatur, GA: Casa Forte Press, 2019.

———. *The Sea Is a Magic Carpet.* London: Peter Davies, 1959.

Philbrick, Nathaniel. *Mayflower: A Story of Courage, Community, and War.* New York: Viking, 2006.

Royal Museums Greenwich. "Longitude Found: The Story of Harrison's Clocks." www .rmg.co.uk/stories/topics/harrisons-clocks-longitude-problem.

Silverman, David J. *This Land Is Their Land: The Wampanoag Indians, Plymouth Colony, and the Troubled History of Thanksgiving.* New York: Bloomsbury, 2019.

Sobel, Dava. *Longitude: The True Story of a Lone Genius Who Solved the Greatest Scientific Problem of His Time.* New York: Walker, 1995.

Time. "Press: Monty's Fighting Editor." May 1, 1944, 86–87.

Upham, Stuart A. *The Illustrated Story of How* Mayflower II_*Was Built.* Second edition. Plymouth, MA: Plimoth Plantation 2018.

Villiers, Alan. *Give Me a Ship to Sail.* London: Hodder & Stoughton, 1958.

———. "How We Sailed the New *Mayflower* to America." *National Geographic*, November 1957, 627–72.

———. Papers. National Library of Australia, Canberra.

———. "We're Coming Over on the *Mayflower*." *National Geographic*, May 1957, 708–28.

Warner Pathé News. "Britain Starts Building a New *Mayflower*." July 27, 1955. www .youtube.com/watch?v=PMDQo5mKaCg.

Winslow, D. Kenelm. *Mayflower Heritage: A Family Record of the Growth of Anglo-American Partnership.* New York: Funk & Wagnalls, 1957.

Winslow, Edward. "A Letter Sent from New-England to a Friend in These Parts." In *Mourt's Relation, or Journal of the Plantation at Plymouth*, edited by Henry Martyn Dexter, 131–42 [60–65]. Boston: John Kimball Wiggin, 1865.

Index

Page references for figures are italicized.

Jamestown, 7, 8, 81, 188, 189, 205, 222
Jarvis, Howard (artist), 183
Jones, Christopher (captain, *Mayflower*), 7, 31, 119, 145, 147, 163
Joseph Conrad, 42, 44, 114, 115, 152, 154
Junker, Jan (crew, *Mayflower II*), 115, 122, 125, 142, *155*, 156, 166, 168, 175
just and equal laws, 7, 9, 17, 211, 225

Kalmar Harbor, 31
Kalmar Nyckel, 222
keel, 31, 39, *41*, 49, 58, 68, 102, 103, 104, 117, 140, 220
keel-haul, 165
Keightley, General Charles (general, British), 78, 80
Kemp, Harry ("Poet of the Dunes"), 170
Kennedy, John Fitzgerald (senator), *180*
Kiefer, Priscilla Alden (descendant, *Mayflower*), 195
King Philip's War, 15
Kirkpatrick, Sir Ivone (senior advisor, Anthony Eden), 57, 77, 80
Kon-Tiki, 12, 129

Lacey, Joe (crew, *Mayflower II*), 125, 150, 152, 165, 175
latitude, 119, 135, 163, 164, 168
Leigh, Vivian (actress), 191, *193*
Leister, Edward (signer, Mayflower Compact), 10

Leming, Reis (airman), 68, 69
letter in a bottle, 134–36, *137*, 144
Lewis, Bob (stowaway), 113
Lewis, John L. (labor organizer), 98, 99
Lewis, Milton (journalist), 184
Life, 3, 18, 49, 87, 125, 154, 156, 159, 174, 178, 179, 181
Lincoln, Abraham (president) 16, 38
Lindsay, Andy (crew, *Mayflower II*), 154, 165, 176
Lloyd, Selwyn (foreign secretary, Britain), 100, 101
Lloyd's of London, 37–38, 93; progress report, 57. *See also* sponsors, construction
Longfellow, Henry Wadsworth (author), 198
longitude, 7, 135, 145, 163, 164
Lowe, John (founder, Project Mayflower), ix, xi, 20, 41, 208; Bletchley Park, 53, 55; focus on wealthy elites, 46; London Exhibition, 90, 111, 204; meets Hornblower, 28, *35*; sale of replica, 200, 201; with Charlton, *22*; with Hornblower and others, *35*; with JFK, *180*
Lucania, 158
Luce, Henry (founder, *Time*), 3
Lugrin, Julian (crew, *Mayflower II*), 125, 140, 176
lying a-hull, 165, *167*

Macmillan, Harold (prime minister, Britain), 79; Aldrich relationship, 88, 89; Bermuda Conference,